Child Protection Practice

Child Protection Practice

Harry Ferguson

palgrave
macmillan

First published 2011 by
PALGRAVE MACMILLAN

Palgrave Macmillan in the UK is an imprint of Macmillan Publishers Limited, registered in England, company number 785998, of Houndmills, Basingstoke, Hampshire RG21 6XS.

Palgrave Macmillan in the US is a division of St Martin's Press LLC, 175 Fifth Avenue, New York, NY 10010.

Palgrave Macmillan is the global academic imprint of the above companies and has companies and representatives throughout the world.

Palgrave® and Macmillan® are registered trademarks in the United States, the United Kingdom, Europe and other countries.

ISBN 978–0–230–24283–8

This book is printed on paper suitable for recycling and made from fully managed and sustained forest sources. Logging, pulping and manufacturing processes are expected to conform to the environmental regulations of the country of origin.

A catalogue record for this book is available from the British Library.

Library of Congress Cataloging-in-Publication Data
Ferguson, Harry (Thomas Harold)
  Child protection practice / Harry Ferguson.
    p.   cm.
  Includes index.
  ISBN 978–0–230–24283–8 (pbk.)
  1. Child abuse—Prevention.   2. Social work with children.
  I. Title.
  HV713.F47 2011
  362.76′7—dc22   2011008061

To the memory of Anne Ferguson-Arnold
25 January 1956–16 January 2008

Contents

Acknowledgements

In writing this book I have relied on the generosity of many people. I cannot thank my editor Catherine Gray enough for all the help she has given me. Catherine encouraged me to write the book, supported and cajoled me into finishing it, read and commented upon every bit of it along the way and has made a huge contribution to its final shape and content. I am also grateful to Katie Rauwerda for her invaluable editorial assistance, and to Maggie Lythgoe for her excellent copy-editing.

Academic colleagues Helen Buckley, Siobhan Laird and Kate Morris read the manuscript and I am grateful to them for the trouble they took and their helpful feedback, as I am to the anonymous reviewers. From practice, Tony Flynn, who is not only a great social worker, manager and leader but a brilliant poet, gave me tremendously helpful feedback and support. I have been lucky to be able to present the ideas developed in this book at numerous conferences and public lectures in recent years, and have been deeply moved by the generosity of the practitioner and academic audiences whose feedback has been hugely beneficial in developing my thinking. The responses of my students have been very helpful in challenging me to clarify my thinking and to try harder to make it accessible. The ideas presented here have also benefited from collaboration and conversations with several friends and colleagues: Andrew Arnold, Alison Arnold, Patrick Ayre, Kenneth Burns, Andrew Cooper, Brid Featherstone, Sarah Goff, Yvon Guest, Fergus Hogan, Paul Hoggett, Joel Kanter, Ravi Kohli, Bill Loach, Barry Luckock, Debby Lynch, Danny Miller, Barry Raynes, Gillian Ruch, Olive Stevenson, Andrew Turnell, John Urry, Jim Wild and Paul Zeal.

The book relies heavily on research I have conducted over a number of years and I am indebted to all the practitioners who opened up their practice and themselves to me and the service users who shared their experiences. Special thanks must go to the social workers and managers in my most recent research into social work practice, who warmly welcomed me into their teams, drove me around in their cars and took me on home visits. It has been an absolute pleasure to be associated with them all and they have taught me so much. I only wish that I could name them all but due to research ethics, they must remain anonymous.

There is a lot in this book about the home and the centrality of what goes on it to social work, so I need to acknowledge the huge contribution those in my own home have made to this book. I cannot thank my partner Claire enough for all her love and support. Ellen, Katie, Ben, Susie, Marc, Lila and Sofia continue to teach me the important things I need to learn about relationships and the joys and challenges of parenting. I'm grateful to Ellen, my 10-year-old daughter, for her help with the cover design and for other insights. As I was writing this book, I discussed some of its content with her. I asked Ellen how she would feel about a social worker investigating her life, relationships and home, including going into her bedroom and having a good look around. 'I wouldn't mind and I don't think children who are being abused would', she said. 'Private places are where you can find out things.' She's right. And my hope is that this book will advance understandings of how such finding out can be effectively done.

In the use of case materials, all names and characteristics that could possibly identify the participants have been changed. While the case studies cover actual events and practices, some details have been changed to protect the anonymity of those involved.

The authors and publishers are grateful to the following publishers and organizations for granting permission to reproduce copyright material in this book: Taylor and Francis Books, UK for the epigraph to Chapter 7, originally from Winnicott, D. (1971) *Playing and Reality*. London, Routledge, p. 41; the Department of Health for the epigraph to Chapter 9, reproduced under the Open Government Licence v1.0.

Every effort has been made to trace all the copyright holders but if any have been inadvertently overlooked the publishers will be pleased to make the necessary arrangements at the first opportunity.

Introduction

In the beginning . . .

It is 4pm on a crisp November afternoon in 1978. I am pacing up and down the road outside the house I intend to visit to investigate a complaint of alleged child abuse. I am a student social worker and it is my first ever home visit. I can hear Elvis Presley's 'The Wonder of You' blaring from behind the front door. I am feeling terrified, anxiously searching my mind to remember what I am supposed to say once the door is answered. And then it is. I check if it is 'Mrs Smith' that I am speaking to and announce who I am and she lets me in. I explain why I am there and Mrs Smith immediately gets upset and starts crying and gets angry that someone has reported her for allegedly leaving her daughter in the home alone. The six-year-old girl who is the subject of the referral is there. I am relieved, as it has been drummed into me that my priority is to see the child and her presence means that I can achieve this on this visit, rather than having to come back another time. I try to calm the atmosphere by suggesting we sit down and discuss things, to which Mrs Smith agrees. We go through the substance of the complaint and she denies there are any problems. I gather myself and ask to see around the home, including upstairs and the bedrooms. This too had been drummed into me by the agency, the National Society for the Prevention of Cruelty to Children (NSPCC), in the couple of months since I came on its training course. There was nothing in the state of the bedrooms or any of the home conditions to cause me concern.

Mr Smith arrived home and my anxiety levels shot up again because he was a big, tattooed, hard-looking man and I was afraid of how he would respond to this unannounced intrusion. Luckily for me, he reserved his anger for imagining tearing apart the person he thought had complained about them. There was a sticky moment when I had to keep explaining that I was not allowed to tell him who had reported it and was not even allowed to tell him if he was suspecting the right neighbour. I advised the parents – or as the agency preferred it, 'warned' them – that it was not acceptable to leave children alone at home and then returned to the office and wrote up my case record. I also wrote, at great length, what happened in a 'process recording', including everything I observed, what was said and how I felt, which was used as the basis for a lengthy supervision with my practice supervisor. I even included detail on the colour and state of the wallpaper. I felt uncomfortable about some of the interactions I observed between mother and child and wrote in my process recording that 'at times they related to one another like six year olds and at others like adults', which the practice teacher thought was insightful and clever, and this helped my confidence and cheered me up. Our feeling was that there were no grounds on which the agency could go back to the family, who themselves did not wish for intervention, and the case was closed.

In the over 30 years since I made this first home visit, some things have changed in social work and child protection. But a great deal about what child protection workers do, or need to do, remains the same, not least in how conducting home visits is central to seeking to protect children. This is a book about those kinds of child protection practices. By 'practice' I am referring to the actual work involved in trying to protect children, the actions, movements, talk that need to go on to ensure that, as far as possible, children are safe. One thing that has changed in the past 30 years is that social workers have to give greater amounts of energy to following procedures and time spent seated at their desks completing computerized records and other admin work (Munro, 2004; Broadhurst et al., 2010a). Yet, in crucial respects, social work remains a professional life spent on the move. If children and adults are to be seen and worked with, everyday practice requires workers to leave their desks, make journeys by transport or on foot, walk the streets and housing estates, and walk into and around the homes where service users live. This book explores the performance of child protection whenever and wherever practitioners are present with children and their parents or carers. It is about the dynamics and methods of face-to-face child protection, especially on home visits, but also at hospitals, clinics, offices and children's and family centres. The book sets out what skilful, authoritative child protection practice has to involve.

Recent decades have seen a relentless catalogue of high-profile cases where children have died despite the involvement of social workers and other professionals. Western governments have responded to these tragedies by putting in place elaborate procedures to try and improve cooperation and communication between the organizations involved, in response to findings that failures in communication were crucial to the increasing risk to children not being spotted. What has been given much less attention is that a crucial reason why attempts to protect these children did not succeed was because social workers and other professionals did not recognize the children's injuries when together with them, not simply in their homes but in the same rooms. The highly influential case of 'Baby Peter' exemplifies how children have literally been in front of professionals yet serious injuries were not picked up and acted upon. At the time of his death in London in 2008 at the age of 17 months, Peter had a broken back and some 50 injuries. The social worker saw the child on a home visit four days before he died. There was chocolate on Peter's face, which the social worker asked to be removed, and cream on his scalp treating an infection. A family friend, on the instruction of the mother, took the child away to clean him up, but never brought him back and the social worker did not follow through on it. Peter was known to be at high risk, having been assessed by professionals to have had non-accidental injuries in the past and he was on the child protection register. The social worker did not herself touch the child while on the visit, and although a paediatrician and a GP saw him in their clinics within a couple of days following this visit and just a day or two before his death, neither of them seems to have examined or even touched Peter either (Haringey, 2008, 2009).

This book is concerned with the dilemmas workers experience about how to manage such situations: What should be made of signs such as when there is chocolate on the face and cream on the child's head? How can workers best get a parent to remove it? How far should workers themselves go in removing the chocolate and cream and directly touching and insisting on seeing the child's body to check for injuries? Where – in the home or elsewhere – is the best place for children to be interviewed alone about their experiences? Many other questions of this kind arise and will be addressed in this book. The remarkable fact is that the literature on social work and child protection has largely failed to address these questions, leaving us bereft of understanding and knowledge about the most complex challenges that child protection practitioners face on a daily basis.

I argue that we need a new way of thinking about the work that social workers and other professionals do to try and keep children safe; I call it 'intimate child protection practice'. The aim of developing a concept of intimate child protection practice is to capture in much more depth the reality that where the work goes on is predominantly in the homes, living rooms, kitchens, bathrooms, bedrooms and gardens of the families that social workers visit, and to evoke the lived experience of what it is like for practitioners to perform child protection in these intimate spaces. The idea of intimate practice also seeks to capture the humanity of the encounter, the fact that it involves facilitating and listening to children's disclosures of any harm that has been perpetrated on them, how they feel about their parents, themselves, their pain and pleasures; discussing their experiences of abuse and arranging medicals that involve the removal of clothing to enable examinations; dealing with the anguish of parents who have harmed their child and may now lose them into care forever; or helping those adults to develop their capacity to care and be safe, nurturing parents. For the professionals, intimate practice demands a range of sophisticated skills, courage and a capacity to use authority directly and wisely, but also tenderness and empathy, all of which requires reserves of mental strength and resilience.

In many respects, evoking intimate practice means little more than giving attention to what professionals already do; the originality of the analysis lies in the fact that most of the literature on child protection has failed to provide this kind of understanding. But it also involves bringing new knowledge and understandings to what is done and challenging professionals, organizations and systems to do things differently. If workers are not practising intimately enough and performing effectively when face to face with children, in their homes or elsewhere, this book sets out why this is so and how it needs to change. The neglect of intimate practice arises from a curious absence from most social work and child protection literature, policy and discussions about practice of any considered attention to the core dynamics, experience and methods of doing the work (Forrester, 2008a, 2008b). Not nearly enough attention is given to the detail of what social workers and other professionals actually *do*, *where* they do it and their *experience* of doing it.

This is most obvious with respect to the practice of home visiting, which is the methodology through which most child protection goes on, yet it is virtually ignored in the literature. The aim of this book is to correct this huge gap in knowledge by focusing on the practices involved in trying to gain access to children and relate effectively to them and their parents and carers in their homes. There is a huge literature on child protection and what is now more fashionably referred to as 'safeguarding'. There are introductory texts, which very usefully cover the law, interagency work, definitions of child abuse and ways of responding to it (Munro, 2002; Corby, 2005; Beckett, 2007). Another group of writers focus on the way that child protection and fears of being blamed for not preventing child deaths dominate childcare services, with the effect that adequate day-to-day family support and preventive work tends to be marginalized or not done (Garrett, 2009; Lonne et al., 2009). Most studies of child protection that have involved researchers observing practitioners doing the work are focused solely on what goes on in the office and analysing the occupational culture and how social workers talk about their clients (Pithouse, 1998; Scourfield, 2003a), or this has been done in tandem with interviewing service users (Buckley, 2003). In some exceptional studies, researchers have left the office and accompanied social workers in their work (Dingwall et al., 1983), or used their own experience as data (de Montingy, 1995), but these studies are not only out of date, they also did not pay systematic attention to the core dynamics and experiences of doing the work, such as home visiting.

A significant factor that has drawn attention away from intimate child protection practice is the increasing concern about the restructuring of social work and child protection since the 1980s, with the emphasis on new rules, procedures, audit, information sharing, interprofessional collaboration and greater accountability as a way of managing the risks of system failures and child deaths. As a result, practitioners are increasingly characterized as 'deskilled' by having to spend more and more time in the office, on their computers, and less and less time with service users (Garrett, 2004a, 2009; Munro, 2004; Webb, 2006; Parton, 2008; Broadhurst et al., 2010a, 2010b). The outcome is what Walker (2004, p. 162) calls 'the subtle yet fundamental shift from the term caseworker to case-manager', except that, with the impact of computerization, it can no longer be deemed so 'subtle'. A focus on the implications of the changing nature of organizations is legitimate because what goes on there is indeed crucial to effective social work and child protection. But to remain rooted in the office means leaving out any sustained attention to the core components of child protection work and what needs to be done, on our terms, to make it as intimate and effective as possible.

The result of this organizational focus is a dominant view of child protection as static and immobile, with the sedentary social worker glued to their desk – and computer – deeply frustrated and unhappy about how the demands of bureaucracy and managers restrict opportunities to spend more time with children and families. We need to go further and consider how the (scarce) time that social workers do have should be used when they are face to face with children and their carers. It does not take long to walk across a living room to directly engage with a child, get a tissue out and wipe some chocolate off their face. But why is this not done, and is it their role and ethically sound practice by a social worker to do it? Suppose social workers and other professionals had all the time they could ever need to spend with children and families, how would and should they best use it? This book seeks to open up a debate and provide some answers to these kinds of questions. For it is impossible for an effective child protection response not to involve human contact and direct relating with children and families. We therefore need to place at the centre of analysis what happens when social workers leave their desks and go on the move to be face to face with children, which invariably means entering the private lives and spaces, the homes, of service users.

How the space where the child lives is viewed, whether or not social workers move around, is central to investigating child maltreatment and keeping children safe. In cases of suspected neglect, the state of the 'home conditions' is fundamental to the assessment of child wellbeing and parenting capacity. I know from my experience as a NSPCC social worker in the 1980s and from my research into the history of child protection that, traditionally, child protection workers used to routinely inspect the entire home where children lived. As well as living rooms, kitchen cupboards would be gazed into, cookers checked out, and bedrooms and the children's sleeping conditions examined. Classic signs of extreme cases were discoveries that children were sleeping on mattresses that had become rotten from bed-wetting, with little or no bedding. Even when the concern was not neglect but other forms of abuse and where there was evidence of quite clean and orderly sitting rooms and kitchens, the determined worker was not supposed to put off investigating the sleeping conditions. There was a belief that it was in bedrooms that the 'truth' of the family's inner life and child welfare were to be found and it often proved to be painfully true. The archives of the NSPCC (where I have spent many years doing research) are replete with photographs of such neglectful conditions, and in the 1950s and 60s, some of these were used in publications to inform and no doubt shock the public about the hidden realities of child cruelty (Allen and Morton, 1961). In my own experience as a social worker, some of the worst conditions I found children living and sleeping in were in homes where the downstairs was okay.

It is striking how little is known about such vital home visiting practices today. My research, based on an approach of shadowing social workers and observing how they actually perform child protection work, from which this book partly draws, suggests that getting into the house is sometimes difficult and that some social workers do insist on looking around the home and seeing children on their own and find these to be challenging and often uncomfortable things to have to do. It takes a clear intellectual understanding of the child protection role, the importance of good authority, and great courage, skill and resilience to go through with what is required to protect children. This book shows how even the most effective workers are sometimes at risk of avoiding carrying out difficult tasks that are essential to ensure children are safe, and examines why such avoidance occurs and how it can be recognized and prevented. As Turnell and Edwards (1999) observe, having to knock on a door and tell a complete stranger that they are under suspicion of maltreating their children is deeply personally and professionally challenging for even the most experienced workers.

The book also addresses other areas that contemporary scandals and research have shown knowledge to be lacking, such as working with fathers/father figures. In the Baby Peter case, for instance, the social workers made little effort to inquire into or engage with the 'stepfather' and the other male lodger who we now know lived there and brutally assaulted the child. I have conducted a number of studies into social care work with men and fathers from which I draw here. Approaches to working with mothers and children have also been the subject of my research and I will draw on some of what I learned about that. This is not, however, a book that seeks to report on a particular research study or findings, but a text about the theory and practice of child protection, which draws on my research conducted over the past 20 years and case studies, as well as other sources of knowledge. It is not a book about child protection in any particular country and my references to policy in particular places are limited. This is not because policy and the contexts of different countries are not important. Chapter 2 in particular shows that they are. Cultural diversity and social class as well as gender and ethnic differences will be considered in the context of the sensitivities involved in engaging with children and families in their homes and other spaces. But far too often the literature on social work is dictated by what the legislation and policy says. It is as if policy *is* the practice. My focus is on practice, on what happens when professionals attempt to protect children and the nature of intimate child protection practice wherever in the western world it goes on. A home visit is a home visit wherever that home is.

Towards intimate child protection practice

The core theoretical argument of the book is that understanding how effective child protection practice is carried out requires a deep analysis of how it is experienced through movement, the body and the emotions. The notion of 'performance' seeks to capture the full range of movements, talk, management of emotions and interactions that are played out during child protection interventions. In elaborating on performing child protection, the book draws on concepts and research about childhood, gender, power, social work and the state and three theoretical strands in particular.

First, because the book focuses on what happens when professionals are face to face with children and families, it is informed by theories that attempt to deepen understandings of 'relational' work. The analysis draws on the perspective of 'relationship-based practice' and ways of thinking about the significance of the emotions in social work (Froggett, 2002; Sudbery, 2002; Trevithick, 2003; Bower, 2005a, Cooper and Lousada, 2005; Ruch, 2007a, 2007b; Howe, 2008). Relationship-based practice seeks to reach a deep understanding of the complexity of human beings, the uniqueness of the person, the problems at hand and what is happening in this case/encounter. It is a 'psychosocial' approach, which focuses on the interaction between the external factors that influence people's life chances and the social conditions they live in and their internal emotional worlds and capacities to be loving, safe, caring individuals (Schofield, 1998; Lefevre, 2010). The 'relational' approach taken here attempts to reach an integrated understanding of individual and structural factors as they interact with each other. This is not a naive approach that ignores power and inequalities but one that explores these 'structural' factors as they are apparent and experienced in and through relationships. It is about the politics of emancipation as expressed in the life of individual service users and families and those who work with them, what I have elsewhere called 'life politics' (Ferguson, 2001, 2009a). The focus of analysis is on the nature of helping relationships as 'the medium through which the practitioner can engage with the complexity of an individual's internal and external worlds and intervene' (Ruch, 2005, p. 113).

A related concept is 'reflective practice'. The aim is to provide knowledge and understanding that can help with critical reflection on the content of the work, so that practitioners can better understand what is going on between them and service users and other professionals, and become aware of emotionally charged experiences and how their values and knowledge base influence their work. The relational approach not only seeks to increase understandings of service users and helping relationships but to provide ways for professionals to have deeper relationships with *themselves* and their own experience. This can be understood in terms of two kinds of reflection: reflection *in* action, which needs to occur when workers are doing the work, for example in the home on the visit, checking how they are feeling and its impact on what needs to done next; and reflection *on* action, which is about looking back over what has just been done, getting support from colleagues and in supervision to critically review how an encounter went and the direction that relationships and cases are taking (Schön, 1983). This enables the book to examine the complex conscious and unconscious processes that go on between workers and service users, which both constrain and enable intimate connections and effective child protection. For instance, the psychodynamic concept of 'containment' (Bion, 1962) will be used to reach a deeper understanding of how social workers work therapeutically with children and families and to outline a model of supervision and staff support and development through which practitioners can be supported to use their minds and bodies to move more and better in performing child protection to the benefit of children, other service users and themselves.

A second strand of theory the book draws on is the new interest in the social sciences in movement, which has come to be known as the study of 'mobilities' (Sheller and Urry, 2006; Creswell, 2006; Urry, 2007; Adey, 2009). Movement has been ignored in the social work literature, as it has been in the social sciences generally (Ferguson, 2008). For sociologist John Urry (2007, p. 43), the study of mobility refers to a 'broad project of establishing a "movement-driven" social science in which movement, potential movement and blocked movement' are understood as central to people's experiences of relationships and everyday life. Utilizing this approach, I argue that movement, potential movement and blocked movement are the very stuff of child protection practice and relate to fundamental issues such as whether professionals move towards children to properly see, touch, hear and walk with them to ensure that they are fully engaged with, here and now, on this home visit, or in this clinic or hospital ward, and the harm to them uncovered. Social work always involves *potential* movement, as professionals need to stay still during encounters, such as when interviewing a child or parent, and be prepared to move around to see the child and the home. However, practitioners are not always mobile when they should be. Drawing on such theory helps the book to show how a key dimension to the risks of children not being protected arises from the ways in which movement is blocked and fails to occur. This can happen on the street, in the hospital ward, and in the service user's home.

Movement (and non-movement) in child protection are linked to the worker's emotions, bodily awareness and lived experience of practice. The requirement to move, to walk up the garden path, knock on the door, enter the home, be face to face with children and their carers and to have to use authority in seeking to check on the child's wellbeing brings up many feelings. In grounding the everyday actions of practice in issues to do with movement, I want to try and capture the adventures and atmospheres of social work and child protection. How social work practice is generally written and talked about lacks atmosphere, as it largely fails to capture the texture, the feel, the lived experiences of where the work goes on and how this impacts on perception and what does (and does not) get done. Urry (2007, p. 73) defines 'atmosphere' as being 'in the relationship of people and objects. It is something sensed often through movement and experienced in a tactile kind of way.' This usefully helps us to focus on how, in having to move to meet their objectives, social workers must engage in highly physical ways with objects such as the street, the service user's home, and children's bodies. This perspective enables us to see afresh and analyse in new ways how the movement of people's bodies, cars, information and activities such as walking and driving are central to child protection practice.

The third strand of social theory informing the book concerns the place of objects and things, or what is called 'material culture', in everyday life. A rich and fascinating set of studies and ideas are available about the place of things such as cars, mobile phones, the internet, buildings and the homes in which we live and the possessions we surround ourselves with (Miller, 2008). Miller (2010), for instance, argues that we need to think about houses as things that are not merely shaped by us in terms of how we decorate and inhabit them. Homes, he argues, shape us and impact on how we live and act. While he does not refer to social work or professional home visiting, I will try to show how such ideas can help us gain new understandings of the meanings that surround homes, what matters to the people who live in them and what happens when professionals like child protection practitioners step into them, and try to make sense of what is going on in them and move around in them. As Miller (2001a, p. 1) argues, 'most of what matters to people is happening behind the closed doors of the private sphere'. I believe this to be as true of child protection practice as it is of people's everyday lives and we are fortunate to now be able to draw on a range of work that provides new ways to make what goes on in private publicly understandable. The creative use of objects plays a vital and undertheorized role in child protection, although the computer is probably the main exception to this. Turnell and Essex (2006) argue for the use in child safety plans of a 'family safety object', which is placed in an agreed place in the house on the understanding that the child is the only one allowed to move it, and that doing so is a way for the child to communicate that they are worried about something. Professionals, non-abusing relatives and other 'safety people' in the child's safety network keep an eye on the safety object and are alerted to concern if they find that it has been moved. Turnell and Essex (2006) give a wonderful example of a boy who chose a rubber fish as his safety object which was put on top of the fridge. The book seeks to develop such insights into the role of objects by addressing the meanings of homes, different rooms, possessions, cars and mobile phones in child protection.

In sum, analysing practice through relationship-based practice, relational theory, a life politics perspective, and the sociology of movement and material culture enables the book to provide new ways of understanding the lived experience of doing social work and child protection as it needs to be done, while 'on the move'. It tries to illuminate and inform the challenges, hazards, adventures, achievements and joys of moving into and through other people's homes and other public spaces and offices to access children and work with their parents and carers, which constitutes the core experience of social work and intimate child protection practice.

The structure and scope of the book

The social work process in child protection involves a number of stages:

- suspicion of child abuse and referral to social work

- investigation/assessment by social work, in conjunction with information gathering and, in some instances, joint working with other agencies

- planning and formal interagency work, including case conferences

- longer term therapeutic and support work with children and families.

The book deals with key aspects of child protection at all these stages. It does so in part in chronological fashion and the earlier chapters are generally more concerned with investigation/assessment and the later chapters give more attention to longer term protection, therapeutic and support work. The reason why a straight chronological approach is not followed is because a thematic approach is also adopted where key issues are discussed as they relate to each stage of the child protection process. Thus the early chapters on home visiting and relating to children cover longer term as well as initial assessment work. The later chapters on working with children and parents are concerned with initial engagement and relationship building, as well as how to intervene over the longer term to develop parenting and achieve child safety. The chapters on working in other spaces like the car, hospitals and offices cover all stages of the child protection process.

The book tries to deepen understandings of the nature and flows of child protection work by breaking down what social workers typically do into visible actions performed in specific contexts and domains of practice: organizations (social work offices, hospitals), journeys (by car, on foot), and the service user's home. Chapters 1 and 2 provide a historical analysis of the origins and development of child protection policy and practices (such as home visiting) from its 19th-century beginnings to the present. Chapter 3 deals with the journeys on foot and by transport that are necessary to get to see the child, including the practice that goes on at doorsteps in literally trying to get into a home. Chapters 4 and 5 cover what goes on during home visits and the movements and actions that are needed if children's safety is to be ensured. Chapter 9 addresses the nature of effective child protection practice in places such as hospitals and social work offices. Organizational matters are also addressed in Chapter 13, which deals with multi-agency working, and Chapter 14 with respect to the role of supervision and organizational support in effective child protection. The issues raised in these chapters are further developed by focusing on work with different family members: Chapters 6, 7 and 8 are devoted to aspects of working with children; Chapters 10 and 11 focus on work with mothers and fathers, while Chapter 12 is concerned with using good authority, working with resistance and involuntary service users. While the domains of organizations, journeys and homes and working with children and parents at different stages of the child protection process are analysed separately, in practice everything is interdependent and connected and some chapters address these cross-cutting themes. Chapters 8 and 14 use the car to draw out the nature of therapeutic approaches and spaces in working with children and in providing support for workers, while Chapters 13 and 14 are thematically linked by a concern with deepening understanding of relationship-based practice in the context of multi-agency working and the creation of genuinely nurturing working environments for child protection workers. Chapter 15 brings together the key themes and arguments of the book by summarizing the actions, movements, forms of talk, the sensory and emotional experiences and levels of support for practitioners that must be achieved in ensuring intimate child protection is practised, as it should be.

1
Knocking on the door of history

I asked the little girl if she went on all right. She said, 'yes, me dada takes me to the "Grand" and to the "pictures" and "Hipperdrome" but he will not buy me any more clothes and boots and I don't like sleeping with him because he hurts me in bed . . . He used to do it to my sister but she went away and then he started to do it to me. He did it on Monday night and 3 times last week . . . It makes me feel bad too and gives me stomach ache. I do not cry much I am too much out of breathe and he says if I tell anyone he will hit me and not take me to the "Grand". I have only told my sister and she said she would tell you. Did she send you?' I told her yes; and she was a good girl to tell me about it.

(from a 1909 child protection case)

These words were spoken by an 11-year-old girl to a child protection social worker in England in 1909. The fact that she was being sexually abused by her father, as well as neglected, serves to show that the problem of child abuse has a long history. What was new at this time was the social work practice that brought this abuse in the family home to light. This is a book about those child protection practices. To begin to outline what these practices involve and to evaluate how child protection can most effectively be done, we need to go back and consider how it began and ask: Why is child protection practice done in the ways that it is? Why, for example, is the home visit so central to its methods? This chapter provides a historical analysis of the emergence of child protection practices, especially the home visit. It shows that the concerns arising from recent high-profile cases are nothing new but have been around for as long as there has been a modern child protection practice. The chapter uses historical case studies to show how, from the outset, gaining access to homes, moving around homes, inspecting them and the children have been crucial practices in protecting children, but we have lost touch with their importance and no longer have a language to adequately describe and understand them. The chapter begins the process that is central to this book of putting us back in touch with this core experience and the practices involved, providing a new set of concepts through which to account for and develop intimate child protection practice.

The beginnings of child protection practice

I will begin by going back 100 years and considering a case of child neglect from 1909, involving the NSPCC, which had been in existence since 1889. It was among hundreds I examined in my historical research. The neglect case involved four children aged 13, 10, 3 and 1, and it was reported by a county court bailiff. The inspector immediately visited the family home and in his case record he wrote:

> The woman and two youngest children were at home, but for more than twenty minutes she refused to open the door, she simply checked me through the window. But, when she did open it and I went inside the hot musty and dirty stench drove me out again and I had to have the back door open too. The woman and two children were as black as tinkers.

Just as it had been since the practice began in 1889, every corner of the house, piece of furniture and artefact possessed by the family are described on the case record:

> The back kitchen windows [were] broken and filled up with sacking and paper in a filthy state. But, the pantry was the gem of the lot, the shelves were so thick with dirt and grease you could peel them off. Then to mend matters, she had swept the kitchen and other place up and instead of taking it up, she simply shut it up in the pantry on the floor. It must have gone on for some time by the look of the heap.

> Up the stairs all thick with dirt and dust. The bedrooms were really shocking. The front room contained broken furniture, bedstead and bedding. The window was broken and then stuffed up with paper. The place could never have been swept of [sic] months perhaps years. The bedding was wet and rotten and falling to pieces and small portions littered the room. The covering consisted of dirty cast-off clothing.

And so it goes on. What is striking is the worker's expression of disgust, horror and incredulity about how people lived and how personal it was and laced with fears – not only for the children, but for workers themselves. What they feared was contamination. As the inspector wrote:

> When I got home I had caught 26 fleas. I had to have a bath and change all clothing. I even had a flea in my hair. I did not see any other class of vermin on the children.

The contamination of the worker is directly connected by him to the contaminating state of the children. Other workers in the case were similarly appalled. The county court bailiff made a statement, saying he had known the family for about three years: 'The smell of the house is so disgusting that I am compelled to smoke to keep the taste out of my mouth.'

This is a classic modern experience in child protection in the way it involves practices that are fundamentally focused on trying to gain access, having to negotiate on doorsteps, deal with resistant and often 'cheeky' and sometimes hostile and violent clients. It is classic too in the mobility involved, moving from the office, to the doorstep, across the threshold and into the home, and moving within people's intimate spaces, including their bedrooms and kitchens, into the most private corners of their lives and selves. This is an early example of what I call 'intimate child protection practice'. It is a deeply bodily experience in which all the senses – sight, smell, touch, hearing – are used and the worker has to manage the impact of the practice on themselves, their own fears and anxieties for their safety, their bodily integrity, and of being contaminated. The abused children were not simply approached as innocent subjects in need of protection but also as objects of fear and disgust because of the perception that they had the power to contaminate. Touch in child protection was deeply problematic, to an extent that there was always a risk of an avoidance of touch, a detachment from the interests of children and a lack of empathy for parents. Yet in this era and well into the late 20th century, workers ploughed on, insisting on going into the depths of people's homes to reach and protect children. This is not to idealize what these early child protection workers did. There was often a coarseness to their approach, a lack of sensitivity and the work was often, by today's standards, crudely racist and sexist. But what is striking is how prepared they were to go into the depths of people's private spaces to 'inspect' and protect children. While developments into the 21st century have seen the emergence of increased awareness of people's rights and the need to avoid being oppressive to them and of a more sensitive and inclusive practice, it has been at the expense of a loss of certainty about the need to go into the depths of people's intimate lives and spaces to protect children.

To fully understand the nature of child protection practice today, we need descriptions and analyses of it that are so vivid you can smell and taste the worker's experience. Where, I want to ask, has the smell of practice gone today? There have been changes over the past 100 years, but at a deep, even primitive level, the smell and bodily experience involved in visiting homes and trying to gain access to children is still there. What has disappeared is our ability to acknowledge it, evoke it and understand it. Our understandings of child protection have been deodorized. The life and soul of the practice, the intimate experience that is at its heart, have been written out of our understandings of what is involved in protecting children.

Home visiting becomes the key method

The most appropriate way to begin this inquiry into how the actual practices of child protection are carried out by living, breathing professional human beings is to accompany social workers from the moment they first had to take to the streets in order to reach their service users.

Child protection practice began in the USA in the 1870s and spread to other parts of the western world such as Australasia and Europe in the 1880s. The NSPCC was founded in 1884 as the London Society for the Prevention of Cruelty to Children (London SPCC). After five years of campaigning by the London SPCC, in 1889 the first ever Prevention of Cruelty to Children Act was passed onto the statute book, giving SPCC social workers, who were known as 'inspectors', new powers to investigate suspected cruelty to children and bring suspected cruel parents before the courts. Because it had so many branches in the UK and Ireland, the London SPCC was renamed the National Society for the Prevention of Cruelty to Children (NSPCC) in 1889. Prior to the emergence of SPCC social workers, attempts to uncover the abuse of children and change parents were made largely by the police, and mainly in public places. Police officers did visit homes to apprehend possible offenders but no attempts were made to work with parents in the home to try and change them or check on the ongoing safety and welfare of the children beyond the initial bringing of the case to court.

This all changed when a new breed of social workers was invented, charged with the legal powers and responsibility to enter homes to protect children from cruelty. From its beginnings in late 19th-century child protection, social workers have walked into what have been regarded as the most unsavoury and dangerous places in society. The investigative brief of child protection workers meant that they were at the forefront of such techniques, going into the slums to root out child cruelty. How the early social workers did this is exemplified by an NSPCC worker's case record in 1898:

> When patrolling various slums, I discovered the four children of Thomas P...They were all sickly, pale faced and greatly distressed in appearance...I examined them and found their clothing swarming with monster lice, their clothing was also filthy and bloodstained. Their bodies a mass of bites and full of eruptions. The house (two rooms) was foul and filthy with dirt and the only bedding was a shakedown.

Workers took to their task with an alacrity that left households perhaps feeling unduly invaded and that the odds were stacked against them. They tore into communities, as we have seen, literally patrolling slums. In the earliest years when the practice was establishing itself, the number of cases brought to light by inspectors themselves was as high as 26%. In the 1880s and 90s, it was common for social workers to follow and take home children they saw on the street who they suspected were abused and neglected, cases the agency referred to as 'cruelties of the street'.

In the 1890s, a lot of work was done on the streets as well as going into the home. Child cruelty was discovered in the home but offending parents were prosecuted and sent to prison. Prosecution rates were as high as 18% of all cases in the 1890s. But by the 1900s, the core approach to practice had changed, and seeing children and supervising families in their homes was regarded as the key way to create change and protect children. By 1901, the prosecution rate had dropped to 15% of cases and was as low as 3% by 1906, stabilizing at even lower levels thereafter, so the vast majority of parents now remained in the home to be worked with. At the same time, the numbers of home visits that inspectors made increased dramatically. In the 1890s, a typical inspector made an average of three home visits per case, and by 1914, the supervision rate had risen to five per case (Ferguson, 2004). 'Supervisions' focused on the family home had become the key way in which social work and child protection were performed. By the early 1900s, the category of 'cruelties of the street' had disappeared from agency records, and the only basis on which investigations could occur was in response to referrals from third parties, with the wellbeing of children investigated in their homes.

The emergence and intensification of home visiting was a key part of a new philosophy of practice implemented by social work, representing a shift in the meanings and ideas of what social intervention was trying to achieve. The imprisonment of parents in the first years of SPCC practice was done within an approach that sought to exclude offenders from society. In the 19th century, the prison was placed on the edge of society and the aims of punishment were 'deterrence', 'retribution' and 'moral reform' (Garland, 1985). The sentences meted out to child cruelty offenders were given a high profile in local newspapers, in part to induce fear and deter others from such criminal behaviour. The retributive aim was for offenders to suffer for their crimes through the deprivation of liberty and physical endurance of hard labour. This, in turn, had a moral aspect to it, as offenders were expected to reflect on, amend and repent their wrongs. From the 1900s, the prison ceased to be the central institution and main sanction and became just one institution among many in an extended network of intervention practices, most of which centred on the home. The probation service and health visiting began around this time, for instance, and social work itself was a key expression of these changes. The concept of 'casework' was born here. It was the principle of moral reformation that defined the core goal of these new social practices. The goals of deterrence and retribution remained but instead of the negative conformity produced by fear, practices like social work were 'henceforth to place their emphasis upon the positive incentives of "hope", with its possibilities of moral regeneration' (Garland, 1985, p. 30). Instead of being cast away in prisons, cruel parents were now approached as social deviants who could be reformed according to the standards of good parenting laid down by society and the state. The aim of child protection social work was to 'enforce parental responsibility', not relieve it (Ferguson, 2004). 'Cruel' parents began to be worked with and their homes and lives investigated in intimate ways in the first manifestations of what, in later decades, would become therapeutically oriented practice.

Inside the home: the child and the house

The significance of home visiting to the aims of child protection was made clear in agency guidance from the outset. In 1904, with regard to 'the child and the house', the NSPCC's practitioner manual (NSPCC, 1904, pp. 7–8) advised:

> As to the necessary access to the house where the ill-used child dwells, this too, like getting access to the child, will depend on determination and tact. No difficulty will be too great where these exist. Mere officialism or bounce will unlock no door either of house or heart. Go with a love for little children; keep yourself well in with it, and practice all the arts of a pure and high intention. Courtesy in a man with authority and power behind him has a wonderful effect. You may destroy the need for a prose-cution by showing to the accused the nobleness of your calling. Two can generally play at the game of bounce, and the owner of the house plays it with all the odds on his side, therefore it is not one in which you are likely to win.
>
> Where a house cannot be got into by consent, the art of seeing through a brick-wall must be cultivated. What a child is suffering in a house may be seen by intenseness of anxiety in a man of trained common sense. He will have eyes in his understanding.

Access to the house and to the abused child was seen as essential and, in many respects, one and the same thing. Playing at 'bounce', or what we today would call 'arrogance' or 'oppressive practice', was a particular cause for concern as it ran contrary to the important prin-ciple of using authority and imposing oneself on clients in a manner that was fair and professional: 'All appearance of fuss and meddle-someness, and, above all, bounce, must be avoided' (NSPCC 1904, p. 47). Using such powers of persuasion was crucial because workers had no legal right to enter a home: 'Entrance to a house, except by the invitation or consent of the occupier, is not lawful, and must not be made without the authority of a warrant' (NSPCC, 1910, p. 55). Being good at child protection depended on the exercise of skill, determi-nation and tact. X-ray eyes to assist with seeing through walls where entry to the home was not allowed also helped, but, as today, proved elusive!

Analysis of the earliest child protection case records shows that the implication of this agency rule that, in practice, home visiting often proved difficult was accurate – not in all cases, but in significant num-bers. This was due to how hard it was to gain the consent of many family members to enter houses, and what happened to workers once in there. A striking feature of the accounts of the workers who made these first child protection home visits is their vividness. In June 1898, an inspector visited a home to inquire into a complaint of child physical abuse by a father. He had known the case since 1891 and the father had had enough of him calling. Visiting at 9.30am:

> I asked to see the beds, but [father] refused to allow me. He again became very abusive and threatened violence. I left the house and again visited at 10.15a.m. and was followed by Police Sgt M… Whilst the Sgt and I was there [the father] behaved as though he was mad – he appeared to be suffering with drink. I saw the sleeping apartment which is fearfully filthy and stinking with accumulated dirt.

The worker goes on to explain what he found on reaching his objective:

> I saw 4 children lying on a mattress and a broken flock bed. There was a dirty quilt for covering. I lifted up the quilt which exposed the children. They were absolutely naked. They had, it is true, fragments of undershirts, but these were so torn and worn, they would not reach a third down the body if they were pulled.
>
> I searched the house for food but could not find a particle.

This shows again how the most intimate features of children's and family's lives were central to the model of child protection practice that was taking shape at this time: the need, which led to a demand, to see where they slept and what they wore or did not wear in bed; and the search around the home for food to see what there was for the children to eat. The ethical issues that arise from such intimate practice are clearly evident in the worker's discovery of the children's 'nakedness', which seemed to cause acute embarrassment, partly because of how exposure of flesh and naked bodies was frowned upon in this Victorian era, but also because, like today, social work practitioners experienced uncertainty about how much of children's bodies it was permissible for them to see and touch as part of best practice.

It shows too how tricky home visiting was because children, mothers and fathers were far from passive in all this. The ways in which the attentions and demands of social workers were resisted is exemplified by this father who tried to stop professionals from trampling all over his home and family. It would be easy to feel sympathy for this impoverished working-class family apparently being walked over by state-empowered officials. There are certainly issues of social class and power that need to be considered here. Inspectors policed the slums, which is where abuse was expected to be found. Families were invariably poor and had either precarious or no housing, and were often mobile. As an inspector said of one family in 1898, they had 'lived . . . in different parts of the town, their selections always being the most degraded localities'. Meanwhile, the philanthropists who supported child protection organizations were from the privileged classes and held respectable local positions, for example as Justices of the Peace. There is a whole tradition of writing in social work and child protection which argues that a crucial aim of such practices was to control the poor (Parton, 1985) and that this remains the case today (Garrett, 2009).

It would be much too simplistic, however, to reduce these issues of power to a 'social control' perspective, which regards the poor as simply being oppressed by social workers. Carolyn Taylor (2008) shows the importance of having a nuanced approach to understanding how power and authority have been used in the past. In addition to social class, it is crucial to take account of factors such as age and gender differences. In the last cited case, it was one of the children who called the inspector in to investigate an alleged assault by this father on their younger sibling, meaning that the worker was there at the request of one of the children. The father eventually admitted assaulting the child with his fist and inflicting a black eye, for which he served five months in prison with hard labour. This shows how an important element of child protection in some cases was how workers were drawn into the strategies devised by those family members who had least social power to resist domination by other, more powerful family members.

It was in the second half of the 19th century that the saying was coined 'An Englishman's home is his castle'. A key achievement of these first child protection workers was to consistently work against that belief by regarding the homes within which children lived as being their space too, which professionals had a right to inspect to ensure that it was safe and nurturing for them. It was in so doing that they had begun to shape what child protection practice was all about. Child protection workers were powerfully symbolic figures. All NSPCC officers were men and wore uniforms. The organization particularly liked to recruit men who had served in the armed services with a proven ability to respect and carry out orders (Behlmer, 1982). The uniform symbolizes the 'disciplined' character of these men, which, as Giddens (1985) shows, has two aspects to it. Within welfare/punishment organizational settings, the uniform has the same implications as in the services, helping to strip individuals of those traits that might interfere with patterns of obedience expected by the organization. Second, the uniform is a potent sign to the public of the distinctiveness of its wearer as a specialist source of statutory powers. Thus the uniform embodied the attempts that were made by the organization to strip child protection workers of autonomy and individuality and develop a standardized organizational response to child abuse. Yet at the same time, these workers were expected to be responsible social actors who had the capacity to assess and judge situations on their own merits.

What gives intimate child protection practice a special reality and authenticity is how, in its formative phase, the practitioners themselves seem to have been caught up in the enthusiasm for it. It shows workers not only keeping up with agency rules and the pace of reform but out-pacing their managers. They take initiatives, develop ideas and begin to conceive of new and varied ways to help children and seek to get parents to reconstruct their lives. This seems to have enabled them to find meaning and excitement in work that was always contentious and invariably emotionally gruelling.

The most painful and challenging dimension of the practice was how it routinely brought workers face to face with the deaths of children. In 1898, an inspector in the north of England received a referral that a child was being neglected. Of his visit to the family, he wrote this in his case record:

> With the man's permission we went upstairs and found all the family have to sleep on one bed which was in a wretched dirty state...back upstairs room absolutely empty.
>
> In a cradle laid a baby Ralph fourteen months old – since dead – in a very ill condition suffering the wife said from pneumonia. The child's face was bedaubed with mucous and dirt, whilst the back door was open exposing the child to a draft. The morning was particularly cold...A few days later the child died.

The notion that professionals have failed at risk children when they die is, historically, quite recent. For much of the 20th century, a child's death was a routine experience for child protection workers. From the beginnings of child protection in 1889 through to 1914 in the UK and Ireland, a staggering 13,613 children died in child protection cases investigated by the NSPCC. Not all these children had, however, been killed by their parents. The figure reflects how such work intersected with the broader social problems of poverty and infant mortality. In many

NSPCC cases, children (like Ralph above) were probably dying anyway from a variety of causes and became caught up in the new powers and classifications of child protection. A key dynamic here was a desire to spread child protection practices across the country to cover entire geographical boundaries. It took 20 years for the NSPCC to provide a service that covered all its territory with practitioners. The existence of child death was actually viewed as a sign that child protection was working *well* because it meant that increasing numbers of vulnerable children were being reached by professionals. The NSPCC even used to publish statistics on these deaths to show how successfully it was reaching children and the value of its work: 'that it is certain that the Society is telling on the life of children' (NSPCC, 1897, p. 38). Deaths were always regretted, but were handled without self-recrimination, while the public tolerated them and professional careers were never threatened because of them. It is hard to believe this today, given the intense criticism of workers and agencies that occurs when children die. Yet right through to the middle of the 20th century, there was no shame for workers involved in cases where children died, when they had done their best to protect children (Ferguson, 2004). I will analyse how and why this changed in the next chapter.

Child protection on the move

In real terms, the developments in child protection meant that the very core of social work was now constituted by home visits and what practitioners were able to achieve through them, while being *mobile*. A modern form of social work and child protection practice was put in place through these developments, which, far from the solidity and all-seeing gaze implied by concepts of social control and surveillance, was essentially 'liquid' in nature (Ferguson, 2008). From early in the 20th century, social work and child protection were on the move. What was seen of service users in their day-to-day lives was achieved by professionals performing home visits for relatively brief periods or by service users visiting social work offices. Child protection had come to rely on getting to know children's experiences through being transient and gaining snapshots of their lives. What has been presented in this chapter should not be regarded as simply a historical account of things that happened 'back then'. We have been analysing how core aspects of child protection practice as it is performed today came into being.

The chapter has shown how child protection practice came to take some of the intimate forms that it does. It has opened up many issues that will be further explored throughout the book, including the problems of intimate contact with (dirty) homes and children and contamination fears and the struggles to gain access to children and move within the home to reach them that have been evident since the practice began. From early on, child protection work had become a professional life on the run as workers followed (and even chased) families around their various addresses. Most often, these struggles were played out on doorsteps and in homes as workers demanded to know what was going on in the private sphere. A whole new professional experience had been opened up by these first generations of child protection workers. They had torn down the walls of privacy and silences that surrounded the Victorian family, stepped into the holes they had made and so were key actors in constituting a whole new social practice of child protection. In doing so, they helped to make real the misery of poverty and human suffering that was once a mystery. They created a social practice that would enable practitioners to search around people's houses and enter their most intimate spaces and desires. Prior to the beginnings of child protection in the 1870s and 80s, the taking of children from their beds was unthinkable. While the nature of their own subjective experience would always be difficult to assess, these practitioners were no mere organizational dupes who simply followed agency rules, but social actors actively constructing the foundations of modern forms of knowledge and a professional culture of child protection practice that would endure for most of the 20th century. They seemed inspired to do this because the agencies for which they worked had instilled in them some vision of the work as a whole and its value not only to children's lives but also to the communities of which it was a part. Moreover, they were deeply respected and had permission from society to practise in this intimate way. But these workers did not do this in any absolute or final sense. They created the conditions that have made possible the continuance of these kinds of encounters and struggles, as practitioners have been following in their footsteps and entering the homes of children and families ever since.

2
Child abuse and the development of child protection policy and practice

Casework is on the move!
(Hollis, 1964, p. 3)

Francis Hollis was quite right. At the time she wrote this in her classic *Casework: A Psychosocial Therapy*, social work practice was becoming ever more dynamic in its responses to problems like child abuse. Indeed, it was in the early 1960s that significant changes in the conceptions of the problem of 'child abuse' began to occur. This chapter brings the analysis of the development of child protection practice and policy into the present. I will characterize a core shift in policy and practice that has occurred in recent decades in terms of a move from an approach based on 'inspection' to a welfare-oriented one based on 'partnership'. This has had mixed implications, on one level increasing the sensitivity with which children and their carers are worked with, on the other leading to greater uncertainty about the legitimacy of authoritative child protection and a lack of understanding of what intimate practice has to involve.

The disappearance of child death in child protection cases

Up to the 1970s, a distinct practice of child protection based on 'inspection' was in evidence, led by the Societies for the Prevention of Cruelty to Children. Chapter 1 set out the form inspection took and conveyed something of what the experience was like for workers, as they performed child protection by stepping into people's homes for the first time. While there was continuity in the practice right through to the 1970s, what did change was the places that were inspected. By 1939, in a case of neglect of two children aged 15 and 12 that was referred by the police, the NSPCC inspector notes in the case record that: 'The home consisted of five rooms in all. There are three bedrooms, kitchen and back kitchen [the bathroom]. It is a council type of house.' With the emergence of social housing, as the 20th century developed, the challenges of child protection practice expanded as the homes of service users generally became larger. There were more rooms for professionals to inspect and more spaces within which families could hide and have secrets.

Up until the 1940s, child protection workers could still expect to have, on average, one child death on their caseload every year. Chapter 1 showed that, in the early period of practice, the deaths of children in child protection cases were commonplace and information about them was routinely made public. Public disclosure of deaths by child protection agencies continued through to the 1930s. By now, however, fewer child protection cases were ending in death. In 1936, the total number of children who died in NSPCC cases was 277. This compared with 1,226 in 1914 (NSPCC, 1936).

Deaths in casework declined for several reasons. Children were becoming generally healthier due to better diet, improved housing conditions, and child welfare services. Deaths in child protection casework declined at the same levels as infant mortality rates. Whereas up to 1914, child protection workers came across many children who were dying of conditions that were linked to diseases, poor housing, nutrition and generally poor public health provision, in the 1930s, child protection had come to surround children who were, by and large, now living anyway. Child deaths also declined due to advances in science and technology, which brought about more effective child protection interventions. Building on the innovation brought about by the bicycle, the motorcycle was in general use in child protection by the 1930s and the car by the 1950s. Changes in the ability to move at speed contributed to a perception that as children could now be reached physically, so it became thinkable that they could be seen more quickly. These developments helped to create the ideal that by acting quickly, professionals not only could but should be able to protect children in time (Ferguson, 2004).

A key influence in these developments was the transformation that occurred in the meaning of childhood and the value placed on children.

Zelizer (1985) shows how the wage-earning child of the 19th-century working classes was a 'non-child', in the sense that they were employed like adults from a relatively young age. The introduction of legislation outlawing child labour and introducing compulsory schooling transformed this 'non-child' into the school-going child who was economically worthless. By the 1930s, children had gained a new sentimental value; while they were now economically 'useless', they were emotionally 'priceless'. The foundations of the characteristics of 'the child' today were put in place – parental dependence, economic and sexual inactivity, and absence of legal and political rights. In the process, 'the death of all children – rich and poor – emerged as an intolerable social loss' and was 'transformed into a public campaign for the preservation of child life' (Zelizer, 1985, p. 27). Avoidable child death became publicly unacceptable and helped constitute the belief that children should be prevented from dying through child protection interventions. This also fed into how information about the deaths that did occur began at this time to be hidden.

By the late 1930s, information about deaths in child protection cases ceased to be made public and had disappeared from view. This did not happen because the problem was 'solved', but because disclosure of such failures to protect children threatened the authority, optimism and trustworthiness of the child protection system. Child protection experts had come to have a powerful belief in the science of their work and the capacity of social work intervention to promote child safety and they were keen to emphasize its successes. On the rare occasions when 'failures' to protect children were publicly disclosed prior to the 1970s, this was not seen as a failure of science but rather of there not being enough scientific knowledge and capability to be able to understand all the risks. The rare cases in which errors were publicly disclosed served, in fact, to expand the influence of childcare experts within the welfare state. This can be seen by the response to the tragic case of Denis O'Neill in the mid-1940s, whose death at the hands of his foster parents had a profound impact on postwar legislation and the development of UK childcare services (Monckton, 1945; Packman, 1981). Social work and childcare experts swept aside any doubts the public had by claims of their successes and with promises that they could succeed even more if the public and the state invested in them and provided for the reaching of new understandings that could promote advances from any constraints not yet properly understood. The lack of disclosure of deaths in child protection cases from the 1940s on meant that when professional failures to protect did occur, knowledge about them was hidden away from public view.

Changing conceptions of child abuse

From the late 19th century up to the 1970s, child neglect dominated in definitions of child maltreatment. Annually, up to 90% of cases were defined as neglect. Neglect took the form of the cases already profiled in Chapter 1, unhygienic homes, poorly cared for children, mothers who were regarded as neglectful because they drank alcohol, and men if they did not go out to work and support their families. 'Ill-treatment' was classified as occurring in some 7% of cases annually, while child sexual abuse accounted for less than 1% of cases. This does not mean that child sexual abuse did not go on. We know from the accounts of adult survivors of child sexual abuse that it did and either they never felt able to disclose it because people would not believe it, or they did disclose it and it was dealt with as something else, usually neglect. In my research into the archives of child protection agencies, I have read cases where girls and young women did disclose child sexual abuse, including father–daughter incest, and the case was taken as neglect because there was evidence of that and it was easier to get through the courts. Some who disclosed sexual abuse were not only disbelieved but punished (Jackson, 2000; Ferguson, 2007).

Until the 1960s, the language used in policy, practice and popular culture concerning harm to children was 'child cruelty'. A new awareness of what came to be called 'child abuse' began to emerge in the 1960s through the pioneering work of medical practitioners such as Henry Kempe. A pediatrician, he deliberately coined the emotive phrase the 'battered child syndrome' to draw attention to how children were seriously harmed and killed by their parents (Kempe et al., 1962). His thesis was that serious and fatal child abuse was denied because it was too painful to contemplate that parents seriously harmed and even killed their children, so people would have to be shocked into recognition of the realities of such abuse. He regarded not only laypeople but professionals who come into contact with children as prone to deny abuse and be complacent about it.

In the 1970s, the term 'battered child' was replaced in policy and practice by 'non-accidental injury to children', known as NAI. At the same time, child sexual abuse began to undergo a significant process of discovery on the strength of the activist work of the women's movement and the work of clinicians who helped bring it to light (Finkelhor, 1984; Driver and Droisen, 1989). Emotional abuse was also identified and included in policy and practice guidance at this time. The term 'child abuse' entered child protection in the 1980s as a generic term to cover physical, sexual and emotional abuse and neglect. While recognition of other forms of abuse has increased significantly, neglect remains the most common form of abuse classified by agencies today (Corby, 2005). Conceptions of child maltreatment have expanded further in the 2000s, as policy now recognizes abuses such as the trafficking of children (DCFS, 2010).

While there were continuities with the past, acknowledgement that serious harm is perpetrated against vulnerable children by parents and other carers involved a distinct shift in recognition compared to conceptions of child abuse based primarily around neglect. As I have shown, prior to the 1960s, child protection workers did have a concept of physical ill-treatment of children, but what Kempe and others began to draw attention to was qualitatively different in the new profile of the abusive parent it produced and how it relied upon much more intense scrutiny of the child's body through the use of X-rays, which revealed past healed bone fractures and other signs of non-accidental injuries. The taking of social histories from the abusive parents began to reveal that most if not all had been abused themselves as children. A psychological profile of the abusive parent emerged, which characterized them as having been traumatized in their own childhoods, and consciously and unconsciously repeating the abuse they received in childhood on their children. The influential concept of 'the intergenerational cycle of child abuse' was coined to account for this and the need for intervention to attempt to break the cycle gained recognition.

The tendency in the 1960s, 70s and 80s was to regard child abuse as a largely psychologically caused phenomenon. Many social work academics were critical of this because it failed to give attention to social conditions and the problems of poverty and stress that characterized so many cases of abuse (Pelton, 1978; Parton, 1985). This critique continues today (Garrett, 2009; Lonne et al., 2010). Theoretical models for understanding physical child abuse and neglect have become more sophisticated and today incorporate a range of causal factors. Research has shown that not all abused children grow up to be abusing parents and 'compensatory factors' in the child's life can make a difference, such as having psychotherapy or counselling as a teenager, and/or having a good relationship with a trusted adult, who may be a relative, or a professional such as teacher, social worker, youth worker and so on (Egeland, 2009).

From inspection to partnership in child protection practice

For most of the 20th century, child protection was conducted through the concept and practice of 'inspection'. Not only children but the entirety of the homes they lived in were routinely inspected by NSPCC inspectors. Although, as I have shown, it was intimate in the sense of entering people's most private spaces, the inspection approach was relatively quick and focused on surfaces, classically levels of cleanliness. It was commendably strong on using authority but lacked intimacy in the more modern sense that I will suggest in this book it needs to. It did not seek, for example, to understand the reasons for the presenting problems or try to resolve them through relationship-based approaches. Doctors were brought in to examine children who were unkempt and whose homes appeared dangerously dirty. This corresponded with the period between 1900 and the 1970s when child neglect dominated casework. Inspectors were caseworkers in the sense that they carried cases, which they investigated and supervised, where needed, on a long-term basis and wrote up their case records. But inspection lacked empathy with the struggles of parents who were poor and, in particular, mothers who had huge burdens to carry.

This began to change after the Second World War when the state took over primary responsibility for social work and child welfare. In the UK, this happened through the establishment in 1948 of local authority children's departments. These social workers, known as childcare officers, had a much stronger statutory brief than before to check on the welfare of children to prevent them coming into care and to work closely with them if they did (Packman, 1981). The theories that were drawn upon to understand and shape helping relationships were drawn from approaches such as psychoanalysis and attachment theory, at the core of which was the potential for the worker to help the service user by addressing their emotional experience by having a close therapeutic relationship with them (Stevenson, 1963; Berry, 1972). The NSPCC remained a key child protection agency, but by the early 1970s, the role of the state as the key service provider was further consolidated when children's departments were replaced by unified social services departments. Child welfare was only one of many responsibilities held by the new generic social workers in social services departments, who also dealt with the elderly, disabled and welfare rights. A new type of local authority social worker emerged from this, quite different from the childcare officers or NSPCC inspectors. The latter had ceased wearing uniforms in the late 1960s, which was a highly symbolic reflection of how professionalism and social work were changing in child protection and the shift in the dominant philosophy of child protection from 'inspection' to 'partnership'.

The value base of partnership and empowerment began to be established when the more 'critical' approach to social work began with the 'radical social work' movement in the early 1970s (Bailey and Brake, 1975; for this perspective in social work today, see Ferguson and Woodward, 2009). It argued that social casework and theories such as psychoanalysis reduced all problems to the individual failings of 'clients', and that power, inequality and poverty had a huge influence on people's life chances and in determining their need for social services. At the same time, social work was professionalizing and its training became embedded in the increasingly popular critical social sciences in the expanding university sector, which critiqued power relations in society and the place of service users, professionals and the state within it. Social work, or at least the traditional ways of doing it through social casework, began to be seen by radicals as part of the problem rather than a possible solution to social ills. In a classic political cartoon of the time, two 'slum kids' hold a conversation: 'We've got rats', says one; 'Shit man', says the other, 'we've got social workers' (Pearson, 1975, p. 133). The radical social work movement helped to engineer an inversion of values. Now social workers were characterized as 'social policemen'; it was they, not their 'problem families', who couldn't be trusted.

In the 1980s, with the influence of feminism and the women's movement, gender, sexism and sexuality reached the radical agenda, while racism (Dominelli, 1997), disability rights (Oliver, 1983, 1996) and gay and lesbian rights would soon follow (Brown, 1997; Hicks, 2000). This kind of critical awareness of tackling discrimination has been crucial in enabling social work to try to respond respectfully to the diverse needs of all social groups. Notions of anti-discriminatory practice, anti-oppressive practice and empowerment became part of the mainstream of theory and practice (Thompson, 1993; Dalrymple and Burke, 2006). As a reflection of this, by the 1990s, it was regarded as more appropriate to speak of 'service users', and since the 2000s, the language of 'experts by experience' (Preston-Shoot, 2007) has been preferred by some. The ethical imperative had become one of needing to include service users within the social work community as 'partners' and to work with them in dignified and empowering ways. As will be shown, this desire to collapse hierarchical power relationships sits uncomfortably with the need to use authority in child protection.

At the heart of policy and practice reform and debates about what constitutes effective, ethical child protection practice has been public disclosure of high-profile cases involving the deaths of children, which occurred despite the attentions of social workers and other professionals. In England, the first such case was that of Maria Colwell who died on 7 January 1973 aged seven, at her home in East Sussex. She was one of nine children and she spent the first five years of her life in the foster care of her aunt but was returned to her mother and stepfather Mr Kepple at the age of six years and eight months, being placed on a supervision order to the local authority. However, Maria was beaten to death by her stepfather in January 1973 and was found to weigh only about three-quarters of what could be expected for her age and height. Kepple was convicted of manslaughter and sentenced to eight years' imprisonment. An inquiry into the role of the social services led to the case gaining attention from the national media and the British government.

This began a process that continues to this day, where media, academic and frontline professional interest in such child protection failures is truly international (Stanley and Goddard, 2002). At one and the same time, professionals and organizations were confronted with new knowledge of risks to children and shocking public disclosures, which showed that child protection systems were failing to protect children from serious abuse and death. These were distressing in their own right because of the sheer extent of trauma and violence that had been perpetrated against children, as each scandal revealed a similar pattern of starved, neglected, physically and sometimes sexually violated children who had suffered multiple injuries from the abuse inflicted on them. They were also shocking in the sense that they appeared to be completely new and to reflect a real decline in professional standards. This misguided sense of newness had its roots in the way that knowledge of child death was, as has been shown, hidden since the late 1930s.

Ironically, at a time when further improvements in child protection practice meant that deaths in child protection work became a rare event, managing the risk of system failure rather than celebrating success or learning from good practice became the defining approach. Since the 1970s, the actual experience of dealing with child abuse deaths among practitioners has been rare and, thankfully, the vast majority of professionals never encounter dead children in their work. The scale of public outcry and discussion of the deaths of individual children has increased dramatically at a time when social workers' actual direct experience of death is very limited. The paradox of contemporary risk anxiety about children and child protection is that it has arisen at a time when generally fewer children die in child protection cases and when child protection systems have never been more elaborate and technically developed. This does not mean that they are good enough, only that, in general, they have never been so sophisticated.

This paradox can be explained in part by changes in the source and meaning of risk. Risk in child protection today is different, in the sense that everyone now knows that whatever is done, there can be no guarantees that children will be safe. Anthony Giddens (1994) calls this 'manufactured risk'. The consequence has been a new concern, an obsession even, with risk. The central importance that 'risk assessment' has taken on in child protection today concerns attempts to bring the future under control and make it safer for children identified as 'at risk' of future harm. Professional systems have become more and more risk averse. Public interest in child protection cases has become immense. Professionals' judgements and authority have been and continue to be pervasively questioned, as every decision is potentially open to public scrutiny and risk laden. One disturbing consequence of these processes has been the emergence of a powerful 'blame culture', both within organizations and in how professionals are routinely pilloried by the general public, public representatives and the media for failing to protect children. This 'blaming system' is targeted particularly at social workers (Parton, 1996). In England, this reached new depths of awfulness in late 2008 with the Baby Peter case, in response to which *The Sun* newspaper ran a petition to have the frontline social workers and managers sacked, which reportedly gained 1.4 million signatures. Sharon Shoesmith, the director of children's services, was summarily sacked from her post by the government and became a public folk devil and was even subjected to death threats.

During the painful cycles and processes social work has gone through in recent decades, it has, at various times, been challenged to be more child-centred by becoming more assertive and comfortable with using statutory powers to keep children safe (London Borough of Brent, 1985). Social work and the professional system more generally responded by endeavouring to take child abuse seriously. One unintended consequence of this was the beginnings of scandals about the overuse of statutory powers and children allegedly wrongly being taken into care. The 'Cleveland affair' in 1987, where 121 children were taken into care by social workers following medical diagnoses of sexual abuse by two paediatricians, led to a major inquiry (Butler-Sloss, 1988) and was followed by similar inquiries in the 1990s (Stanley and Manthorpe, 2004).

These contradictory developments of social workers being found either not doing enough to protect or protecting too forcefully had a major influence on legislative reform. As Parton's exemplary analysis of recent developments in child welfare and protection shows, in England the 1989 Children Act enshrined principles that encouraged an approach based on negotiation with families and involving parents and children in agreed plans. Professionals were strongly encouraged to work in partnership with parents and young people. The focus was not simply on child protection, as the legislation set out the role of the state in supporting families with children 'in need'. The use of care proceedings and emergency interventions were to be kept to a minimum (Parton, 2007). While an ethic of partnership work embedded itself in practice, the impact of child deaths and the pressure to avoid making mistakes and blame led to the work being dominated by child protection concerns. Cases that did not cross a threshold of 'significant harm' to children struggled to gain attention.

By the mid-1990s, practice had shifted to focusing on investigations into child abuse to an extent that was viewed as too one dimensional. Investigations were deemed to be largely focused on incidents of alleged abuse, with insufficient attempts being made to gain an understanding of the wider history and social context of children and families' experiences and needs. Where no evidence of incidents of abuse were found, too many families were left without services and feeling aggrieved, even where vulnerability and need were apparent (DHSS, 1995). This does not necessarily mean that the standard of child protection investigations themselves were good, that social work had mastered this challenging activity. It was an outcome-led judgement about how a focus on child protection prevented a wider concept of child welfare and family support applying in practice. Attempts followed to 'refocus' policy and practice towards family support and a broader concept of need and the 'whole child'. The use of assessment frameworks was encouraged, exemplified by the *Framework for the Assessment of Children in Need and their Families*, which was introduced in England and Wales in 2000 (DH, 2000; National Assembly for Wales/Home Office, 2001). Similar models have developed across the western world (Buckley et al., 2006; Rose, 2010). The assessment framework is based on an ecological model, which directs workers to gather information on a range of domains affecting children's lives: the child's developmental needs, parenting capacity, and family and environmental factors. These are represented visually in a triangle to show how each domain interrelates and that there is a systemic element to children's experiences and how assessments should be done. The intention is not just to inquire into a particular event or incident but to reach as deep as possible an understanding of the child's world (Horwath, 2010). Recent policy developments have further consolidated a shift to a 'whole systems' and partnership approach. The Children Act 2004 in England placed statutory obligations on agencies to cooperate in 'safeguarding' children. New forms of integrated working have been developed based on the policy of *Every Child Matters* (www.dcsf.gov.uk/everychildmatters), in which 'being safe' is one of five outcomes. The language of policy and practice was changed to that of 'safeguarding', a term intending to capture the wider goals of promoting child wellbeing, of which protection was just one (Parton, 2006).

There are some commendable features to these developments. Revised *Working Together* guidelines for all professionals in England and Wales now require that children are seen by social workers on their own, the first time this has been so explicitly spelled out in policy and guidance (DCSF, 2010). However, a major downside is a loss of focus on the core meanings and tasks of child protection. The assessment framework is so focused on 'need' that, bizarrely, it does not mention the word 'risk' at all (Calder, 2008a). The movement away from using the language of 'child protection' has been deeply problematic and contributed to a systematic failure to focus on what child protection practice has to involve. The influence of the ideals of working in 'partnership' has chimed well with social work's value base of empowerment. There are, however, signs that this may be beginning to change, as the sheer enormity of the difficulties presented by working with resistant and hostile parents and carers in cases ending in the deaths of children has forced itself onto the policy agenda (Laming, 2009).

One consequence of these developments has been a general lack of clarity about the use of power and authority in social work and how – or indeed if – their use can be reconciled with achieving empowerment/partnership. Analysis of the use of authority has not been grounded enough in consideration of the actual tasks that social workers have to carry out – such as getting parents to agree to their children being seen on their own and having their homes inspected – while having to try and develop relationships with service users that are as respectful and equal as possible. A series of studies by Trevor Spratt and colleagues over a decade (Spratt, 2000, 2001, 2008; Hayes and Spratt, 2008; Spratt and Devaney, 2008) show that social workers constantly grapple with the dilemmas of how to provide 'care' and/or 'control', family support and/or child protection, and how difficult it is to achieve care over control in a context where there is pressure from the media, public and managers to avoid taking risks in case professionals are seen to fail to protect children. In developing such insights, what is needed is a nuanced understanding of the ethical dimensions of social work and child protection that incorporates the exercise of what I shall call 'good authority'.

The retreat from intimacy and face-to-face practice

The overwhelming response by welfare states to child deaths and other system failures has been to seek bureaucratic solutions by introducing more and more laws, procedures and guidelines. The more risk and uncertainty have been exposed, the greater the attempts to close the gaps in practice through administrative changes. Since the emergence of child abuse inquiries in the 1970s, a focus on the risks caused by ineffective professional systems has been deeply influential. Policy makers came to regard the key factor in why professionals did not protect children as arising from failures by agencies to communicate vital information that could have brought the abuse to light. The DHSS inquiry report into Maria Colwell's death argued that failures in the interagency system were largely accountable for Maria's (avoidable) death from abuse: 'Maria fell through the welfare net . . . primarily because of communication failures' (DHSS, 1974a). DHSS guidelines for working with non-accidental injury to children quickly followed, in which a primary emphasis was placed on the process and procedures of interagency work: 'The outcome of any case will depend on the communicating skills of the professionals involved as much as their expertise' (DHSS, 1974b). A new emphasis was placed on the interprofessional child protection system as being the crucial variable in the effective management of cases.

The DHSS comment 'as much as their expertise' suggests that perhaps face-to-face practice issues with children and parents required equal attention in the development of policy and practice. But this has not been the case. This is not to say that practice issues have been completely ignored, but that they have been systematically downgraded in favour of an interprofessional communication agenda. Some 35 years after the Maria Colwell case, the Baby Peter case provides a revealing example of how this emphasis on interprofessional communication has been used to try to explain too much. A striking feature of the case was how Peter's mother and the men who lived in the home managed to deceive and manipulate professionals by covering up the child's injuries and also the fact that the men (who were abusing him) lived in the house. When the head of Ofsted, the UK agency responsible for inspecting the quality of social work practice, was asked in an interview what social workers are meant to do about such deception, she said their inspectors had found that, in the London borough of Haringey where the Baby Peter case occurred, health and social care professionals and the police did not communicate well enough with each other. But the key point is that before any information can be shared, *someone has to find that information*. And to do that, you have to go and see the child and carers and, in the process, try and figure out their genuineness and whether any deception may be occurring by trying to get to the 'truth' by entering into the kinds of unpredictable encounters, invariably on home visits, that lie at the heart of child protection practice.

The dominant perspective in commentary on the state of social work today suggests that practitioners' skills are being eroded by procedures and audit and having to spend too much time at their desks and computers and not enough time with service users. This is exacerbated by the increased emphasis on 'joined-up' working, interagency collaboration and social workers' case management role. Moreover, it is argued, the time spent with service users is increasingly determined by what the procedures decree should be done, rather than this flowing from the intuitive actions of professionals (Munro, 2004, 2005; Parton, 2006, 2008; Broadhurst et al., 2010a, 2010b). This has occurred alongside new philosophies of welfare that emphasize direct regulation of practice and 'care planning', all facilitated by increased capacities to process and store information about service users and practice that have arisen through computerization and IT (Webb, 2006). New opportunities are available to monitor staff through the use of data banks and assessment and other frameworks, which both shape and record their work (Garrett, 2004a). The resulting time pressures and necessity to spend so much time in the office create risks that children will not be protected, which have their origins in poorly designed and managed systems

(Munro, 2010). These analyses of the development and implications of complex professional systems and managerial responses have made an important contribution to knowledge by identifying what can be called the 'systemic risks' that contribute to problems in protecting children. But it is crucial that the nature of practice and the risks involved are also understood in terms of detailed analyses of the *doing* of child protection face to face with service users, what I call 'practice risks'. This is to turn attention to intimate child protection and the experiences professionals have and the decisions they take on home visits, in hospitals and clinics, and the day-to-day actions and movements they do or do not make to relate to and protect children.

Conclusion

While there have been significant changes to social work in the 130 years or so covered in the first two chapters, what has struggled to be transmitted in the transition to new theories and organizational arrangements is a coherent vision of what child protection has to involve. The challenge was, and in many respects remains, to combine the best of the model of authoritative practice inherent in inspection with the compassion and ethical virtues advanced in radical/critical practice and notions of partnership, and the psychodynamic, relationship-based practice approach so skilfully developed by earlier generations of academics and social workers such as childcare officers. As I have shown, several factors have interfered with the transmission of this knowledge and practice wisdom and hindered the development of intimate practice.

Due to the increases in bureaucracy and accountability mapped out in this chapter, the dominant image of social work today is of static practitioners bound to their desks. But social workers *have* to leave their desks and go on the move to see service users if they are ever to do much good. Such a focus on practice also brings into view the responses and contributions of service users, which are hugely significant in shaping what occurs and the unpredictability of practice (Evans and Harris, 2004). The form that social work and child protection take in advanced modern societies must be understood in terms of the *flow* of mobile practices between public and private worlds, organizations and service users, the office and the home. At the heart of this is the sensual body of the practitioner on the move. We need a new language to capture the sphere of activity and actions that go on beyond the office, on the street, in the car, while doing the home visit, while with the child, where the worker is outside the organization and most often acting alone. Every practitioner always carries the expectations, constraints and enabling features of organizations with them even when they are not actually in the office. But practitioners' performances and experiences in those places beyond the office are unique to them and cannot be reduced simply to what the system allows. Our aim must be to reach a deep understanding of social workers' experiences of what happens when they leave their desks and go on the move to try to protect children in their homes and other intimate spaces.

3

Streets, housing estates, doorsteps: getting to the home

Did I knock hard enough?
(social worker)

The above question was asked of me by a social worker who I shadowed on a home visit. She had received no reply for two minutes so knocked again and after the third knocking the mother eventually came to the door. The worker was investigating a referral of alleged physical abuse and neglect and she had to be very determined to get into that house to see the children. She succeeded, but only after experiencing moments of worry and existential dread as she stood on the doorstep completely uncertain about whether she could get in at all and what she would face if she did. The question 'Did I knock hard enough?' seems so mundane and relates to such an elementary aspect of child protection practice. Yet it is spot on for drawing our attention to the courage, skill and knowledge that are needed to perform child protection effectively – to get the body working by, in this instance, getting the fist to hit the wood of the door with sufficient power – attributes that have gone largely unexamined in the child protection literature. The risks of not doing this elementary work well enough are expressed in the well-known social work in-joke concerning the temptation to execute the 'quiet knock' so that the parents do not hear you, and you can leave feeling relieved and able to say that at least you tried to get in.

To properly capture what social work and child protection involve doing, it is necessary to 'go with the flow' of how its practices are performed from day to day. We must follow the modern-day practitioner as they leave the office, make a journey by car or on foot, walk to the doorstep and (try to) gain access to the service user's home, walk into and within the home, and then make the return journey. Social work is the lead agency in child protection and it is to social work departments that referrals of concern are made. To make a legitimate inquiry into suspected child abuse, a report from a member of the public or other professional is needed. This is not always a straightforward process, as decisions have to be taken by 'duty' social workers and their managers or at multi-agency meetings about the level of need or risk involved and whether it warrants a direct investigation by social work. The general drift in recent years has been towards getting agencies other than social work who are in contact with children to take more responsibility for trying to safeguard them before passing their concerns on to social work. In the UK, the Common Assessment Framework was introduced in the mid-2000s for all agencies to use in assessing their concerns and designing and delivering interventions (DCSF, 2009). Generally, it is only when those concerns reach levels of acute need or risk of significant harm to children that social work gets involved. It is not my purpose here to analyse this process of referral definition, but to begin from the point at which that process has been completed and a decision made that direct contact with the child is necessary, which normally involves making a home visit.

Child protection practice, as undertaken through home visits, contains a number of dimensions/stages/challenges:

- Getting there (in time)
- Getting in
- Getting parents/carers to work with you
- Getting access to and engaging with the child to ensure their safety
- Getting around the home, checking bedrooms and kitchens
- Getting out
- Getting back (to the office, your home)
- Getting it down on paper and getting in touch with other professionals
- Getting support and insight into the experience through supervision.

This chapter deals with the initial steps (quite literally) in performing child protection, getting to the place where the child is. This usually happens by taking a car journey, be it to the street and front gate outside the home, or to the edge of the high-rise housing estate, from which point there is still significant walking to be done. This may seem like an unusual thing to focus on, an unnecessary distraction even. Surely, it can be argued, the important thing to focus on is the actual meeting between worker and child? But walking and travel to get to the child are a key component of what social workers do, and what happens on these journeys is important in shaping the worker's experience and the eventual encounter with the child and parents. More crucially still, what happens on the doorstep of the home actually forms part of the encounter in terms of what goes on and whether the worker gets to see the child at all.

Walking the walk in child protection

> Is it not truly extraordinary to realise that ever since men have walked, no-one has ever asked why they walk, how they walk, whether they walk, whether they might walk better, what they achieve by walking, whether they might not have the means to regulate, change or analyse their walk: questions that bear on all systems of philosophy, psychology and politics with which the world is preoccupied? (Honoré de Balzac, 1833, cited in Ingold, 2004, p. 315)

Balzac is referring here to the neglect of attention to the nature of walking by people in general. Although written some 178 years ago, he could just as easily be writing about social work today. His questions have great relevance for our understanding of child protection, and the risks and rewards involved. We need to ask ourselves why social workers walk, how they walk, whether they walk at all, or in what situations do they not walk enough, how they might walk better, and when and where does it matter? The aim of such an inquiry is to help provide knowledge that can increase social workers' capacity to reflect on and analyse the nature and quality of the movements they have to take so that practice at its best can be better understood and achieved and, where necessary, improved.

Social work involves travelling to and around different kinds of environments, some pleasant, some much less so. Travelling can mean a sense of freedom from office routines and management; an experience of fun, adventure and excitement that seems important to practitioners in making the work meaningful. Walking around the kinds of typically disadvantaged public places that social workers routinely face can involve having to negotiate conditions that assault the senses – unpleasant smells, refuse, poor lighting, aggressive dogs, as well as actual threats from service users and/or other residents. These comments are not meant to stereotype disadvantaged communities and service users. Such conditions are an indictment of a society that fails to provide decent housing for its most vulnerable citizens. The effect 'on the ground', however, is that social work often involves walking in an atmosphere of tension and, at times, menace, pervaded by uncertainty, anxiety, fear and sometimes a sense of adventure. Urry (2007, p. 88) identifies adventure as a key aspect of the mobile experience of modern life: 'There are some walks that involve moments of adventure when the body is put through its paces and the bare body painfully physicalizes its relationship with the external world.' The adventure of social work involves walking along rural backwaters and lanes, city streets, housing estates, up the stairway of high-rise flats, up the path to the home; crossing the threshold, walking around as well as sitting while in the home; and then getting out again. Even walking from the office to the car to make the journey can provoke anticipation and deep emotion.

In my research into how social work practitioners experience and go about doing child protection, I have been struck by how deeply physically and emotionally demanding the work is even before the worker meets the service user. Even getting to the doorstep of the home can involve workers in taking significant risks. The level of danger social workers can feel in some high-rise housing estates is such that they will not agree to leave their car and walk up to the flat unless a family member comes down to meet them and escorts them up the stairs/lift to the family home. I have been told of housing estates with lifts where infected hypodermic needles have reputedly been pressed in beside the lift button with the intention of harming visiting professionals. One social worker I accompanied to a home visit, on foot along inner-city streets half a mile from the office, told me she always walked now because it was safer than taking her car. She had been made to stop her car by a gang of youths who tried to hijack it as they were trying to escape the police. Luckily for her, the police arrived in time. She cannot now drive on these streets for fear of assault or of her car being damaged or stolen. Walking did not seem to me like much of a relief from these risks. The area was very poor and the streets populated by gangs and some very ill-looking people who appeared to be needing a drugs' fix. The visit we were on was not successful as there was no one in and the social worker and I parted ways. On my return, I was propositioned by a woman who asked me if I'd 'like some company?' Walking these streets required hypervigilance and was emotionally draining.

Public housing estates can be intimidating for different reasons. They are places that often have a particular atmosphere and their design results in very few people typically being out and about in their public spaces. This lack of people can lead to an intangible, uneasy feeling that something is wrong, and a sense of danger and insecurity (Halgreen, 2004). Social workers know this feeling well and it is often made worse by the fear that it is the recognizable presence of their car and themselves on the estate that is causing the uneasy quiet. A common fear is that retribution, if not visited upon them, will be taken out on their car, which is important as a secure base for them to return to and escape from the menacing, hostile environment. Worrying about your car as well as your own safety has a psychic toll on workers (Smith, 2003). Research suggests that the more people there are in public places, the safer people feel (Urry, 2007). But, for social workers, the presence of people can also be viewed as potentially hazardous. The Laming Report (2003, p. 91) into why professionals did not prevent the death from abuse of eight-year-old Victoria Climbié gives an example of an encounter that occurred when two social work staff were looking for Victoria and her carers:

> Ms Bridgeman and Ms Hobbs spoke to a number of people hanging around outside the premises, some of whom were drinking alcohol. They asked where room 10 was, if anybody knew who lived there, and if there was anyone upstairs. The people they spoke to informed them that the family had moved away about a week ago. This was of course true, as Kouao [Victoria's great aunt and carer] and Victoria had moved in with Manning [Kouao's boyfriend] on or about 6 July 1999. However, Ms Bridgeman agreed in evidence that she should not have relied on this information. They went upstairs to room 10 and knocked on the door. There was no answer. They asked people they had spoken to earlier if they had any concerns about the family, but none were raised.

Contrary to the criticism made here, this seemed like quite a robust piece of investigative work. The workers asked around people in the neighbourhood and actually checked for themselves whether Victoria and her family were at home. It may be that the workers were thought to be wrong for placing undue emphasis on the feedback that no concerns were raised about the family. The criticism that the workers 'should not have relied on such information' involves a rational interpretation, however, of their thinking, experience and actions. What happens if we take full account of the emotions and risk in exploring why workers rely on certain information and perceptions in particular circumstances? From this perspective, the professional response described above was likely to have been influenced by the workers' feelings of fear and unease in being in an unfamiliar environment in which groups of people were consuming alcohol and may be indifferent towards you, or friendly, but who equally may distrust and want to attack and punish you.

There is a significant literature on walking, which can help to deepen our understandings of the complexities of the challenges professionals face. Tim Ingold's fascinating work on the human foot shows how differently the world can look when perceived through the feet and not the head. Social science, he argues in a wonderful turn of phrase, is 'head over heels', in that it biases what is 'seen' through the eyes, ears and the mind and ignores or downplays touch, the feet and lower body. People behave and perceive things in particular ways because of the deep relationship that exists between our minds and our bodies. People don't only perceive things through their minds when they sit still and think. They interpret things while they are in motion, and walking is a way in which people acquire knowledge of the world. It is through our feet, in contact with the ground, that we are most fundamentally and continually 'in touch' with our surroundings (Ingold, 2004, p. 330; see also Lewis, 2001). What happens in social work and child protection writing, and the above quote from the Laming Report exemplifies this, is that the mind and body, thinking and action/movement are cut off from one another. The implications for social work theory are that we need accounts of how practitioners experience their work, perceive their service users and make decisions while on the move that are literally grounded; how they think on their feet, or even *through* their feet and other parts of the body.

This means that thinking, walking and getting the body to move cannot simply be understood on a commonsense level and are much more complex and difficult than is usually recognized. It is what Merleau-Ponty (1962, p. 235) calls the 'lived body' that is significant here:

> My body is the seat or rather the very actuality of the phenomenon of expression ... [It] is the fabric into which all objects are woven, and it is, at least in relation to the perceived world, the greatest instrument of my 'comprehension'.

It is not, then, simply a matter of the mind telling the body what to do but recognizing that bodily experiences deeply influence how and what we are able to think and do. The aim of an atmospheric inquiry into social work is to understand much more about the lived body of social workers and how they comprehend things as they are in motion and move through public spaces and then into the private lives and spaces of service users.

Doorsteps and knocking on the door

The adventure of social work and child protection amounts to much more than the unknown in terms of physical threats or actual violence from aggressive service users, significant as that is. It is characterized by feelings of excitement, dread, fear, often extreme anxiety, thrill and adrenaline rushes. Such an intense mixture of feelings is often present in the same moment, and is part of the routine experience of social work, often referred to as the 'buzz'. As a social worker in one of my research studies exemplified it: 'You get on a high from it, you get a buzz from all the activity and going out and . . . there is a buzz about it, about being busy and on the go.'

The experience of the car and its dynamism in transporting the worker to the place of danger/risk is a fundamental part of the adventure, especially when the use of speed is called for in response to serious referrals. But nowhere is the buzz of the adventure more deeply felt than when walking up the garden path or stairway and knocking on the door. Doorsteps and the encounters that go on at them are hugely significant but neglected places where important social work goes on. Like the NSPCC inspector in Chapter 1 from 1909 who was 'cheeked' at the door by the mother for 20 minutes, practitioners do experience parents who resist giving them permission to enter the home, and, on occasion, they do not succeed in getting in at all. This is a vivid example of how blocked movement occurs in child protection, which can have tragic consequences for the child. One of the most memorable cases I worked with goes back to the early 1980s; I can still feel the reverberations of stress in my body from what it was like to try and get in and how disgusting it smelled and felt like once inside. I visited weekly for two years and on virtually every visit the father met me at the door and verbally accosted me before allowing me in. Some of it was playful and invariably creative, in that among many words, the greeting always contained 'Paddy' (because I'm Irish) and 'fuck' (or variations of it, 'fucker' or 'fuck head', because I was a social worker). The word 'off' was sometimes the only other word added, which was a pretty sure sign he was having a bad day.

I never did as he asked, but stayed on the doorstep and fought out with him the right to be allowed access to see his children. It was a doorstep ritual he clearly needed to go through. It symbolized his need to constantly negotiate power and assert his rights and desire to protect his family and probably his masculinity. The most extreme and frightening battle we had occurred when I visited after I had taken his three-year-old child into emergency care due to unexplained bruising. He opened the door and, in the midst of loudly verbally abusing me on the doorstep, shouted into his wife, 'Shall I hit him?' I was sure she would say 'Yes, please do!' because she was always complaining about me visiting, but instead she came out and pulled him in, saying, 'Get in here, you silly bugger!' He replied, 'Okay, you can come in but you won't get out without getting your fucking head knocked off.' And in I went. Before the end of the visit, he had got out the family photos and showed them to me. His son was eventually returned to him on a supervision order and I visited for another year, after which, because things had improved, the order was revoked. When I told him I did not need to visit any more, to my amazement he expressed extreme disappointment, saying I was the only person who ever came to see them.

This family taught me a great deal about the deeply ambivalent relationships some service users have with social workers, how in a context of great parenting problems, poverty, social isolation and a pattern of resolving problems through violence, he both hated and desired my visits and our relationship. He taught me about my own investment in a dangerous kind of macho social work, where getting in at any cost, even under the threat of having your head knocked off, became a kind of victory not only for needing to see the children and the home, but something to boost my masculine pride. This was dangerous practice on my behalf – I should not have visited alone after taking his child into care – and should be expunged from individual and team behaviours. Greater support for staff and routine assessment of the risks to them of visiting happens today through 'lone worker' policies. However, what constitutes an acceptable risk for workers to take remains a tricky question.

This father correctly understood (and literally acted upon) the vital importance of the doorstep as a transitional space, a threshold between my public world and his and the family's private life. The reasons why the doorstep, hallway and porch are where some telling failures to properly access children have occurred has to do with how parents use the physical structure of the home to enable them to prevent social workers gaining access to and properly seeing children and also the meaning of these transitional domestic spaces. By drawing on anthropology, we can understand these problems as not simply about feckless incompetent practitioners but in part a product of the ambiguous space where they happen. Home visiting involves stepping across a boundary into another world and can be understood in terms of making transitions and what anthropologists call 'liminality'. This refers to an 'in-between' state, a sense of normlessness that arises from moving from one state to another (Turner, 1969, 1974). The doorstep, hallway and porch are in-between, 'liminal' spaces because they are neither in nor out (Rosselin, 1999). Everyday life depends on the maintenance of order and routine, and spaces where there is an absence of such order are experienced as dangerous. Within them, we experience the world differently, we quite literally do not know where we stand. This affects perception, making it much less reliable. As Rosselin (1999, p. 53) explains:

> The concept of the threshold is a prime concept in traditional anthropology. It is connected with the work of famous French and British scholars, such as the seminal work of the Frenchman Arnold Van Gennep ([1909] 1981) and his British followers Mary Douglas (1979) and Victor Turner (1960). According to Van Gennep, society is like a house with rooms and corridors. Thresholds symbolize beginnings of new statuses. The 'dangerous' act of crossing the threshold is for that reason controlled by ritual, similar to the popular ritual performed by the bridegroom who carries his bride over the threshold of their first home together.

The importance of these points lies in their implications for how practice goes on at doorsteps. Failure to gain entry to the home does not always mean being totally prevented from seeing the child. Eight-year-old Khyra Ishaq starved to death in Birmingham, England despite countless attempts by social workers to get into the home to see her. She was brought to the door by her mother and social workers were given sight of Khyra there. That is as close as they got to her. Her emaciated state was deliberately concealed by the loose clothing she was dressed in, and because no one got close enough to touch or lift her, the neglect went unseen (Birmingham Safeguarding Children's Board, 2010). It is no mere accident or coincidence that professionals have failed to protect children when they have got no further than dealing with them on doorsteps and in hallways. It is not just that they do not get to see enough of the child on the doorstep, but also that the encounter takes place in a zone that causes a loss of focus because of blurred boundaries and uncertain rituals.

I have explored with social workers in research their day-to-day experiences of practice on the doorstep and here a social worker gives a vivid example:

> I've thought of a case, actually, where I couldn't get in ... And the referral came via housing, that the child had been left. I think the gas man went round to the house and knocked on the door and the child, who I think was three, tried to post the keys through the door, implying that he was left home alone. And the gas man said, 'No', you know, 'you stay there. Don't post the keys through.' I think the gas man called the police. But by the time the police got there the parent was back. So the issues were around the child being left home alone. And so when I went to the house ... The family weren't known to us previously, so I didn't have any contact numbers and I don't know why I decided not to write to her and let her know, but I just went round and she lived in a block so there was a buzzer and mum was so angry. 'I'm not letting you in. Go away. Go away. I don't need no social workers.' I said, 'Can I just come up for five minutes?' And she let me in the first door but she wouldn't let me into the flat and she kind of hovered by the flat door and I said, 'We've received information that you've left a child alone.' 'My child wasn't left alone. My brother was there.' She was very angry and I tried to say, 'Well, I just need to explore this with you. I just need to make sure that you are aware of the possible dangers and what harm your child could come to if he was left home alone.' I said, 'Is your child here?' and she said, 'Yeah, he's in there.' I said, 'I need to see him.' 'What do you need to see my child for?' I said, 'It's part of the assessment. We have to see the children.' There's kind of two doors to the flat, so she was at one door and she let the child come to the other door. And all I could do was wave at him. And he waved back and looked quite happy and quite used to mum shouting, but she wouldn't let me into the flat at all. She was getting angrier and angrier. I tried to find out what GP she was registered with just so that I could do checks. 'What do you want to speak to my GP for?', like really, really angry. And I think she just got angrier and angrier and I eventually had to give up and go. I did checks with the GP and I think she was newly registered. So I shared the information and had some case discussion. And I'd seen the child and our concerns didn't warrant enough for us to force our way in. So I just closed the case. But then it came back because the child was registered at nursery but wasn't attending nursery and the case was allocated to [colleague's name].

One of the real hazards of such doorstep encounters is that the glimpse of the child from a distance is taken as sufficient to be able to say that the core condition of practice, that the child must be seen, has been met. What this worker managed to see of the child meant something of value. He was alive 'and looked quite happy', and had a demeanour of not appearing upset by his mother's shouting, which could, of course, also give grounds for concern. The social worker's persistence at trying to get in was admirable and she seemed to take matters to the limits of what the parent would allow on this occasion and this was good practice. But to rationalize closing the case in some measure on the basis that 'I'd seen the child' is not acceptable, because 'seeing' the child from a distance is simply not good enough. I am not suggesting that the worker could have gone further in this encounter in getting the mother's permission to gain access and real engagement with the child. My point is that it should have been openly acknowledged that the child had *not* been engaged with and the risks assessed. The decision might still have been the same if those involved felt that the social work concerns did not warrant them 'forcing their way in'. But the reality of not engaging with the child should have been acknowledged and this could have formed the basis for a more honest appraisal of what might still be needed to check their welfare more thoroughly.

Although getting into the home can often be straightforward, as the parent(s) or carers invite the social worker in to discuss their concerns, where it becomes more difficult to get in, workers need strategies to gain cooperation. One is to offer to leave soon after you get in:

> I have got one case where the mother was reluctant to allow me in ... She was initially reluctant because it was unannounced. We received information from the police that the house was in a complete state and it was a drugs den and it had been raided. So I took another worker with me. And mum was initially very shocked and the police obviously hadn't informed her that they were going to refer to us. And you could see that she felt quite put out and so I said, 'I won't take up much of your time. I just need to get some information from you but we can organise it for another day if that's more convenient. But can I just come in for five minutes?', because I think you can always do that. You can get in and then if they're not comfortable, you can organise another time to come back.

The appropriateness of such a response depends entirely on the presenting situation. It is only justifiable to leave in this manner if this does not jeopardize seeing the child and gathering adequate information and evidence concerning their safety and wellbeing.

One way workers deal with the tensions of investigating serious concerns for children is to avoid unannounced visits and make announced ones by alerting the family of their intention to visit in advance of it.

The extent to which this is possible depends a great deal on the level of urgency, because if a visit is needed straightaway, there isn't time to forewarn the family. Another factor in weighing up whether to announce your intention to call is the wisdom of giving the family advance warning, which gives them an opportunity to stage-manage what the worker can see and to coach the children on what to disclose on the visit. In Chapter 4, I suggest that in long-term cases where there are child protection plans, unannounced visits are crucial to ensuring that the reality of the children's world is discovered – walked into – by the worker, without an opportunity to stage-manage. In new referrals, there is still some scope for prior announcements but these are too often done to make workers feel better and less anxious. I therefore advocate keeping them to a minimum.

Conclusion

Child protection work involves walking in different atmospheres, some pleasant and welcoming, some much more hostile. It is vital that the full extent of these challenging and often risk-laden experiences is taken into account by managers and organizations. Workers need to prepare mentally for each encounter and be fully alert to what is going on around them and on their guard, constantly monitoring and reflecting on the impact of the physical and emotional demands of the work on their capacity to be child-centred. The threat on the street, the stairs of the high-rise flat and the doorstep can be so intense that entry to the service user's home can seem like a relief. This may be momentary or, when the atmosphere is more welcoming, a longer term comfort. Yet the move into the private domain is not an escape from atmospheres but rather a stepping into them. All homes and the relationships within them have atmospheres and how professionals manage stepping into and negotiating them is at the core of performing social work and child protection. For all the risks, atmospheres and adventures that walking in public involves, having reached and stepped into the service user's home, the adventure is only just beginning.

4

The home visit: crossing the threshold

For a considerable period in the history of casework the home visit was largely taken for granted and no commentator seems to have considered it advantageous to describe or analyse the obvious.

(Timms, 1964, p. 194)

Although it is almost 50 years since Noel Timms wrote this, his words could not be more relevant to social work and child protection today. Despite being the core place where face-to-face work goes on and the heart of child protection, the home visit has been almost completely ignored in analyses of practice. Having already dealt with getting there and knocking on the door, it is time to step inside and get straight into the heart of the child's life and home. This chapter begins to consider how child protection is performed in the home by drawing on social workers' accounts of their experiences and examining scenes from home visiting practices in child death inquiry reports. It identifies a core problem of contemporary child protection as being social workers (and other professionals) not moving in rooms or around houses enough to meaningfully engage with children. To correct this, new understandings are needed of the dynamics of practice and homes in child protection.

Making sense of the home and suspected child abuse

While the home visit has been the core method of social work for going on 140 years, it is no less important to social work today. Without it, social work could not exist. Or put another way, while some significant work can be done when social workers are absent and at a distance from service users – information gathering, interprofessional discussions, assessment of need/risk and advocacy – helping and protecting people demands making human contact with them, to meet. While some interviews take place in offices, clinics and hospitals (discussed in detail in Chapter 9), the main way social workers become present with children and families is to go to where they live. The most important reason for this is that the family home is where the majority of children live and so often is a central reason why social workers are involved at all, such as where there are concerns about child neglect due to poor 'home conditions'. More generally, promoting children's welfare and safety means assessing and working on family relationships and parenting skills in their natural surroundings, their home.

The meaning of 'home' has been the focus of investigation by a range of disciplines, including history, geography, urban studies, housing studies, architecture, anthropology and sociology (see, for instance, Saunders, 1990; Miller, 2001b). Yet it has been virtually ignored by social work, despite the home visit being central to its practices, and the importance of the home as a place that provides meaning and security in people's lives (Webb, 2006. For an excellent example of the centrality of the home in social work with adults, see Jones with Powell, 2007).

A social worker's first task on gaining entry to the home is to explain to the parent(s) or other carers why they are there. Much will depend on whether the social worker is expected, whether it is an announced or unannounced visit, and at what stage in the process the visit is taking place. If it is a first ever visit, clearly there will be significant explaining and introductory work to be done. As one social worker explained to me:

> I think it depends whether it's unannounced or not. If you do it unannounced, it can be quite tricky because you then have to introduce yourself so that you say where you're from, say that you've received some information and can you come in to discuss the information because you don't really want to talk about such things on the doorstep. And that can be quite difficult because you've caught the parents off guard... I had one parent, she got really, really upset and she was crying and it was just really awkward because you then felt really bad for causing her so much distress. But I think some visits you have to do unannounced. So if it's a family, I think it's easier if it's a family that's known to us, that's had an assessment done before, because, obviously, they're more familiar with the protocol, and it's always easier if the referrer has told the family, then they know.

The guiding principle of responding to all referrals and all child protection investigative work is that workers must be honest with family members about their role, the concerns being looked into and the possible consequences of the intervention. This is not as obvious as it seems. A social worker told me recently that her tactic for getting to see upstairs in a home is to ask if she can use the toilet and then to have a peek in the bedrooms as well as the bathroom/toilet. This may save the worker the trouble of having to go through the struggle of asking the parent's permission, but is not acceptable practice because it is fundamentally dishonest.

A social worker has to complete a number of tasks and processes in order to meet the core goal of inquiring into the concerns for the children that have led to the intervention. In an initial investigation and assessment, parents and other possibly significant adults must be interviewed about the concern expressed, for example whether they leave their children alone, hit them as suggested and so on. The worker will be guided by a knowledge base and the use of assessment frameworks, which cover the child's development, attachment and psychological wellbeing, the carers' parenting skills, the environment and wider family relationships (DH, 2000). The child or children who are the subject of the referral need to be seen and, if it is appropriate to their age and understanding, interviewed. Babies and infants must be seen and the quality of care they receive assessed. The wellbeing of any siblings not named in the referral must also be checked out (Holland, 2004). From the moment the encounter begins on the doorstep and the worker gains access to the home, they should be making assessments of the parents, their responses, observing what is going on, how the child and other family members relate to one another, and how the children relate to the worker.

While it is commonly stated that the core task in child protection is that 'children must be seen', putting this into practice in ways that ensure meaningful engagement occurs with children has often proved difficult. A telling example of the problems that arise on home visits during the early stages of a case comes from the report of the inquiry into the death of four-year-old Kimberley Carlile. There had been concerns about possible non-accidental injuries to Kimberley, whose parents, Mrs Carlile and Mr Hall, were resistant to the intervention of the social worker, Martin Ruddock. The following extract is taken from the report of the inquiry into Kimberley's death:

> When Mr Ruddock arrived at the Carlile home Mr Hall was clearly expecting the visit as he opened the door. From the outset his demeanour was not so friendly as on the occasion of the 12 March meeting. Mr Ruddock was ushered into the living room on the first floor; no-one else was present.

Mrs Carlile, who was then 3 or 4 months pregnant, was said to be asleep upstairs, and so was the youngest child, Z. The other children were also upstairs, playing quietly. Mr Hall was quick to reassert his hostility to Social Services and his desire to want from social workers nothing more than for the family to be left alone. He went on to express strong feelings about the involvement of all the agencies. He was not angry; he was not emotional; his talk was not aggressive. But he was insistent, to the point of uncompromising emphasis, that the family was quite capable of coping with its own problems and in their own good time. Mr Ruddock concluded in his statement to us: 'Overall I would describe his demeanour as assertive rather than angry or intemperate.' Having ourselves seen and heard Mr Hall, we think that 'assertive' is too mild. We think that many people in Mr Ruddock's position would have found Mr Hall intimidating. But he apparently did not. (London Borough of Greenwich, 1987, p. 115)

There is an important implication here that workers may become so used to being intimidated that they become desensitized to it and cease to fully recognize or minimize it and its toxic effects (Stanley and Goddard, 2002). The report goes on to comment on the 'technique' adopted by the social worker to try and get the man to engage, which was to recall an earlier constructive meeting with the family, reminding him that the family had previously conceded that Kimberley had behavioural problems that called for professional help. But this engagement strategy did not work:

The discussion veered away from the need for Social Services to have Kimberley medically examined, and reverted to the question of official intervention. Mr Hall was testing the strict legal entitlement of Mr Ruddock to impose himself on the family for the protection of children. The discussion degenerated into repetitiveness. The angularity of Mr Hall's stance sharpened, rather than softened. He became unyielding to the point where it was being made clear that access to Kimberley (or any of the other children) was being stubbornly and unreasonably refused. Towards the end of the visit Mr Ruddock was permitted to peep through the small glass panel at the top of the door to one of the children's bedrooms. Two children were on the floor, between the beds, with their backs to the door. All that could be seen was the back of one young head and the top of another, one smaller than the other. That was all that was visible of either child. Reflecting now on the incident, Mr Ruddock cannot even be sure that the younger child was in fact Kimberley. The two children could have been X and Y [her siblings]. Even if the younger child was Kimberley, to all intents and purposes she was an 'unseen' child. Like a little glow-worm glimmering in the dark, Kimberley's body provided no more than the barest glance. (London Borough of Greenwich, 1987, p. 115)

The social worker told the inquiry that while he acknowledged that his sighting of Kimberley was totally inadequate child protection practice, he was

> positively reassured by the fact that he was allowed to look through the glass window by Mr Hall who could not have known in advance how much of Kimberley (if indeed it was her) would be seen. Mr Ruddock argued that Mr Hall must have realized that there was a good chance of a good look at Kimberley and that would have defeated all his efforts at concealment of Kimberley's wounds. (p. 115)

The report argues that this is not convincing and that this man was not endangering his concealment of Kimberley's bruising and battering by allowing a look through the glass window of a door sealing off the onlooker from the children: 'Even if Mr Ruddock had obtained a frontal view it is unlikely that he would have observed any signs of child abuse' (p. 116). Indeed, a month earlier, he had seen her 'in the flesh, at close distance and over a lengthy period of time' but did not observe any physical injury on her: 'His observations were limited to the colour (or rather discolourment) of her skin and her demeanour.' The report concludes:

> We are confident in saying that Mr Ruddock was in no position to draw any inference from the permission to gain a glimpse of Kimberley other than to conclude that he was being hoodwinked. All that we have said at the end of the last chapter applies with like force to the visit of 14 April. Even at the risk of being accused of indulging in boring repetitiveness, we must repeat that, when investigating a case of child abuse, the child *must* be seen. (London Borough of Greenwich, 1987, p. 116)

These remarkably vivid extracts from an account of a difficult home visit raise several key issues that are central to child protection practice and this book. It shows how the context where the practice goes on is crucial to shaping what happens, in this instance how this father tactically used the physical structure of the home to prevent the social worker having proper sight of the child. It demonstrates just how hard it is to put into practice principles concerning the need to engage with children, what it might mean to 'see' a child and that seeing (from a distance) is never enough. It also shows that social workers have a key role in detecting evidence of injuries and harm to children through the use of touch, but that this is also the responsibility of the medical practitioner through an examination. Also revealed is the kind of parental hostility and resistance that social workers can experience when trying to see children, and the challenges they face in trying to see through when they are 'being hoodwinked'. These key dimensions to child protection in the home are usually ignored in the literature, but they will be addressed in depth throughout this book.

How the home is used to block intimate practice

The interpretation of the Carlile report is a rational one, arguing that the worker should have been able to see through the deception, simply by being aware of the possibility of it, and then acted to see the child properly. The problems with this kind of interpretation can be further examined through another case example. In child protection, even (or often especially) when families and professionals are well known to each other, problems in accessing children within the home have been enacted time and time again in child death inquiry cases. A vivid illustration of the problems that arise on home visits in long-term cases where the family are well known occurred in the case of five-year-old Jasmine Beckford, who had been seriously physically abused and taken into care and was returned to live at home on trial. The following lengthy extract is from the report of the inquiry into Jasmine's death, featuring the social worker Ms Wahlstrom, Jasmine's mother Beverley Lorrington and father Morris Beckford:

> On 12 March 1984 Ms Wahlstrom saw Jasmine alive for the last time...
> Ms Wahlstrom's own entry [in the case file] for this occasion is headed:
> 'Home Visit as arranged'. Beverley Lorrington opened the front door and
> showed Ms Wahlstrom into the downstairs front room. Ms Wahlstrom
> enquired about the children, and Beverley took her upstairs. We have seen
> a drawing of the room, which was sparsely furnished. It shows the posi-
> tioning of the furniture and children. We have also seen photographs of
> this room and other rooms in the house, including the kitchen, taken by
> the police on 5 or 6 July. They were spotlessly clean, reflecting Morris
> Beckford's obsessive cleanliness that he ruthlessly imposed on Beverley
> Lorrington. Jasmine (dressed in jeans) and Louise were both sitting on
> the floor watching 'Jungle Book' on a hired video. Chantelle was sitting
> in a babysitter. When Ms Wahlstrom came into the 'playroom', Jasmine
> did get up but took only a step or two towards the bedstead, upon which
> she probably used to prop herself. She did not walk across the room and
> was not heard to say anything. She remained in that position for some
> moments and then continued watching the film. Ms Wahlstrom proceeded

to have a conversation with Beverley Lorrington in which she admitted that she no longer took Jasmine to nursery class, the reason given being that she had been 'off school for a while with a bad cold and got out of the habit of going to school'... Morris Beckford returned home and the three adults went downstairs. Altogether Ms Wahlstrom was in the playroom for 20 minutes and in the home for 45 minutes.

...

Ms Wahlstrom's record of the children's health and welfare was that 'all three appeared well and happy'. Before us, she amended that phrase to 'calm and collected'. The grounds for those generalised words are not apparent. We have stated in Chapter 7 that we find that on that day Jasmine was recovering from a fracture of her thigh and would have walked with an abnormal gait. Since she did not perform any purposeful act of mobility, her healing bone fracture would not have been noticed. Ms Wahlstrom also explained to us – and we accept her description – that Beverley Lorrington was waving her arm about so that Jasmine was partially obscured from sight, Miss Lorrington standing between the two of them in the playroom. If Ms Wahlstrom had carried out the elementary task of walking with Jasmine, or talking to her, even in her mother's presence, the fact of child abuse would have been all too apparent. We think that Ms Wahlstrom was gravely in error in doing no more than have a cursory glance at the children in front of the television set. Her visit did not accord with the basic requirement of ensuring the welfare of children. She was grossly negligent. We conclude, moreover, that the visit was stage-managed by the Beckford parents who had been given five days' notice of the impending visit and thus had ample opportunity to arrange the sitting of the children and the unrevealing clothes worn by Jasmine. Indeed, Morris Beckford said as much in his written statement to the Inquiry. Ms Wahlstrom should have been alive to such parental ruses to conceal the effects of child abuse. (London Borough of Brent, 1985, pp. 125–6)

Once again I have chosen this long extract because it is quite remarkable in the detail of its description of the home and what went on during the visit. It typifies how in such cases the children's bodies were moved about by parents and carers in tactical ways to conceal their injuries. The same happened to professionals. Parents have manipulated the placement of their bodies on doorsteps and within rooms to prevent them from properly seeing, touching, listening or talking to injured children. Professionals have effectively been rendered immobile, stopped from moving and properly engaging.

An important thing to focus on in making sense of such practice is the social worker's state of mind in such situations. What might it have been?

What would it have taken for the social worker in the Carlile case to have insisted on seeing Kimberley close up? What would it have taken for the social worker in the Beckford case to have got up and moved around the place, to have walked across the room to properly see, talk to, touch, play with, hear the child? Did she even know that such movement was a key part of performing effective child protection? I suspect she did not.

At this stage in the Beckford case, the social worker had made over 50 unsuccessful attempts to gain access to the children. Morris Beckford hated social workers and he and Beverley Lorrington were often hostile to them (both were brought up in care). The social worker is likely to have been gripped by fear and anxiety, and the hate the parents felt towards her was probably palpable. In the grip of such feelings, the worker became 'stuck' to the spot and immobilized. However, the way that practice is written about in these inquiry reports is that the emotions and lived experience of practice are ignored, and practice is talked about as though social workers just have to make up their minds to do something, such as engage directly with the child, and then get on with it. Children are seen as being allowed to die either because the proper organizational structures, rules or guidance are not in place to direct workers to make such decisions, or because of breakdowns in the communication of information between professionals, which meant that they didn't realize the danger to the child. But following on from my argument in Chapter 3, it is the 'lived body' (Merleau-Ponty, 1962), not (just) the rational mind and procedures that shape action and what does and doesn't get seen and done. We need to understand much more about how the body and mind of the practitioner moving into the lives and spaces of service users are affected by the experience of doing social work, and how the senses and emotions impact on perception and workers' and service users' capacities to relate to one another. Thinking about practice in terms of movement can help us to develop a different kind of understanding of child protection and theory of practice based on the core question of how does the (professional) body move through spaces (such as the home), or become immobilized and fail to move (enough)?

The importance of movement in protecting children

In answering such questions and making sense of what goes right and wrong on home visits, it is crucial to understand that social work practice and the walks and other activities undertaken in the service user's home are not the same as those performed in other places, such as the street, the social work office, hospital ward or clinic. This is because of the nature and meanings of homes and professionals' experiences of them and the actions of the service users who live in them. To begin with – literally to gain access to a house – as I began to show in Chapter 3, home visiting involves stepping across a boundary into another world, a liminal space, and entering the particular atmosphere created by the family.

The house is a space that provides opportunities for family members to keep aspects of their lives and parts of themselves hidden by attempting to stage-manage what the professional gets to see and know. As we have seen, (injured) children and social workers can be placed in positions in the room that obscure the injuries and what the professional can actually see. Adults as well as children can be hidden, such as when the presence of abusive fathers or father figures is kept secret by mothers – the man hides in the bedroom or discretely leaves through the back door as the social worker walks in the front. In child sexual abuse cases, all domestic spaces where the child can be isolated by the abuser and not seen are danger zones, including garages and garden sheds (Calder and Peake, 2001). A student social worker who had extensive experience of working with children in residential care recently told me of a case where two children she looked after were in care because they were sexually abused by their father. They were allowed home at weekends on condition that the man was not allowed anywhere near them or the home. Social workers were quite vigilant in checking on him not being in the house and the children spent several, apparently successful, weekends at home until one of them disclosed that their father was living at home the entire time and continuing to sexually abuse them. At the time the children were taken into care, he had taken up residence in the garden shed, which no professional ever looked in, so as to deliberately avoid detection. Sure enough, when social workers investigated, they found a bed and other possessions of the father in the shed. The children were never returned home again. Turnell and Essex (2006, p. 118) rightly stress how important it is that professionals' safety planning includes clear statements to the family about 'who is where in the house, garden, garage, etc., when the children are home'.

Anthropologist Daniel Miller (2010) argues that we need to think about houses as having 'agency', by which he means the house is an object that influences how we act, that acts upon us as well as us acting upon it. We tend to think of houses as things that we have control over, do up, shape to our tastes. Even if we do not own it, the assumption is that we have control over the home and can personalize it and 'make it a place of our own'. The home is central to the objects that make up our lives, what Miller calls 'material culture'. He challenges us to consider how such objects are crucial to making us what we are:

> We think that we, human subjects, are free agents who can do this or that to the material culture we possess. But inevitably we can't. Objects can be obdurate little beasts, that fall from the mantelpiece and break, that refuse to grow in shady spots in the garden, that cause us to trip, and that crash their systems just as we were about to type something genuinely interesting. If, in all such cases, they are clearly not reflecting the agency that is represented by us, then it seems reasonable to start talking in terms of the agency represented by them – the gremlins ... Things do things to us, and not just the things we want them to do. (Miller, 2010, p. 94)

Miller gives the example of how most people live in homes that are much older then they are. Compared to the house, we are transient. This creates a sense that the house has its own powers and properties that lie beyond us. The power of the home is significant when it is someone else's house because we enter it as strangers to its contours and meanings. What is entered is not an empty shell but a space that contains the atmospheres and reverberations of the lives of those who live there. Social workers face not just the human agency of those who live in the house, but their agency in the context of the power of the house itself. As occupiers of the home, service users have the capacity to use the property as well as themselves to block or enable how practitioners work. Workers face the double whammy of the house and its inhabitants combining all their potential to influence what they can see and do in the home.

A key implication of this is that workers need to have a deep understanding of how the home can be used to shape how practice is done and to block access to children and risky individuals (like violent men). Workers and their agencies must develop counter-strategies and use their own capacity to act in overcoming how service users turn the agency of their homes to their advantage. This is why movement and the necessity of walking around rooms and homes to establish the wellbeing of children has to be taken as one standard of good social work. Effective child protection practice has to involve not only professional mobility to reach the child but ensuring that children move. Engaging in ordinary mobility with children – as the Jasmine Beckford case painfully showed – is a way of spotting child abuse, even if it only amounts to taking a few steps with them. Static, immobilized practice places the child at (higher) risk.

An obvious but still remarkable feature of practice in the home is that there is not much space to move in, even when gardens and sheds are included, as they must be. Walks in the home are very short and whether or not children are protected routinely comes down to professionals taking or not taking a few short steps so as to engage with the child, establish who is resident there and the home conditions. But the tighter, reduced amount of space does not make actually moving in the home any easier. It may, as I have already begun to show, have the opposite effect.

The impact of domestic space being so enclosed is another reason why practising in service user's homes is not the same as doing so in public places. Ingold (2007) refers to how walking outdoors is 'enwinded', meaning that it is inseparable from direct experience of the weather and fresh air. Pathways get formed outdoors through the interaction of (wet) weather and the impact of footprints repetitively made on the earth. Walks in service users' homes go on in quite different enclosed environments characterized by the absence of (fresh) air. It is the family's air, their atmospheres that must be breathed in by workers. The extracts from the historical case files in Chapter 1 exemplify how the history of social work as told through case files is replete with complaints from social workers about the smells they must breathe in and the impact of dirt on their bodies and practice.

A huge practice risk here is how disgust prevents workers from getting close to, engaging with or touching children. When the social work staff, referred to in Chapter 3, finally found Victoria Climbié at home, they did not directly engage with her or touch her and two social workers and a police officer subsequently (and independently of one another) refused to visit the home as they believed Victoria had scabies, a contagious disease (Laming, 2003). This shows that whatever workers' good intentions are prior to arrival at the visit, every fibre of the lived body can tell them to get out of the home into the street, the fresh air and the car, back to safety as fast as they can. Even for the most seasoned professionals, direct engagement and touch in conditions that provoke disgust are deeply problematic, and unless its effect is fully acknowledged, this causes workers to distance themselves and detach from abused children. Workers are often unaware of these avoidances, and good supervision is essential in helping them to express the disgust and other difficult emotions they feel and become fully aware of their non-engagement with children.

Some atmospheres in the home are experienced consciously and physically, through sight, smells, noise and touch that 'hit you in the face'. Sensing atmospheres always occurs intuitively, but where the physical signs of risk (such as dirty home conditions) are less overt, it is essential to use and rely on intuition and trust 'gut feelings' to make sense of the experiences that are swirling around and unconsciously entering the mind and body. Thus, in the Beckford example given earlier in the chapter, the fact that the home was spotlessly clean was not a sign of wellbeing and good parenting but a source of discomfort for workers as it reflected Morris Beckford's obsessive cleanliness that he ruthlessly imposed on Beverley Lorrington. In obsessively clean homes occupied by resistant involuntary clients, an atmosphere exists where it is the social worker who is made to feel like a contaminating agent, like dirt. While the Beckfords were socially disadvantaged, this is a common atmosphere and experience in investigations into middle-class homes.

Performing child protection involves the use of different kinds of movements, gestures and activities. A walk will take the worker up close to the child, but other actions are necessary if direct contact is to be made: bending down, lifting up, jumping and twisting in play, using the hands and touching. This does not, of course, mean that good practice has to involve ceaseless movement. Sitting with the service user and engaging in lengthy discussion are essential to good interviewing, as is being calm and still and observing interactions and relationships in the family. Being immobile during significant segments of the encounter is essential to good practice. The requirement to actively engage with children and their home means that, at some point during a visit, the worker must move around the house and engage directly with the child and their home conditions, including investigating with their own eyes who is living there. Equally, when the child is seen in the hospital or clinic, workers need to perform a meaningful act of mobility with them. Meaningful acts of mobility with children will vary depending on their age and stage of development. With an infant who is not yet walking, it has to involve, at a minimum, the worker moving and picking the child up, acts that can be performed in informal ways such as through play, or more formally as part of an explicit arrangement where parents and carers know that such contact is part of the safeguarding role and, where possible, give their consent. I return to the issue of touch at greater length in Chapter 7.

Conclusion

Effective child protection work involves talking, listening, empathizing and observing, as well as the skilful management of mobility and immobility, movement and stillness, transferring between being seated and still and periods of being on one's feet and actively engaging with the home environment and children. In practice, these are fluid processes and skilful work involves managing the tensions and 'flux' that arise between mobility and immobility. Urry (2007) proposes that the metaphor of 'flux' is more appropriate than 'flow' when speaking of mobile phenomena because uninterrupted flows of practices rarely happen. Flux well expresses the dynamics and tensions between movement and non-movement or blocked movement that characterize child protection practice.

The emphasis on child protection practice as a purely rational activity where the onus is on social workers to follow agency rules is misplaced. As this chapter has shown, social workers can lose sight of the child because of their state of mind and their bodily experiences, in a context where the home can be tactically used against professionals to conceal the truth of children's suffering. Professionals have to build an awareness of these dynamics and the crucial role that moving towards children and moving with them in the home has to play in keeping them safe.

5

Bedrooms, kitchens and more intimate spaces

One thing that is very noticeable is that the worst squalors are never downstairs. You might visit quite a number of houses, even amongst the poorest of the unemployed, and bring away a wrong impression. These people, you might reflect, cannot be so badly off if they still have a fair amount of furniture and crockery. But it is in the rooms upstairs that the gauntness of poverty really discloses itself.

(Orwell, 1962, p. 53)

This chapter develops the exploration begun in Chapter 4 of the dynamics of the home and what happens when professionals step into it and service users' lives. It takes the analysis further by going even more deeply into the child's home – into the most intimate corners of their existence – and considers how social workers experience making difficult requests to see children, the home and how they deal with what they find there. The above quote from George Orwell was written in the 1930s as part of his famous visits to the northern English town of Wigan to discover how the poor actually lived. While poverty is often a factor in child abuse cases, in inspecting spaces such as people's bedrooms, social workers are looking for other things relating to the quality of care provided for the child. But Orwell's point equally applies: intimate spaces like bedrooms can reveal surprising things that otherwise remain hidden. As the historical case examples featured in Chapter 1 showed, moving around the home and checking on bedrooms and other intimate spaces was once regarded as best practice. As was suggested in Chapter 2, in recent years, attention to this element of child protection has fallen into decline and rarely features in policy or accounts of practice. This is despite the need for it having been starkly revealed in cases where children have died or been seriously harmed.

The chapter considers in more detail what performing child protection practice in the home needs to involve, how it can best be done by social workers and other professionals and what enables as well as blocks it. The notion of 'performance' once again seeks to capture the active component of child protection as enacted by the practitioner, through talk, gestures, movements and being still. It is also intended to capture what is experienced by workers in their bodies and senses when they relate to service users in the home. Moving into people's physical spaces also means going into the interior of their emotional lives and this has to involve an examination of the worker's inner life and unconscious as well as conscious experience.

Seeking to engage with children and inspect the home

Home visiting can be pleasurable, particularly when the worker is broadly welcome and the service user recognizes a need for them to be there, or at least when there is no overt hostility and resistance. There are few more interesting jobs than spending your time going from home to home meeting children, parents, relatives, neighbours, and gaining insights into how people live. As one social worker I interviewed said:

> I try and remember that it is actually a privilege, that I do wield a lot of power, and I still find it incredibly stimulating to think about it like that, because I am being paid for and employed by the state to go into the parts of society that most people don't really imagine exist, very often like to think exist, so I consider it a privilege that I'm doing that. And I find it absolutely fascinating to go into these places and discover what actually is going on in these people's lives, and it's incredibly stimulating to then know I am being paid for and supported in my job, and I want to see behind that, I want to see what goes on for these families, and try and really see what life is like for some of these children, to make a clear decision about whether they're safe or happy or we should be worried, or anything like that.

It can also be very tough: if the family do not want you there; if they intimidate, threaten and even assault you; when you witness arguments between family members and experience their emotional pain; and if the home conditions are poor and it is unpleasant to be among the smells and dirt. Even when it is enjoyable, social workers regard certain elements of home visiting as difficult and always at or near the top of the list is the breaching of the family's privacy. Workers are deeply conscious of being in the family's space and that they have no absolute legal right to insist on being there, unless they have the grounds of high suspicion of risk to seek a court order. The following quote from a social worker is typical:

> It's not always nice, it's quite often that the family feel like you're impos-
> ing upon them, saying 'who are you to come in and sniff around my
> house?', which I appreciate. But, like I said, it's difficult...it's perhaps
> going over again what the concerns are and then explaining why you
> need this, need to report that you've seen this, the kid's bedrooms
> and so on. So it's not always the nicest of things to ask but we have
> to do it.

The extent of workers' feelings of discomfort around boundaries and privacy and whether they can overcome it depends a great deal on what role they see for themselves. In terms of the language and concepts being developed in this book, the issue is how intimate they are prepared to be in entering family members' most private spaces and getting as physically close as possible to children to ensure they are safe.

In general, most activity on home visits seems to take place in the sitting or living room. It can be the kitchen, but the living room is usually where the (comfortable) seating is (or, in some homes, the only seating) and where it is possible to sit and conduct the interview. The living room also tends to be the most accessible room in terms of how the home in western societies is structured. Visitors naturally flow into it on entering the home. Thus far we have been hanging around mainly at doorsteps and in sitting rooms, that is, downstairs. In terms of the model of intimate practice I am advancing in this book, the living room (or downstairs room) is best framed as the place where the child protection encounter normally starts. It is likely to be the main stage on which the performance is conducted, but there are other rooms – what, after sociologist Ervin Goffman (1959), can be called 'back stages' – that have to be performed in too.

A core aim of all child protection practice is to reach an understanding of the child's world, experience and wellbeing and to respond accordingly. The primary rationale for seeing around the entire home is to be able to examine the standard of care being provided and to gain an appreciation of the child's world through the space they inhabit. One social worker describes the importance of this:

> I have not checked sometimes in houses that are very kind of clean and
> well presented. But that's awful, because I have checked in houses where

it's been very clean and well presented and a child's bedroom says a lot in social work. There was one case where it was all about emotional abuse and the child and family who I was working with, his bedroom was really sparse. It was just basically a bed and a box and a TV, whereas the sister's bedroom had photos, lots of knick-knacks and pillows and it was really nice, whereas in his bedroom, there was just nothing there, no personality in the room at all. So that was quite a big indication as to his role within the family.

This is indicative of how bedrooms can give important insights into the truth of children's experiences and their role and treatment within the family. As another worker expressed it, seeing the bedrooms enables you to see what the parents' priorities are. If their own bedroom is well resourced and cared for but the children's, or one of the children's, are not, this is a vital clue as to how the children are regarded and treated. The same is true of checking fridges and kitchen cupboards. If, as happens, all that is found in the fridge is alcohol and there is no milk and other essentials for children, this constitutes skewed priorities and points to child neglect.

Where there are concerns about child neglect and a lack of food, checking fridges can throw up some surprising things. This social worker explains his recent experience of inspecting the fridge to see what provisions were in:

[Mother] was at the fridge and she had lots of boxes in there, and to be honest I thought 'that is a lot of boxes', so I just happened to pick one up and it was empty. They were all empty. And I said to her about that and she said, 'Oh I just haven't got round to chucking them away.' I said, 'Well why did you put them back in the fridge', and she said, 'Oh I don't know.' And that child now is, well unfortunately the child is not with her anymore, the child's with the grandparents because the mum was using heroin, she was smoking heroin in front of her little girl, but she's with her grandparents now.

Little wonder that doing work of this unique kind can make workers as well as those on the receiving end uncomfortable. Some do not look around the home at all. Even when they know they should really be doing it, some avoid it. They are so confused about their role and focused on service user rights and protecting privacy that, on ideological grounds, they do not see it as a legitimate part of their practice. The latter involves a serious error: regarding the parent/carer/adult as the service user. This is not to say that all children and young people regard the attentions of social workers who make sure to directly engage with them while in the same room as them or the worker's visit into their bedroom as acceptable or welcome. Rather, it means that the task must be conducted with the child's best interests as the primary concern, which has to include fully experiencing the spaces in which they live.

While some practitioners recognize that looking around the entire house and the children's bedrooms can be helpful, they do not do this on all occasions:

> I think the general feel is that first and foremost if there has been a referral, if there's been concerns regarding the state of the home, and if there is a really dirty house, and the children ... then yes, that's quite a common thing that you're going to ask to see about the house and see upstairs. But like I said, every time we step in, it might well be that you go into the home and it's just not appropriate at that time. I think everyone just has their own feeling, and you do know within the first few minutes in the house how the visit's going to go.

Those social workers who believe in going right into the depths of the service user's home do so in order to fully understand the child's world and root out children's suffering. Practitioners need to go about the work in ethical ways by maximizing the scope there is for empathy and negotiation with family members. The meanings of home and of particular rooms differ from culture to culture. Culturally sensitive practice requires workers to understand and respect the norms of families concerning where to expect to be able go in the home to conduct interviews and so on. But respecting people's culture does not mean that certain rooms can be no-go areas. The worker needs to use their authority in culturally sensitive ways while insisting on their need to see whatever is necessary of the home and children to ensure they are safe.

The styles and strategies used to request access to children and different parts of the house differ from worker to worker. If it is imposed in a dictatorial way that alienates parents (and children), it can create more resistance than might occur if more empathy for their predicament was shown (Forrester et al., 2008b). Some workers take the approach of leaving the difficult questions until late in the interview:

> Once we'd got comfy sort of thing, I would probably towards the end of the meeting say, 'Will it be alright if I have a look at the children's bedrooms?' And judging on how we have been getting on ... And if the

house is immaculate, I would probably not worry quite so much about that, but if it's a bit grubby...

The notion of 'getting comfy' involves an attempt to have developed at least some measure of acceptance by the parents of the need to carry out such an in-depth inquiry. Another approach is to use their intuition to decide how far to go in seeking to see around the home on this particular visit. Where parents resist strongly as part of trying to come to terms with the referral and the intervention, some workers make a judgement that it would be better not to push it on this occasion but to come back another time and do it:

> Whenever we want to speak to children on their own, which is obviously what we always ask to do, but sometimes on that first initial visit it's just not appropriate and so you have to then maybe on the second visit ask, or maybe whenever you're leaving say 'On my next visit I'm going to ask this.' But it's always easier to drop it in at the beginning of the conversation, you know, if I'm going to speak with mum on her own to let her know that within the first few minutes of arriving at the house and say, 'OK, I'll speak to you both and then if it's possible can I speak to...?' So that they're aware and they know that it's coming up, rather than just saying, 'OK, can you leave the room now', you know, it's not going to work.

The logic of this strategy of asking the hard questions early is to get them out of the way and deal with any fallout from them:

> Again it depends, if I know it's going to be a real difficult thing, like I had to ask a mum early this week about the father of her child, he's not had any contact since birth, but I needed to know who he was because we need to sort of be in contact with him because his daughter's asking about him, I knew that was going to be difficult. So I had a long visit and it was something I saved till the end, once we'd actually kind of built up a good relationship and had a good talk, and she then had a clear understanding of why I needed to know the father's name. But most of the time I think it's the other way round, in that if I have any sense there's going to be difficult issues to talk about, then I do it right at the beginning, get them out of the way, nice and open, and then it's quite nice to think 'there you go, that's it', and you can see the fallout from it, because the most frustrating thing is...you think you've got [to the end of the interview] and then right at the end, he goes, 'Oh yes, uncle so and so has been having contact with him.' Uncle so and so is a known paedophile and so then you have to start all over again.

Going into families' intimate spaces and facing unbearable feelings

However, practitioners do not always ask and do as they should, and the complexity of the tasks and the feelings they give rise to are such that the risk of avoidance of difficult subjects routinely arises. An example from my research will help to show how this happens. A social worker I shadowed visited to inquire into an anonymous referral about a 7-year-old girl whose mother it was alleged goes out for long stretches at night and leaves her in the house, possibly cared for by her 16-year-old son. The children's father did not live with them and had sporadic contact. It was claimed that the girl is heard to scream out at night at times like 2am, she has a neglected appearance at home and school and her mother sends her out to do the shopping at a local store. The family lived on a council estate and had four dogs, which were at the gate beside the front door, barking and trying to get at the social worker. The mother willingly let the social worker in and denied it all, claiming it to be a malicious referral. She said that when she goes out, her daughter is always looked after by her 16-year-old brother. The latter said he does have some of his mates around when he is babysitting and denied this was a problem for his younger sibling, who is asleep in bed when her mother goes out. The social worker suggested that this babysitting arrangement may not be fair to or in the best interests of the 7-year-old. The mother was open to the social worker seeing the child and said she could come back and see her later after she gets home from school, but the social worker arranged to come back two working days later to see her.

The social worker did not try to return to see the child that day, even though she returned straight to the office and did not have other visits to make. Nor did she ask to see around the home, telling me after the visit that she did not feel comfortable asking to see the bedrooms, even though she felt that the home conditions and nature of the concern for the child justified it. She could not really explain why she didn't go through with it, it was just the uncomfortable feeling she had while in the home: 'I try to work with families in ways that equalize the power that I have. It's difficult.' She said she does ask to see the bedrooms, not in every case, but if the home conditions and 'feel' of the home suggest it is needed. She does feel uncomfortable doing it, and has known herself that, on occasion, she avoids doing it. In some cases, she has gone back to see the children and their bedrooms after having recognized the need to do so. The social worker's philosophy was that

> The child's bedroom tells you a lot. It shows how much they care about him or her and what they are prepared to do for the child. It doesn't take much money to provide a clean bed and make a child comfortable.

In not seeing through on this philosophy, the social worker had admitted to an avoidance. She said she would probably try to see the bedrooms when she makes the return visit. The fact that she didn't see the child and try to look around the home on that day is questionable practice. The time gap gave the mother the opportunity and time to work on the seven-year-old child and her story, should she wish to, and probably clean up. This prevents social workers from uncovering the reality of children's lives and any harm that may have been done to them and to use this evidence as the basis for an assessment that can be used to motivate the parent(s) to change.

In my experience of observing and interviewing social workers, when given permission to talk about the difficulty of the work, they will admit to having practised avoidance of this kind. Avoidance is not the same as forgetting, which involves something slipping the mind. Avoidance can happen in several areas: not asking to see the children or, when it is requested, not following through by insisting on it; not requesting to interview the children on their own; not asking questions about especially delicate and personal subjects; not asking about fathers, cohabitees, or who is resident with the child; not requesting to see around the home, including the kitchen and bedrooms. Social workers don't intend to avoid things, and like the social worker in the above example, they sometimes go back and make up for what they have not done. However, some do not face up to the avoidance or go back. Indeed, some are not even fully aware of what they have not done. This can be because they lack the necessary knowledge and skills as they were never properly trained to do the activity in the first place; or they feel they do not have time; or they know what they should be doing but decide against it; or the avoidance of issues occurs at an unconscious level.

A vitally important but peculiarly underrecognized reason why core practices in child protection are avoided is because they are so difficult. A lot of the difficulty can be explained by just how hard it can be to overcome a feeling of being overly intrusive in someone's home. It's all the more difficult when parents use their hostility and the home to stage-manage what the worker gets to see, as discussed in Chapter 4. A hugely important source of the difficulty lies in the emotional pain and unbearable feelings that doing child protection work brings up (Cooper and Lousada, 2005). You don't ask or follow through on seeing children or around homes because you are too afraid of what you might unearth and the consequences of having to deal with it, for you personally and the child, the family and the organization. The crucial thing to try and bear in mind, however, is that the consequences for the child of professional inaction may be far worse than anything the worker has to go through. But, in those fateful moments when they are in the home and face to face with service users, it is enormously difficult for workers to think straight enough to become aware of unbearable feelings and how they are causing avoidance. Psychological defence mechanisms are at work, which result in justifications for not doing things. It is crucial, then, to understand the unconscious as well as conscious states of mind that arise in these situations.

To fully understand the dynamics of workers' psychological states when carrying out such practices, it is necessary to evoke the strangeness and unpredictability of what can happen when workers meet service users in their most intimate spaces. In Chapter 4, I suggested that what goes on in the worker's mind and body is not fully under their control and is influenced by unconscious factors. A central insight from the growth of theoretical work on the home is that it should not be regarded as a neutral space, but one that is bursting with symbolic meanings and emotions. Stepping into the child's life, their home, means entering the family's space, system, energies, smells, sounds, movements, an entire atmosphere and this transition across a boundary causes disorientation. As one social worker in my research put it: 'The house is just a tip, it's full of, it's like a time warp to go into the house.' Gathering yourself and your self-composure and creating the conditions of calmness and 'order' in the home that enable the core tasks of child-centred practice to be carried out require personal resources, a capacity for deep reflection and a highly skilled performance.

As I showed in Chapter 3, such transitions and disorientation can be understood in terms of entering that 'in-between' state of normlessness that anthropologists call 'liminality'. Liminality tends to be a temporary stage, which recedes once a sense of orientation to the new conditions and 'order' has been achieved. The doorstep and hallway, as Chapter 3 showed, are classic in-between spaces, being on the boundary between being in and out. Once the worker is clearly on the inside and in the rooms of the home itself, things have a chance to settle – although they may not.

Given the particularities of child protection, I shall replace the anthropological language of liminality with the terminology of 'professional insecurity'. This refers to trouble in feeling grounded and comfortable in your own skin. Comfortable here is not about being able to stretch out and relax, 'putting your feet up', as one would do in one's own home, but is meant in the professional sense of having a sufficient sense of security to be able to think clearly and have the presence of body and mind to conduct an effective intervention. Discomfort concerns difficulties for the worker in managing their own feelings and making sense of what seems to be going on in the family and the atmosphere in the home. The examples given in this book from child death inquiry reports and research are illustrative of how social workers and other professionals experience professional insecurity and lose (or never gain) their focus on the child's safety.

In a similar spirit to that of 'atmosphere', the kind of language needed to make sense of these experiences, the 'something' that happens when worker meets service user when home visiting, is to be found in the metaphor of 'reverberation', drawn from the work of Gaston Bachelard. In *The Poetics of Space* (1969), Bachelard argues that it is necessary to understand the sensuous nature of domestic space. Houses are lived through one's body and its memories. We all tend to have a deep emotional attachment to our home and the notion of what a home is. Classically, the home we lived in at birth and as children holds special meanings and memories. The metaphor of reverberation suggests an immediacy in how the characteristics of houses and those in them physically affect us and are part of us. What Bachelard evokes is a sense of unpredictability and deep emotional and psychological responses in our experiences of our own and others' homes. Reverberation helps us to articulate how professionals step into spaces that are pervaded by complex meanings and atmospheres and how homes trigger memories and emotions in us that we may not understand or even be fully conscious of.

The further and deeper practitioners go into homes, the riskier and harder child protection practice gets, and the more reverberations there are to cope with and the more prone the worker is to experiencing professional insecurity. Let me give an example from my own practice experience. Many years ago I did a home visit to a case that concerned low-level childcare problems/query neglect. A man answered the door who was the father of the children. I asked him if I could speak to him about the children and he told me his wife was upstairs in bed. I asked him if I could go up and see her and he grunted and pointed up the stairs. I went up the stairs and entered the bedroom, to find the woman in bed completely submerged under the covers. I spoke to her and got a murmured response. I persevered, encouraging her to uncover her head so that we could talk. She persisted in remaining covered and I asked her why she was in bed. 'I'm depressed', she replied, 'I want to die.' Without thinking, I immediately responded: 'So why don't you kill yourself then!' She responded equally quickly with: 'Don't worry, I've tried', at which point she emerged from under the blankets (these were pre-duvet days). I sat on the edge of the double bed and we talked. I remember vividly the feeling of shock and shame I felt the minute those words 'So why don't you kill yourself then' came out of my mouth. I'm a social worker, I kept thinking, I'm supposed to encourage people to live better lives not die. I said and did many stupid things in my time as a social worker, but this is right up there at the top of the stupidity charts. The reason I am being so open about this faux pas is because it is the kind of unexpected behaviour that holds clues for us in trying to reach deeper understandings of how the environment we are in reverberates through us and influences why we do and say certain things.

I can now understand it as precisely the kind of behaviour that arises from an experience that triggers unconscious feelings. In that moment, standing in that bedroom, unconsciously I was back as an eight-year-old boy feeling anxious and helpless witnessing my mother who was unwell in bed. She turned out to be fine but something about this encounter took me back there, and its location in the bedroom was crucial to my conscious and unconscious responses. Had this woman been stretched out covered by a blanket on the settee in the sitting room, I doubt that I would have responded as ineptly I did. All of us have a history of domestic spaces and particular rooms represent the people, events and emotions we experienced in them, which are imprinted in our memories and psyches. These submerged feelings pop up when we don't expect them and unplanned things are said and done. This means that every worker has an unconscious as well as a conscious relationship to rooms in homes and how they behave in them, which reverberates through them and influences how they work with children and families and which they need to come to understand. A valuable exercise for students and practitioners is to reflect on what different rooms in homes mean to them and what might be lurking in the shadows waiting to come to the surface when they least expect it.

Something else I learned from this kind of messy encounter is that the kinds of mistakes or Freudian slips where stupid, inappropriate things are said and done are not necessarily destructive. This woman and I went on to have quite a good working relationship and her mental health did improve. I'm not at all sure if I can claim any particular credit for that – for a start I was not alone in working with her as she also had a psychiatrist – but I do have a hunch that the intimate experience we shared in her bedroom and my crude honesty possibly helped to create trust very quickly. I'm not at all advocating such a direct and insensitive approach to service users, rather my point is that these slip-ups will happen and the key thing is to admit to them and learn from them – as much about ourselves as about family members. This is a crucial component of good reflective practice. Workers should be given permission in supervision and case discussions to admit to the absurd, the stupidest thing(s) they have said and done, as a basis for learning from it about themselves as well as the child and family.

Psychoanalyst and writer Brett Kahr (2009) has studied the impact of the unconscious and issues to do with sexuality on how psychotherapists go about their work and the extent to which couples counsellors raise the issue of sex with their clients. Contrary to the popular stereotype that psychoanalysts are preoccupied with sex (Freud did after all regard psychosexual development as central to the human condition), many couples counsellors do not in fact raise sexual matters with their clients, despite sex being regarded by them as a key issue in couple relationships. This, Kahr argues, can be due to how therapists can take on the couple's own reluctance to talk about sexuality, which they do not state overtly but unconsciously project onto the worker, who then does not ask. But inhibitions also arise from other matters:

> Fewer aspects of human behaviour produce more anxiety than sexuality. After all, sexual behaviour and sexual fantasy can produce our greatest bodily and psychological pleasures, but sexual behaviour and its fantasmatic antecedents can also result in abuse, rape, even torture and lust murder. And the anxiety around sexuality – an overarching aspect of human experience which can create life or cause death – will be reflected not only in the general population, but among experts and professionals as well. Frank discussion about sexual matters generates very primitive, archaic fears about our own conception. (Kahr, 2009, p. 16)

While psychotherapists have to endure these fears and defences in the comfort of their own consulting rooms, social workers are faced with the enormous challenge of not only discussing relevant intimate matters with service users but going into the very spaces where sexuality and intimacy at their most private and sacred are practised. For children, this can include where violence has been perpetrated. These issues go well beyond just sexual abuse, given that social workers enter children's bedrooms to inquire into all kinds of harm to them. While their role is in key respects quite different, social workers are even more prone to the same kinds of avoidance as counsellors, given that their engagement with the child and family takes place in the home and its most intimate spaces.

The unconscious processes and unbearable feelings, in part triggered by the place where the practice goes on, play a significant but usually unrecognized part in why children are not properly engaged with and protected. The key issue, then, is for organizations to find ways of supporting workers in recognizing their professional insecurities and feelings. They need to be able to bear them sufficiently to overcome avoidance, confront difficult things, and perform the actions that are so vital to protecting children.

Conclusion

The chapter has examined some of the kinds of experiences of other people's homes that are at the heart of performing social work and child protection and which good practice involves working through. This is enormously difficult work and it is little wonder that workers' reluctance to act to challenge parents is a common finding in reviews of cases where children have died or been seriously harmed (Brandon et al., 2008). As many critics of the child protection system have pointed out, too much bureaucracy limits the time and energy that can be devoted to relating to children (Munro, 2005; Broadhurst et al., 2010a; 2010b), while problems in interagency communication often mean that social workers do not have access to the full story of risk for the child. But the most significant and yet least understood aspects of what social workers and other professionals can do in child protection occur when practitioners leave their desks and offices and interact with service users in their homes, where professionals are required to be proactive. For when things go wrong and abused children are missed, something always happens that blocks professionals' performance of direct engagement with the child, of which the worker's own resistance and avoidance of the unbearable feelings and difficult aspects of the work are a part.

A crucial question that needs to be asked of social workers by supervisors and peers is: 'Tell me about the atmosphere and what reverberates within you about this child/adult/home/family?' Reflection on it can deepen understandings of the dynamics of relationships with children and parents/carers and how free or constrained professionals feel to move around and take control of encounters, and what can immobilize them in performing the actions that are essential to doing effective child protection.

6

Relating to children

Whatever form the organisation of the social services takes, direct personal communication between social workers and children about their problems is indispensable.

(DHSS, 1974a, p. 76)

It should go without saying that the child needs to be at the centre of child protection. It has to be said because children are so often lost sight of and not properly related to, and this can have tragic consequences. Attempts to ensure child protection professionals focus more effectively on the child have periodically been developed in policy and have always been in tension with protecting the rights of parents and the family to privacy. The most recent manifestation of this in England, for instance, is that revised government guidance issued in 2010 places a specific requirement on social workers to see children alone when assessing their needs and promoting their safety (DCSF, 2010). But what does 'seeing' children mean, where should they be seen, how can this be achieved and what do we know about how best to work with children and young people to ensure they are safe? This chapter explores these questions through the notion of 'relating' to children. This terminology has been chosen because it captures a range of stages of work, from 'accessing' children and initial 'engagement' with them, to longer term therapeutic and support work. It also includes different activities: observing, talking, listening, walking and playing with children. In total, the notion of relating to children seeks to account for the key experiences and elements of what occurs and needs to happen in relationship-based work with them.

In many respects, relating to children in child protection permeates this entire book and many examples and issues involved in investigation, assessment and long-term work have already been considered. There are also some excellent books on communicating and working with children

(Brandon et al., 1998; Jones, 2003; Lefevre, 2010). So I am again being selective here in focusing on the issues with respect to the core concerns of this book: space, intimate practice and the impact of lived experience and different environments on how children are related to. This and Chapters 7 and 8 are thematically linked in addressing the influence of different environments on where children are seen and related to, and how practitioners use themselves and their skills in doing so. Chapter 7 is about the nature and importance of touch in keeping children safe, Chapter 8 deals with the car as a neglected space for therapeutic practice, while this chapter considers the merits of the home, schools and family centres as spaces to relate to children.

Making contact with children

As far as possible, all contact with children should be planned. Prior to going to where the child is, be it their home, school, family centre, hospital or other place, the social worker needs to have a strategy for how to make contact with them. On new referrals, this intervention strategy will be worked out with the support of their manager and in collaboration with other agencies who know the child and family. Such 'strategy discussions' are at the heart of coordinated child protection work. In long-term work where there is a child protection plan, the worker must be clear about the aims of every visit to the child and what must be done to ensure they are safe. These are always age and ability specific, but generally will include clarity about: who and what they need to see in and of the home; what they should be seeking to see of children's bodies to check their wellbeing; what degree of movement by (and with) the child and tactile contact they need to have; and what they need to be talking to the child about.

Practitioners tend to have standard introductions to children worked out, which explain their role, the aims of the meeting, and set ground rules about limited confidentiality. This involves explaining that because their role is to keep the child safe, if they hear anything that suggests the child is at risk, the social worker cannot keep this to themselves but must discuss it with other professionals and, at an appropriate point that ensures the child's safety, with the parents. In responding to children with disabilities, it is essential that social workers provide whatever help with communication the child needs. This ensures that the child's experience is fully and clearly communicated and understood (Kitson and Clawson, 2007). Kitson and Clawson (2007) show how disabled children are more vulnerable to abuse than their non-abused peers. Reasons include because their body is handled routinely by different carers, they spend time away from home, and the child is targeted by abusers because they appear less likely to complain successfully to others. Kitson and Clawson (2007, p. 176) point out that

> if the child does not have the choice of words, symbols or signs to tell what happened, does not feel they are being listened to or is not given access to a person to tell, the information will not be made available.

Disabled children and young people use a wide range of communication systems and if workers do not adequately understand the issues, they need to involve experts who do.

Practitioners also usually have a repertoire of techniques to try and get children to talk and interact with them that they have developed and refined through experience. Lefevre (2010) summarizes what research suggests are the qualities children like to see in social workers and other professionals:

- Outgoing, approachable, easy to talk to
- Not stuck up or too formal
- Able to get on with children and adults
- Capable of understanding 'the ways and thoughts of kids'
- Good listeners
- Have a good sense of humour
- Good at calming people down when they are upset
- Not judging others, trying to understand.

But however much protecting children requires professionals to take initiatives on their behalf, young people must not be regarded as merely waiting for the professional adult to decide when to speak to them and direct where it should happen. Children are social actors who have rights and capacities, which differ according to their age, stage of development and abilities. Establishing meaningful contact and developing helping relationships with children depends on the extent to which children and young people feel that their rights and abilities are being respected (Bell, 2002).

Gaining parental permission to interview their child is one thing, gaining the child's cooperation another. As one social worker put it:

> This again is different with each practitioner and different with each case, and every child and every young person. It may well be that quite often you'll go into the house and a child or young person doesn't want to speak with you on their own, it'll be that mum or dad gave permission, but whenever you ask the child or young person, they refuse to meet you or refuse to see you.

When this happens, the social worker explained:

> Well if they refuse to see you…quite often that would be on an initial visit, I'm thinking of my own experience, and then once you visit maybe a second or third time and build up that relationship, then it's usual they'll come, they're quite happy to meet with you.

The process outlined by this social worker of relating directly with the child on their own after the professional has enabled them to get to know them a little and at least some trust has developed is broadly viewed as a desirable approach (Lefevre, 2010). This is only possible if the level of the concern in the case allows for some time to be devoted to relationship building. Even when children agree to be seen alone, some express their reluctance to engage by saying little or nothing. Several factors influence whether children and young people feel able to speak to professionals, including the extent to which they regard themselves as having a problem, previous negative experiences of such encounters, or being coerced or pressurized by parents beforehand not to (Jones, 2003). When they do speak, the worker must be alert to how they may have been coached by parents or other carers to give a positive view of their experience that is in stark contrast to the reality, as happened, for example, in the Victoria Climbié case (Laming, 2003).

However, the extent to which the social worker can accept the choice made by the child or young person to not engage depends on the nature of the concern being looked into and the level of risk they are thought to be at. Where the child is a suspected victim of physical abuse or serious neglect, their choices will be limited. They will require medical examination as well as being spoken to alone, and where the severity of the abuse or neglect require it, this will involve a formal social worker–police interview to establish their wellbeing and safety. In cases of suspected sexual abuse, the child will have to be interviewed jointly by the police and social workers. Evidence of physical harm following sexual abuse is much less common, because penetration of the child's body may not have happened as part of the abuse, or where it did, there may not have been marks, or where there was penetrative abuse, the sometimes extended time lapse between the abusive acts and their coming to light means that the physical signs will have gone. Much then depends on what the child verbally discloses. This is why so much effort has been put into developing well-appointed, child-friendly interviewing suites and joint police–social worker interview approaches, which need to be forensically sound enough to provide permissible evidence in court (no leading questions or suggestive comments), while trying to lessen the impact on the child of such a potentially traumatic experience. All efforts must be put into ensuring that the child does not have to be interviewed more than is necessary (Butler-Sloss, 1988).

Where to relate to children on their own

In day-to-day child protection work, social workers have to find ways of seeing children on their own as part of investigations, assessments and long-term safety work. Where and when to see children alone often presents agonizing dilemmas for social workers, who need to give careful thought to the timing and when it feels right to do it and where to do it: in the child's home, in school or elsewhere? Much will depend on what stage the case is at in the child protection process. At a minimum, all children who are the subjects of child protection referrals, who have the appropriate age and understanding, need to be related to as part of the initial investigation and seen on other occasions during the assessment phase. In cases of substantiated concern where children are on child protection plans, regular contact alone with them must take place to check on their safety and wellbeing, and as part of the therapeutic input.

My research suggests that many social workers decide to conduct some assessment interviews with the child in the home, very often in their bedroom. Places such as schools and children's and family centres are also used. Several factors influence the choice of location and it is difficult to identify a definite position among social workers on what is the best place, due to the uniqueness of each situation. This is nicely articulated by a social worker:

I think we have less direct contact than it would be nice to have time to do, and in a way it kind of loads our visits [because] in those times you have to do quite a lot. But then part of I hope the skill of a social worker and our training is that when you do then have direct, one-to-one contact with children, you are able to make them at ease and you engage in an age-appropriate way, and you ask questions which they understand, and you are able to gauge how much they understand that and what kind of level of honesty you're getting from them sometimes in their responses. And so there's no easy answer to how you engage children in those situations because it depends whether there's a mum stalking outside the door of the bedroom you're sitting talking to them in. Or whether they've got their little brother there, because they won't speak to you without their little brother there, and so there's always a relatively unique dynamic to it, so there's no simple answer to that. And for me again part of the stimulation of it is that the privilege of it is it's always unique, you're always remembering that it's someone's own lives that you're dealing with, so I say part of the question I'll always try and ask is: How is it feeling for them? As a man, as a social worker, as a council employee, how are they feeling about me being there, what can I do to try and get the most accurate, honest appraisal of how things are for them out of them.

The self-monitoring and questioning this male social worker engages in is the kind of excellent reflective practice that is required here if the influence of gender, ethnicity, ability and the setting where the contact with the child occurs are to be taken into account. Some of the dilemmas and dangers of relating to children on their own in their home are exemplified by a case from my research that involved three children, aged 2, 8 and 11. Their mother had allegedly been drunk and had gone out with the 2-year-old, leaving the 8- and the 11-year-old at home, expecting a 17-year-old babysitter who didn't show up. The mother was picked up by the police on the roadside at two o'clock in the morning because she appeared to be falling over drunk and had her 2-year-old with her in the buggy.

Following a referral by the police, the social worker assessed the family. She found the home conditions to be comfortable, with no grounds for concern. She requested to see the 8-year-old girl and her 11-year-old brother together without their mother in their bedroom, to which their mother consented. They disclosed nothing that caused her concern. The subsequent case conference did not place the children on a child protection plan or the child protection register. There was an advocate for the children at the meeting to whom the children had made statements that were read out to the conference and which were really positive. Social

work remained involved due to the severity of the initial reported incident and it was transferred to a long-term worker. A couple of weeks
later, the mother went into school drunk again, the school reported it
and the social worker visited the home and found the mother very drunk.
The social worker followed up that incident by seeing and interviewing
the children at school. The 8-year-old disclosed that her mother regularly goes out between 3 and 9pm to the pub, she sometimes doesn't feed
them, she sometimes drops the 2-year-old when she's drunk, swears at
him and pulls his legs, and that she hits all three of them.

In the light of what was now known, the original social worker was full
of regret and self-recrimination about how she handled the first referral:

> I'd only had the case for 19 days, but I spoke to the children alone in
> their bedrooms and I should have spoken to them in school. But the case
> was transferred [to a long-term worker] and one of the children has now
> disclosed quite a horrific amount of abuse at home and I didn't pick up on
> it because I spoke to the children at home and not in school.

The social worker concedes that 'I guess they could have not disclosed
for a number of reasons', but returns to the view that she saw them alone
in the wrong place:

> So what I should have done, I should have gone into school and seen the
> children in school because it would have been a safer place for them to talk
> about bad things at home. But instead I spoke to them in their bedroom
> and I spoke to them together as well... in their bedroom with the door
> shut and they obviously didn't feel comfortable to disclose.

I think the social worker is right to have reached this conclusion
about how cases with that type and severity of problem should be
handled. Yet she was also using hindsight too freely to beat herself
up. There is no guarantee that in response to the first referral the children would have disclosed abuse if interviewed in school. As Jones
(2003) observes, schools can have inhibiting effects on children if
they identify them as places where they are spoken to by adults to
be told off. It is also significant that the long-term social worker had
the benefit of the second referral, a somewhat longer known history of
concerns to relate to the children about, and a slightly longer relationship between them and social work (albeit different practitioners), and
perhaps benefited from more trust being built up. The second worker
may have found the children in a state of readiness to talk about

their experiences that they simply were not at before. It is, of course, also possible that the lack of disclosure at the first bedroom interview was because it was poorly conducted. I was not present so have no way of knowing. Yet the conclusion that the environment of the home, with the mother who was the alleged abuser downstairs, inhibited the children's capacity to be open and honest about their experience is inescapable.

The social worker thought she 'didn't speak to them in school probably because I'd seen enough of them at home and I was a bit busy with other cases'. Ultimately, she felt that interviews with children were done at home to save time:

> I think if the child makes a direct disclosure in school we always see the child in school. There are instances where you do always see the child in school, you do always speak to them alone and you don't need the parents' permission. In fact, it's generally best without the parents. But . . . if you can do a visit after four o'clock and then if you see the parents and the children and the home conditions and you can speak to the children . . . obviously they'd be school age so we'd see them after school. But that's the most efficient way to do it, because, depending on what the issues are and the case, sometimes you do need to see the parents alone, so you could follow that up with a visit to school. It's almost the most efficient way to do it because you see everyone in one visit, rather than seeing the parents, then seeing the children [at school], then seeing the parents and the children together. But . . . it's not always the best for the child so I now will make an effort to see children in school.

This points to the huge challenges social workers face when the demands of high caseloads and paperwork threaten to pull them away from a capacity to be available to children and to practise therapeutically when with them. The assessment here was completed in the space of just 19 days, not necessarily because this was regarded as sufficient to find out all there was to know, but because the contact with the children was fitted into a series of time-limited, procedurally driven tasks within which whatever contact occurred with the children had to be good enough. On top of interviewing the parents and gathering information from other professionals, it does not seem unusual for assessments to be based on one or two 10–15-minute meetings with the children. This can lead to assessments that are too partial and consequently unsafe and lacking in therapeutic benefit for children. Social workers need to be able to keep going back to see the child so as to reach a point where it feels like everything there is to know about them has been established for the purposes of effective child protection in the short and long term.

I shall return to the time issues below, but so far as where practice should be done, the easiest way out of these dilemmas would indeed appear to be not to see children alone at home when their suspected abusive parent(s) or carers are also in the house, or at least not to base the assessment entirely on that meeting. Social workers do sometimes employ the approach of going elsewhere to engage with the child. As another worker articulates it:

> Where you can go down and meet with a child or young person and do some work with them in a setting where there's some space and security, rather than at home where they don't feel able to inform me, maybe there's just too many distractions, or mum and dad are there, or it's just more difficult, and sometimes then it's easier to meet them in the setting of school.

Interviewing children in secure places that are known to them, such as schools or family centres, is probably the ideal here. While schools can be inhibiting environments, for the abused child it can be a 'secure base' (Gilligan, 1998), within which they can have a lot of trust in their class teacher or a special needs school worker, and social workers can use this as a resource by doing joint interviews. The more serious the suspected abuse, the less reliable the home is as a place to interview children. The more proximate a suspected abuser, the less appropriate it is to interview a child in their vicinity. Even if reassured by professionals that they cannot be heard beyond the room with the door closed – false reassurance surely, given the scope there is for parents to listen in behind closed doors – children may still fear that they can be heard by parents or other family members. The abused child's experience of home will be that it is controlled by adults who seem all-powerful, and this control is written into the very architecture of the place. The child will rightly know or suspect that 'the walls have ears' and this inhibits what they are prepared to say. This is another example of the dynamic discussed in Chapter 4 of the building, the home, having 'agency' and power in how it exerts an influence over those in it. When it is the site of danger and trauma as much if not more than love and nurturance for children, the fear and risk they experience is felt to lie in the walls and very timbers of the home. True freedom to speak and act must come beyond the home's walls. It is vital that workers consider what the home and particular rooms in it may mean to children and the likely impact of any other adults who are in the home, even if they are not in the same room when the interview is going on. The presence in the home of non-abusing adults who the child trusts can have a consoling effect, making it a more congenial space to risk disclosing any harm they are experiencing. The argument in Chapter 5 concerning the emotional impact and unpredictability of the bedroom as a space in which to do this sensitive work is another reason for caution about whether it and the home are the best place to relate to children alone.

Yet there are too many variables at play to make it appropriate to insist on a blanket rule that children should never be related to alone at home. So much depends on the situation. Where the adult who is in the home is a non-abusing parent and the perpetrator is not there, it is likely to be acceptable to relate to the child there. Some feel that if the level of concern is low, just seeing the child at home is justified. Social workers sometimes have to make compromises and be pragmatic and try to speak to children when and where they can, such as when the impact of parental resistance means the worker decides to engage with children there and then when the opportunity arises. This should not mean making unacceptable compromises, but the reality is that there are no easy answers and workers have to manage the risk of getting it wrong. It is only acceptable for social workers to communicate with children alone in their homes if the potential flaws of this are fully recognized and other ways of checking on their wellbeing are included in investigations, assessments and built in to longer term child protection plans, for example seeing them elsewhere, such as at school or family centres.

Skill, play and body technique in relating to children

In critiquing the impact of high caseloads and bureaucracy, we must be careful not to place too much emphasis on limited time as the key or only variable influencing how social workers relate to children. It is also necessary to focus on the quality of the contact and relating to children that is possible and required. It is spending quality time with children that matters. Once again, workers adopt varying approaches when relating to children and young people and different styles are in evidence. These are determined by workers' level of experience, knowledge, training, their personality and how they are as a person, what they feel comfortable doing.

Some workers conduct the session sitting on chairs, settees or beds at an appropriate distance from children using talk. Children, especially younger ones, may not remain seated in these situations and get up and move around, but the worker remains seated and essentially still. Then there are workers who are playful and go down to the children's level, quite literally in terms of getting on the floor and communicating and playing with them. Sitting on the floor can be a particularly useful way of engaging a child/young person who is reluctant to talk. I have interviewed some social workers who will spend most or all of the time with the child on the floor, even while engaging with the parent(s), because this gives children more opportunity to engage with the worker on their level. I have no way of knowing how common it is to conduct an entire interview while sitting on the floor, but suspect it is not usual. My impression is that those who do it tend to have experience of working in environments where free association with children was encouraged, such as family support services and children's centres.

Writers from academic and practitioner backgrounds recommend that workers carry with them toys and other communication aids to use with children (Brandon et al., 1998; Lefevre, 2010; Koprowska, 2010). Many exercises and techniques are available. Turnell and Essex (2006) show the value of getting children to create words and pictures of their home to describe their experiences and what danger and safety means to them. The 'three houses tool' enables information to be gathered that supports risk assessment by getting children to draw houses that represent their worries, strengths and dreams, that is, the kind of home they would like to live in (Weld, 2008). Levels of skill, confidence, experience, training and organizational support determine how prepared – in every sense – workers are to relate in creative ways to children (Lefevre, 2010). Some highly thoughtful and committed social workers have told me that their personal style of working does not involve sitting on floors or using art- or play-based communication with children. They do not feel comfortable doing it. This discomfort does not derive from any intellectual or ideological objection but in some measure from their inner selves, the body positions and techniques they prefer and how difficult they would find it to drop down to the floor. It just doesn't feel right; the resistance is visceral, lived in the very fibre and being of their bodies and souls. They literally cannot bring themselves to do it. This is especially pronounced when they are in service users' private space, on home visits. These workers are also much less likely to be tactile with children, a theme I discuss at length in the next chapter. Whether or not this motionless practice is a problem depends on how effective the approach they do adopt is in enabling the child to communicate their experience. Workers who prefer this style may have other talents and communicative competences that could make them as effective as their more playful, freely moving colleagues. But their bodily inhibitions, their 'stiffness', brings the risk of them not moving sufficiently enough to reach children's level and see through on the actions needed to ensure protection (discussed in Chapters 4 and 5).

Relating to children in spaces beyond the home

When harm to a child or young person has been substantiated, social workers and other professionals need to work creatively in seeing them not only on their own, but with their parents. At various points during short- or long-term interventions, the entire family also have to be worked with together. Examples of such work are provided in several other chapters. In the final part of this chapter, I want to focus on one-to-one intervention work with children and young people where it not seen as appropriate to do it inside the home. This will help to draw out further the particularities of the home and what other spaces have to offer. Children may not feel safe being worked with at home for reasons other than the proximity of an abuser. The home may be part of their problem, and meaningful therapeutic work is best done in an explicitly nurturing environment.

Louise is 13 and has an 11-year-old sister and 10-year-old brother. The family live in social housing in a densely populated urban area. In the 12 years they have been married, Louise's parents have lived in three of the most marginalized areas of the city, but, as her mother Deirdre explains, 'nowhere was ever as bad as where we live now'. Their story exemplifies the daily struggles of living in poverty and social disadvantage. As Louise's father Robert expresses it: 'I live in a dump. I live in a ghetto. It's kind of as simple as that.' They live their lives surrounded by 'drug pushers, gun carriers, child abusers and joy riders'. As Deirdre characterizes it:

> Our next door neighbour pushes drugs. The neighbour behind on the other side of us, we're in the middle of a block of neighbours, they're alcoholics. It's just total destruction everywhere you turn. A lot of anger, a lot of hurt, a lot of resentment in people, you know. People, they are good

people, but they're going through an awful lot of pain, especially the kids. The kids in our area are very angry kids, you know. They only know how to act with violence. Like you have this constant situation of violence so it's actually like living in a ghetto in America.

She believes the routine violence and hostility they have to confront in the neighbourhood has its roots in poverty and people simply not having enough money to feed their children. Once, their dream as parents was to be able to move out of the area to live in the country, but due to poverty they now feel stuck in the ghetto. There is concern now for the children who have become isolated in their own home and back garden, because of their fear and the parents' unwillingness to allow them to be bullied on the street by drug-pushing neighbours. Louise witnessed a neighbour threatening to kill their dog by placing a gun in its mouth. Louise's teacher is concerned that she is losing her confidence and becoming withdrawn. Louise has disclosed sexual abuse by a non-family member and there has been an incident of domestic abuse by Louise's father against her mother. Thus it was not all about the extreme pressures arising from poverty, and it was known that Robert was abused as a child.

Because it is located in a neighbourhood that, to the family, resembles a war zone, the deep insecurity of the family home is part of the young person's problem. The family were seen there but the real therapeutic and support work went on at a local family centre. As the family centre worker puts it:

> This centre is situated in the middle of the edge. That we're living very much, if you can live, in the middle and the conversations that we have here are with people who are living on the edge of society, who are living in disadvantage.

Louise felt that she herself had benefited from attending the centre and especially the individual work that was done with her:

> And it really helps too... They listen here. They're actually really good listeners. You know, someone other than your family to talk to. There's someone else that's not against you like, there's one more at least. And when you come here, we do arts and crafts and we just, they have a bean bag in there that you punch and all that, that relieves you and lets out your anger. The way you are feeling depends on what happens before you come in. Sometimes you'd be feeling low, sometimes you'd be really happy. So I have a scrapbook that I have locked up and all my, you know, anger

and all that stuff, all that's in it. So I, I don't think anybody else has that, it's just something that [centre worker] thought I should do. So I did. [female centre worker]'s really nice and so is [male centre worker]! They're both wonderful.

This bears out Schofield and Brown's (1999) argument that spaces like family centres and their staff play a vital role as a secure base for vulnerable young people. The centre also provided family therapy sessions to all the family together and saw the parents as a couple and individually. Robert was helped with the trauma of his childhood abuse. This work was primarily aimed at building the children's resilience by dealing with the impact of the trauma they had experienced, preventing domestic abuse and stopping the parents from imploding further in the face of such extreme social disadvantage. This 13-year-old young person clearly valued the highly skilled work that was done with her, the creative resources of bean bags and art and play materials the centre could provide, the deeply meaningful therapeutic relationships she developed with the workers, all set within the secure base of the centre itself. This could not change the appalling circumstances of poverty and the unsafe neighbourhood, but it helped the young person and other family members to build their internal resources to cope. The intervention was also a means of dealing with the individual characteristics, destructive patterns of emotional response and behaviours through which the parents and children conducted their relationships. It enabled a family at high risk of cracking under pressure to stay together, averting the ultimate tragedy of parents and children who have so little of material value in their lives losing all that is emotionally precious to them.

Conclusion

This chapter has shown the importance of the environment where children are seen in influencing whether they feel sufficiently secure and safe enough to disclose their experience and gain help with their trauma. Every worker must be supported through education and training to reach a level of ability where they can relate creatively to children, using a range of body techniques on home visits and in other spaces. This depends on gaining the self-knowledge that brings understanding of their comfort zones and what is stopping them from going beyond them in what they are prepared to ask, see and are able to hear. It requires recognition of and overcoming their avoidance of painful issues and the impact of particular environments on how secure the worker and the child are able to feel. Workers need organizational structures and managers who can ensure that they have the time that is needed to have meaningful relationships with children and that they develop the capacity to get into a state of mind and body that enables the time that is spent with children to be as focused and productive as the child needs it to be.

7

The importance of touch in protecting children

> We now know that it does matter how a baby is held and handled.
> (Winnicott, 1971, p. 141)

Relating to children in social work and child protection is always non-verbal as well as verbal. The younger the child, the less scope there is to conduct discussion-based interviews and the more the child or infant must be heard to speak, as it were, through their body. On top of gathering the parents'/carers' views of the child, communication must go on through observation of the child and touch. Touch has, in many respects, become deeply problematic and even taboo in working with children and this chapter argues for the importance of touch in child protection work. I distinguish medical examinations from what I call 'professional touch', which should be considered a routine part of day-to-day practice that keeps children safe.

A brief history of touch in child welfare

From its beginnings, touch has represented a problem for child protection practitioners, although the reasons for this have changed somewhat over time. Chapter 1 included a case study from 1909 where the worker expressed clearly his fears of being contaminated by the children and home he had just come into contact with. In a remarkable passage from the 1910 edition of the NSPCC procedural manual, under the heading 'Cleansing of the Hands', workers were advised of hygiene rules:

> To avoid risks to the health of himself or other persons, an Inspector should at all times, in cases where there is any likelihood of there being any disease

of an infectious or contagious nature, and also after handling a dead child, take precautions for the thorough cleansing of the hands. It is best to use a carbolic soap for washing the hands after dealing with such cases. The hands should always be well-cared for, and any cuts or abrasions have suitable dressing applied in order to keep the wound free from the chance of contamination. The nails should be kept clipped quite short, and no dirt allowed to accumulate under them. (NSPCC, 1910, pp. 42–3)

For a variety of complex reasons, which I have analysed elsewhere (see Ferguson, 2004), social workers at this time began to view neglectful families as not only harmful to children but as a source of pollution and a personal and social risk. A major preoccupation with germs and dirt and a dread of internal pollution found its way into child protection discourse. By 1914, doctors were being routinely called in to examine suspected abused and neglected children and their homes. This attitude remained for most of the 20th century.

The rapid development of professional social work after the Second World War saw another, more humane approach to touch emerge. This was influenced by new understandings in psychology and child development based on the work of John Bowlby (1951) on attachment and others such as Clare Winnicott (1963) and Donald Winnicott (1953, 1957). Practice and the needs of children and families was now talked about through the language of relationship, holding, touch. Juliet Berry, in a wonderful 1972 book *Social Work with Children*, captures this beautifully:

> Apart from the non-verbal communication of literally holding a distressed child, there are many ways of symbolising encircling warmth – one possibility is to keep a rug in the car. Children certainly understand such symbols. (Berry, 1972, p. 55)

Here, touch is part of what marks out the common humanity between worker and child. Touch, appropriately applied, heals (Lefevre, 2010). But the experience and language of contamination and disgust in child protection lived on. In fact, after the Second World War, it intensified and was not only evident in child protection case files but in public statements and books such as Allen and Morton's 1961 classic history of the NSPCC, *This is Your Child*. They quote an estimate that between 6 and 7% of children in the UK 'are at some time during their childhood so neglected or ill-treated' (p. 62) as to require intervention. Of these cases, they wrote:

It is almost impossible to describe the conditions of acute neglect, filth, degradation and stench in which many of those children exist. No descriptive writing can bring to mind the air of total disorder, the lack of warmth or comfort, or the smell of the saturated beds, unwashed people, absence of feminine hygiene, and putrefying food that add up to the truly neglected household. (Allen and Morton, 1961, pp. 62–3)

Six years earlier, in his book *The Prevention of Cruelty to Children*, Leslie Housden did, in fact, try to describe the smell of practice:

From such matters as these, it is easy to pass to the next criteria of the Hopeless Home. The Smell. Easy to pass to it but much more difficult to convey its character in writing. It is a curious mixture of dirt, ill-ventilation, bugs and body excretions. No one can accurately describe it. It is very slightly sweet, yet almost acrid, and invariably revolting. I cannot get used to it, yet on only one occasion have I found it quite unbearable. (Housden, 1955, p. 172)

From the 1970s, attention to disgust and the smell of practice in social work and child protection largely disappears. This was in part due to how notions of partnership and empowerment became influential in policy and practice, as discussed in Chapter 2. Out of a concern to respect service users, most of who were already disadvantaged, it became difficult to publicly admit to feeling disgusted in your dealings with families. On one level, this was entirely appropriate, given that, as the above quotations show, there was a tradition of families being judged in such unkind, persecutory ways. But while we can all agree that being kind and humane towards marginalized families is a good and desirable thing, the problem is that, in the gritty reality of practice, social workers do, in some cases, experience disgust due to the smells and dirt they encounter. In my experience of observing practice and teaching, this does get some informal recognition among practitioners in remarks like: 'wipe your feet on the way out!' The poor and disgusting home conditions that workers experience are the subjects of stories that are told in offices, often just after the worker has been on a home visit. I heard one practitioner talk in graphic detail about how she refuses offers of cups of tea in some homes. This was not, as I expected, due to the often heard reason of not wanting to drink out of the family's dirty cups, but because she knew she had an appointment soon after to see a 'dirty' family and she did not want to have a need to use their toilet. But although there is a culture of such informal talk about dirt and smell, no clear acknowledgement or coherent understanding exist about its implications for avoiding touch and the development of the kinds of tactile, intimate relationships that are necessary to protect children.

Another reason the focus moved away from discussing such intimate experiences of practice is the attention that came to be given to inter-agency communication. A further factor that has driven professionals away from using touch and talking about it is the emergence of child sexual abuse as a social problem and the spectre that has intensi-fied through the 1990s and 2000s of professionals' fear of allegations (Piper and Stronach, 2008). Policies based on averting risk to profes-sionals as well as children have resulted in 'no touch' policies in many professional services working with children. Yet the issue of touch in social work and child protection has been peculiarly neglected. There now seems to be something of a taboo on touching and on talking about it.

This arises in a context where deeply troubling cultural norms have quickly developed, in which no one, it seems, wants or feels able to touch children these days, especially if they are not related to them. A fear of contact with children is, in part, a product of how it has increasingly been regulated by the state through criminal records checks. Significant changes have occurred aimed at trying to eliminate risk from childhood, which have resulted in children having much less unsupervised contact with adults and the outside world. In 1971, 8 out of 10 children aged seven or eight went to school on their own, but by 1990, this figure had dropped to less than 1 in 10. In 1971, the average seven-year-old was making trips to their friends or to the shops on their own. By 1990, that freedom was being withheld until the age of 10, meaning that, in the space of just 19 years, children had lost up to three years of freedom of movement. These trends have undoubtedly intensified in the past 20 years. One effect is that today parents spend much more time looking after their children than in the past. One study found it has increased from 25 minutes per day in 1975 to 99 minutes in 2000, and one of the reasons is the fear of letting children play unsupervised (Gill, 2007).

Without doubt, greater respect for the integrity of children's bodies and their rights not to be touched arbitrarily by adults has contributed to fewer children being inappropriately handled and sexually abused out-side the family. But this kind of attitude and fear of touch now runs so deep in western culture that, as I shall go on to show, it is influenc-ing professional practice in undesirable ways that limit the capacity of professionals to protect children.

The troubling absence of touch in child protection today

Social workers and other professionals are routinely in situations where touch has an important role to play in helping children. Within this, the challenges of workers experiencing disgust and fearing to touch children due to the risk of contamination remain as significant as ever in practice. A compelling example is evident in the Baby Peter case:

> On 30th July 2007 all the children were seen on a planned home visit by the social worker on their own and with Ms A [Peter's mother]. Peter was in the buggy, alert and smiling but overtired. His ear was sore and slightly inflamed. He had white cream on the top of his head and Ms A thought the infection had improved. Peter's face was smeared with chocolate and the social worker asked that it be cleaned off. The family friend took him away to do so and he did not reappear before the social worker left. Ms A said she had a GP appointment and mentioned grab marks on Peter. She was worried about being accused of harming him. (Haringey, 2009, p. 13)

In some respects, this was almost a good piece of practice. The social worker saw the two older children on their own, and although we are not told where, it was clearly in the home. On the basis of the analysis in Chapter 6 of the implications of where children are interviewed, the value of seeing children in such an unsafe environment is highly questionable. She saw Peter too, from a distance at least, and was presumably concerned enough to want to see more of him, so asked for his face to be cleaned. She did not, however, follow through on it when the family friend did not bring Peter back. It is now known that the chocolate was deliberately placed on Peter's face to conceal injuries and that Peter's mother had a cohabitee and another man resident in the home and she hid their presence from social workers although they were abusing Peter.

The poignancy of this scene is all the greater, given that three days later Peter was dead. This was the last time the social worker saw him alive. At the time of his death, the over 50 injuries he had on his body included a broken back, and a tooth was found in his stomach, which is assumed to have been knocked out by a blow. It is certain that the child had serious injuries when in the social worker's presence. In the last two days of his life, that is, after the social worker's home visit, a paediatrician saw Peter but did not examine him for injuries. His GP also saw him a day or so before he died and described him as being in 'a sorry state' (p. 20). But he did not examine him either. Peter had an infected scalp, which is why he had the white cream on his head when the social worker visited. His childminder, who had been given a key role in the child protection plan, had refused to look after him any longer due to the infection. The painful truth is that no one touched Peter. He was an object of disgust and professionals as well as childminders feared contamination by him.

As I alluded to in Chapter 4, the same happened to Victoria Climbié who had scabies, because of which two social workers and a police officer (independently of one another) refused to even visit the home. At least one other social worker couldn't get away from Victoria quickly enough when she came to the office because of her condition. Very early on in the case, some seven months before she died, she was actually described by the duty social worker as being like one of the 'adverts you see for Action Aid' (Laming, 2003, p. 54). Far from regarding the distance this put between professionals and Victoria as a problem, the report describes this social worker's concern for her health and safety as 'understandable' (Laming, 2003). None of the workers in Victoria's case appear to have discussed their contamination fears with colleagues, although one police officer did make efforts to raise it, but with little support. She simply failed to visit Victoria or to propose an alternative strategy for dealing with her fears. This painfully demonstrates the real dangers of workers not being able to discuss uncomfortable feelings.

In preserving the memory and dignity of Peter and Victoria, we need to avoid the risk of sentimentalizing how they were viewed and approached when alive, a risk that is compounded by the sheer awfulness of their deaths. Like Peter, Victoria was a child on the margins. She was home-less, incontinent, unkempt and smelly; she wore a wig, she was black and spoke in a foreign language. Media reporting of the Baby Peter case was full of lurid descriptions of his dirty and diseased state and filthy home conditions. As the BBC put it, in the run-up to his death Baby P was 'alive with nits and scabs from healing injuries' (1 December 2008). The painful truth is that these children generate mixed emotions that make it hard for professionals to get close to them. While the unkempt state of the children and the home is real, this detachment is not because of anything the children themselves do, but because of professionals' need to dis-tance themselves. It feels safer to do so because they fear contamination by the child and their family.

These fears are compounded by how such families are regarded as dangerous 'others', to be feared and, both literally and metaphorically, handled carefully. It is important to understand that disgust is not just a personal reaction and choice that we decide for ourselves but is socially constructed. Sociologists have shown how disgust and fear of the 'other' arise from a combination of social and psychological processes (Douglas, 1992; Joffe, 1999). The persistent stigmatizing of the poor and demonization of groups such as asylum seekers and economic migrants (like Victoria) by government and the media make them into outsiders and marginalized 'others' against which the purity of 'us', the decent and the civilized, is secured. At the psychological level, direct contact with such outsiders is experienced as a contaminating threat to the integrity of the self. If that individual, like Baby Peter and Victoria Climbié, literally has an infectious disease and is also neglected and smells due to poor care and hygiene, then the drive to avoid them further increases. More intensely still, there occurs a powerful, even irresistible, drive to exclude them through what Douglas (1966) calls 'purity and pollution rituals'. It is not too fanciful to suggest that, at some level, individuals and systems are glad to see the back of them so as to restore their own purity and cleanliness and that of society. As the Laming Report (2003) notes with cruel irony, while workers would not visit Victoria at home, they were content to let her stay there in her apparently contaminating environment.

These factors meant that it would have taken an enormous amount for Baby Peter's social worker to have seen through all the deception and to have insisted on the child being brought back and his face being seen clean, or to have touched and cleaned the child's face herself, and to have inquired more deeply into the presence of men in the home and inspected it for physical signs of them, toothbrushes, shaving gear and so on. But becoming aware of and working through these difficulties is what is required of intimate child protection practice.

The nature of touch

There are several lessons to drawn from the above analysis. A crucial one is the need to define touch and to justify its use ethically in child protection today. Touch in child protection takes two forms: medical examinations, and what I will call 'professional touch'. Medical examinations need to be carried out by qualified practitioners and must be thorough, focused not just on the presenting suspicious marks or bruises but also looking for signs of injuries on other parts of the body. This usually involves the medical or health practitioner seeing the child undressed. This examination most often takes place in a GP surgery or hospital ward or clinic, but, where appropriate, can be performed by health visitors on home visits. In one case I shadowed, the social worker did a joint home visit with the health visitor who, about two-thirds of the way through the 45-minute meeting, asked if she could see the eight-year-old child upstairs in the bedroom. The social worker accompanied the health visitor, the mother and her daughter upstairs. As the social worker explained:

> The health visitor said, 'Let's have a look and see if you're sore', and got her completely undressed...mum was there and I didn't take any part in that.
>
> ...
>
> I would feel most uncomfortable about undressing a child. I'm just trying to think if I've ever asked someone to undress their child...Not really, no...I mean maybe if there's a visible bruise I have. But not just on the off chance. And even at a medical, if you take a child for a medical, probably at the point where the child is getting undressed, I wouldn't stay, I'd leave the doctor with the nurse, with the parents.

What I call 'professional touch' is distinguished from medical or health examinations by how it involves contact with the child through ordinary greetings and social interaction such as lifting a toddler to say hello, or through play, hand-holding while going on walks, and cleaning normally exposed parts of the body, like the face. Professional touch, then, is focused on day-to-day interactions and involves a less overtly forensic approach to trying to discover harm to children than an examination, but paradoxically it may lead to the discovery of abuse that would otherwise have remained hidden.

As I am using the concept, professional touch also incorporates an understanding of touch as humane and nurturing. Touch is a way of expressing care and promoting healing for children, as part of ethical good practice. Finding a language through which this quality of care can be better understood, valued and developed is vital. In his book *The Renewal of Generosity: Illness, Medicine and How to Live*, sociologist Arthur Frank argues that best practice in health and social care is characterized by the most basic of human practices such as touch, which must be used in a sensitive manner that conveys generosity:

> Care is enacted in gestures that can console far beyond what they accomplish as practical components of treatment. For touch to console and thus to heal, it must be more than efficient. Touch must be generous, seeking

contact with a person as much as it seeks to effect some task. Generosity is the resonance of touch, endowing the act with a capacity to give beyond its practical significance. (Frank, 2004, p. 6)

It is not simply, then, that touch needs to be central to working to protect children, but 'generous' touch that must be achieved. Generous touch is the medium through which the worker in the earlier quotation from Judith Berry provided 'encircling warmth' when 'holding' a distressed child. This is what Michelle Lefevre (2010, p. 209) calls using 'touch to communicate comfort' in working with children and young people. It is interesting to note that in some areas of social work, physical intimacy and touch in the form of hugging is virtually regarded as good practice. In a study of palliative care social work, service users and carers interviewed for the study disliked bureaucratic social work where the emphasis was visibly on completing forms. Several service users mentioned being hugged by their social workers: ' "She'll give us a hug, and that does for me, an awful lot" (wife of a cancer patient)' (Beresford et al., 2007, p. 91). The researchers found that:

No service user mentioned finding hugging uncomfortable or inappropriate; in fact one woman told us that her social worker doesn't do hugs and she was very sorry about this, as she would have appreciated a hug from the social worker whose support she prized highly. (Beresford et al., 2007, p. 91)

Comforting touch infused with generosity was seen as part of a process of establishing meaningful, deep relationships characterized by trust and intimacy:

'They may have the skill but there has to be that bond as well, there has to be that trust and relationship' (man patient, white UK, 50 yrs old). (Beresford et al., 2007, p. 88)

With rare exceptions (Lefevre, 2010, pp. 208–10), there is no comparable discussion of touch in child protection. Service users in child protection – children as well as adults – are, it seems, untouchable now. I have heard social work students relate their experiences of placements in adult care, where there was almost a felt obligation to show compassion for and generosity towards older people by touching them on the hand or placing an arm around them, and then going into child protection placements, where touching service users was actively discouraged.

This is deeply regrettable. Because of its humane, generous and forensic dimensions, professional touch has as important a role to play in child protection as medical examinations, and in some situations is as vital as what can be observed and communicated through talk. Evidence of this has already been shown through the Baby Peter illustration above and other professional failures, such as not taking Jasmine Beckford by the hand for even a short a walk across the room, which could have revealed her broken leg.

There are, of course, significant ethical issues at play in terms of when it is legitimate and safe to touch a service user, especially when it is a child. Over the past few years, I have given many papers at conferences and workshops on child protection practice, covering the dynamics of face-to-face work. Of all the contentious issues this gives rise to, none provokes more heated feelings, argument and debate than touch. What should the role of touch be in child protection? Is it legitimate, and if so when, for social workers to touch children? Or parents? When I first began inviting professionals to reflect on such questions, I felt especially nervous because I had no definitive answer myself to what the proper use of touch is and I feared being put on the spot to provide one. I soon began to discover that far from being expected to have definitive answers, the issue is characterized by a lot of confusion, tremendous uncertainty and often deep fears and anxiety. Many social workers and other professionals had never talked about it in public. At the same time, people generally have strong and opposing views on touch, which are often passionately expressed, even though they have not had the opportunity to think it through very much at all. This discovery was in itself an important finding, as it reflected the way that, in a climate of fear and risk anxiety about inappropriate contact with children, touch by professionals has become taboo (Piper and Stronach, 2008). Some admitted to using touch a lot in their practice but said they would never say it out loud for fear of being seen as dangerous to children. Many claim that touch is not allowed, but then cannot identify the policy or guidance that says this is so. It turns out that the prohibition on touch they imagine to exist comes from their own assumptions and fears, the messages they pick up from the defensive, risk-averse organizations they work in, and their personal resistance to doing it. While in such sessions, I have always advanced a pro-touch position. I have learned that enabling professionals to have the debate is, in itself, crucial to helping them clarify their feelings about it and reaching a deeper understanding of the role of touch in keeping children safe. This is my aim here also.

Practising touch

In my experience, there is a significant variation in approaches to touching among practitioners. Some workers do touch sometimes, some never do. A common belief is that whether or not to touch is an individual choice, as opposed to something that must be routinely incorporated as part of best practice. As one social worker exemplified it:

> Everyone's different again, and it's what you feel comfortable with as an individual yourself, but I would shake the little boy's hand and that would be it, or things like that ... everyone's different, you know.

The following is typical of the kinds of stories I have heard. A social worker told me about her team manager going on a home visit and how she only came to realize that a toddler was seriously underweight due to neglect by picking the child up. The child was wearing loose clothing that concealed her emaciated body, which the team leader would not have become aware of without picking her up. This she did in a playful, 'Come here till I see you', 'How are you today?', kind of way. The social work team discussed the team leader's experience at a staff meeting and came to the collective view that some people are more 'touchy-feely' than others, so it should be up to individuals to decide whether to touch children or not, depending on the level of comfort they feel with it, how tactile a person they are. The social worker was curious to know what I made of their decision.

My view is that the position adopted by this social work team was wrong and goes against what is required for effective child protection practice. Whether or not workers should be prepared to touch children must not be an optional, personally decided thing. Every worker should be prepared to touch children as a routine part of their practice and do so without question when certain situations require it. The social work team was correct that we all have different comfort levels with touch, but not being a tactile kind of person can never be a justifiable reason to avoid touch. Our professional duty is to understand what makes us feel the way we do about touch, to want to do it or avoid it. As part of developing a capacity for intimate practice, workers need to come to a deep self-understanding of what their relationship to touch is and how tactile a person they are and find ways to correct for it, if need be. Some people will come to understand that their pattern is to touch too freely or too much, or too quickly. Professional touch differs from touch in personal relationships and its boundaries and rituals need to be learned. At the other extreme are those who avoid touch, who don't even like shaking hands, never mind hugging or comforting a distressed person by stroking their hand.

Culture is another vital component. When I was growing up in Ireland in the 1960s and 70s, generally speaking, physical intimacy was not expressed freely in the families I knew, while in public there was a lot of back-slapping among men and some strong handshaking. The assumption was that it was a sign of good character to have a firm handshake; men with limp ones were not to be trusted. This shows how gender and sexuality are big factors in these matters – note the homophobia in the fear of gayness implied in limp handshakes. Given the legacy of sexism and inappropriate touching so many women have to deal with, their experiences of and feelings about touch should always be respected.

Some social workers regard their preparedness to touch as influenced by culture, where nationality is seen as either encouraging or disallowing it, while others regard it as to do with their personality and character, how tactile they are as a person. Some see it as a mixture of both:

> If he [the child] is very confident about it, if the child initiates it I would, but only if the child initiated it. Because maybe that's more about me as a person, I'm like a very English person . . . and actually I'm not a very tactile person.

Here Englishness is seen as synonymous with detachment and keeping a physical distance, not being 'touchy-feely'. This quote also exemplifies how some workers place great emphasis on the child's actions and how forthcoming they are at initiating contact with the worker. If the child physically touches them, gets up on their knee or whatever, they are more likely to flow with that and allow the contact. But for the worker to instigate such contact, especially too early on in the relationship, is regarded as much more difficult and problematic. Within this perspective, workers argue that there is a need for the child to develop trust in them before they feel it is appropriate to lift them up or touch them and for the parents to regard them as trustworthy as well:

> I would find that quite difficult on a first visit, maybe when I'd got to know the family better, yes, then I might, but not on a first visit I wouldn't. I think people are quite wary about social workers, and they would be quite angry if a social worker breezed into their house and picked up their child.

The impact of past experiences also influences what workers feel able and prepared to do. This is especially true when it involves criticism from a parent for what they regard as overintrusive contact with their child and an infringement of the parents' rights to determine the nature of professional contact with their child. These tensions are exemplified by a story a social worker told me about being in a home with an infant who was crying in his cot and wanting to be taken out, but the child's mother did not want him moved:

> So sometimes I play it by ear. I remember once feeling very cross with myself when I used to work with a mother and child and she said he was a chatterbox, wanting to be picked up. And she said no, I'm leaving him there so that he can just get used to being by himself for a bit, and he wasn't being abandoned, or anything like that. There were lots of people in the room, lots of people giving him attention, which she said was what she wanted, and then she left the room and he went on and on at me to pick him up, so I picked him up in the end. And then she came back and this wasn't what she wanted, and I felt I shouldn't have done that, he was her baby, I should have asked, so I do ask permission before I touch people's children.

This sensitivity to the child and parents, building trust and the timing of a particular kind of intimate contact is appropriate. Yet possible problems with it and dilemmas remain. It is not appropriate for it always to be the child's responsibility to initiate tactile (or other) contact with the worker. For workers, initiating tactile involvement with the child must always be on the agenda. While this may be trickier early on in investigations and assessments, it must always be included as an option and needs to be an element of longer term work where children are on child protection plans. This means workers incorporating into plans such things as their need to take children by the hand for walks, to make it plain to parents that picking up a baby or infant is part of relating to them and checking their wellbeing. As Lefevre (2010, p. 208) says, 'the appropriateness of touch is, then, *based on the help the child or young person needs*'. As she points out, some children and young people do not want to be touched and even if they did accept it, it is inappropriate. For instance, children who have been sexually abused may experience it as unsafe and the beginning of a process of being groomed for abuse.

Physical touch can never be without limits and boundaries and must also be done in the company of a parent or other adult. As one social worker observed: 'Sometimes children are much too overfriendly and you think this isn't right, sometimes they're quite shy.' Even where it is the child who initiates the physical contact, it is the worker who is responsible for setting the boundaries of acceptable behaviour. This necessitates asking the parent if it is okay to allow the child to have the contact, and in situations where the child's touching is inappropriate, the worker needs to tactfully put a stop to the physical contact. The child's reactions to the worker must be used in a reflective way to gain insight into their wellbeing and problems. As Michelle Lefevre has observed of her own experience of children who have initiated affection towards her:

> This has usually tended to happen with children I have not known for very long and who have been neglected and/or sexualised. They have responded to my friendliness in a way that has illuminated their emotional hunger or lack of clarity about boundaries. Practitioners should aim to find a way of managing such situations which ends physical contact as quickly as possible but also does not shame or reject the child. (Lefevre, 2010, p. 209)

Being prepared to touch children (and their carers)

Social workers must always be prepared to appropriately touch the children with whom they work. Being 'prepared' means three things. First, that they have clearly thought through the ethics of touch and how touch should be done, realizing its humane possibilities. Second, that they have done the introspective work on themselves that enables them to identify how tactile they are as a person so that they may adjust their behaviour accordingly and be prepared for touching as and when it is necessary. And finally, that they understand that problems with touch and disgust are acceptable parts of being human and need to be owned up to as a basis for working through and beyond them, so as to be able to have as close as possible relationships with children (and their carers) and engage in tactile ways as and when necessary. If they do not touch children themselves, they should ensure that other professionals do it.

It is widely known and discussed how access to children – and, by implication, touch – by adults who are not related to children is increasingly regulated by the state and forbidden, through procedures such as criminal records checks. But it is deeply concerning when even those professionals who can reasonably be expected to touch someone else's child don't do it and are confused as to whether the practice is socially and politically condoned and whether they have a professional and ethical right to do it. This withdrawal of touch is a crucial part of the drift in recent decades towards professional detachment from children and their carers and a child protection practice that is non-relational and lacking in intimacy.

In advocating a tactile child protection practice, I am not, of course, suggesting that workers should *always* touch. Vital issues surround when it is legitimate to touch. Nor does it mean that it should always be the social worker who does it. In some circumstances, as I have shown, it will be more appropriate for the health visitor or doctor to do it. Or for a female worker to do it. What I am arguing against is the no touch policy and attitude that governs how some practitioners, managers and even whole organizations think and behave. At a conference, an experienced child protection manager/adviser argued passionately against my pro-touch position, insisting that what I am arguing for is 'dangerous'. Her reasoning was that too many practitioners have been victims of allegations of inappropriate touch. Social workers, she said, do not have time to develop relationships that allow for the development of trust and creation of appropriate opportunities for touch to be initiated and its meaning and intention understood. In response, other social workers took what I have been calling in this chapter the humane, generous perspective and argued that it is essential for practitioners to touch children if they are to keep them safe and have meaningfully comforting relationships with them.

The view that 'we haven't got time' to have relationships that permit touch is a common one. But social work and other professions need to be clear about what they can and should do with whatever time they have got. It does not take long to walk across a room to engage with a child. The act of touching can be performed in seconds. It is correct to say that touching must go on in the context of a process in an encounter. When initiated by the worker, it should be negotiated with the parent/carer and with the child, where they have the capacity to understand. So, for instance, directly checking the wellbeing of a child who is across the room from you in his buggy with chocolate on his face requires a preparatory process in the interview, which involves observing, assessing information and raising relevant issues for discussion, before moving towards the child. This act should not be performed arbitrarily or in a vacuum but in dialogue with the child and mother: 'I'm just wondering about Peter, is it okay if I take him out of the buggy?' and moving towards the child while saying it and making some eye contact with the parent(s). It is important to make eye contact with the child, while talking and gesturing towards them when approaching and reaching the buggy. On arrival, physically reaching towards the child, and in a playful, reassuring tone touching his hand, hair, perhaps a little ticklishly, but always with kindliness. And then picking him up and either having his mother clean his face or getting her to give you a cloth to do it with, or using the wet wipes or tissues you brought with you. In cases where there has been an assessment and there is a child protection plan in place, these actions should be part of it. It should not be a shock to a parent that the worker wishes to engage in a tactile manner with their child.

Conclusion

Given its humanity, there will be limits to the extent to which the use of touch can always be anticipated and prior permission gained. Touch is one of those dimensions of human practice that is so universal and normal that to mention and draw attention to it can cause more suspicions and problems than would occur if the person just got on with it. But while professional touch should be no less humane than that by laypeople, it is distinguished by its ethics and the need for negotiation and consent. Professional touch is a skill that rests on the creative integration of tactile contact performed simply and generously in everyday natural ways, but with determination in the realization that its use is a vital part of what keeps children safe and feeling cared about and loved.

8

The car as a space for therapeutic practice

So it seems that when you set out for a car ride you never know where you will get to, or what will turn up on the way.

(Winnicott, 1963, p. 51)

As earlier chapters have shown, social workers and other professionals regularly have to relate to children and other family members in their most intimate spaces: living rooms, kitchens, bedrooms. A key aim of this book is to enter these spaces where practice is actually done in order to deepen understandings of the encounters between professionals and children, parents and other carers that go on in them, but where research and writing about child protection have previously failed to go. This chapter focuses on another crucial, and neglected, space where child protection work goes on: the car. There is, in fact, no more intimate space in which practice goes on, in the sense of the small enclosure and close proximity that the car forces on its occupants. When the space of the car is given the detailed attention it deserves in social work, it emerges as much more than a one-ton object that enables the worker to reach the child and get from A to B. The car is a site of practice where vitally important opportunities for meaningful communication and therapeutic work with children arise, as the quote above encapsulates. It is a space where vulnerable children make significant disclosures and 'therapeutic journeys' go on, in every sense, whether it is during drives that are undertaken as part of ongoing casework, or when children experience hugely significant 'moves' into care, changing placement or other life changes. The car is important for workers too, as a secure base to retreat to from the demands of home visits, aggressive service users and office politics, and as a space to gain supervision and support from managers who have accompanied them on difficult visits.

In the social sciences, the car is becoming recognized for the central place it occupies in contemporary life and subjected to detailed analysis (Miller, 2001b; Dant, 2004; Featherstone et al., 2005; Cresswell, 2006; Urry, 2007). The fact that the role and meanings of the car in welfare practices today have been largely ignored seems to reflect an assumption that what happens between leaving the office and arriving at the home visit, taking children out on drives, and the return journey to the office is wasted time, or perhaps 'non-time'. Research shows that the assumption that travel time is wasted time is increasingly mistaken (Laurier, 2004; Lyons and Urry, 2005). This chapter draws on such insights from mobility studies, together with theoretical ideas from psychodynamic and relationship-based practice, which enable due attention to be given to therapeutic processes and working with the emotions. The car focuses attention on the implications for practice of what Adrian Ward (2008, p. 181) calls 'the in-between times', and the place of those times in the longer term relationship with the child and the promotion of their welfare. The car is an important object for study in its own right in child protection and can help us to make sense of and theorize the nature of therapeutic relationships in social work and child protection practice.

The emergence of the car in social work

To fully appreciate the meanings and significance of the car in child protection, we need to begin by imagining a time when it did not exist. From its beginnings in the 1880s through to the end of that century, practitioners used horse-drawn cabs and trains to travel to see their clients. Horse-drawn cabs were in use up to the 1920s (for an image of this, see Ferguson, 2010, p. 125). The reach of practice was local and its tempo slow. The bicycle began to change this (Kern, 1983) when it came into universal use in social work in the late 1890s and 1900s. It stretched the reach of practice, resulting in celebrations of these new powers among child protection workers, who, it was noted, were now travelling over one million miles a year and could reach children in otherwise inaccessible districts (NSPCC, 1901). The motorcycle was in general use in child protection by the 1930s and the systematic use of the car in social work dates from the 1950s. The car gave practitioners a new flexibility and autonomy to move (at speed) when and as they pleased, as it separated social work from the train timetable or waiting for a horse-drawn cab (Urry, 2007).

The car also afforded new opportunities to transport people and objects and to help service users in practical ways. One photograph from the 1950s depicts a child protection worker standing proudly beside his car, the interior and exterior of which was loaded with a family's belongings, demonstrating the capacity that now existed for social workers to move people and their belongings (Ferguson, 2010, p. 127).

By the 1970s, car use had become so central to social work that gaining employment usually depended on having one. Today, functioning without a car has become virtually unthinkable, as car use in general has grown exponentially (Featherstone et al., 2005). The need to travel faster and more often has also arisen from the emergence of new knowledge about risk, especially since physical child abuse and the prevention of death became the central preoccupation of social work in the 1970s and pro-tecting children in time took on more urgent meanings (Ferguson, 2004). While the environmental implications of such extensive and growing car use – at least in petrol-driven models – may be dire, the future of effective child protection work is inextricably bound up with auto-mobility.

Moving stories: the car in child protection practice

At the heart of social work and welfare practices is a requirement to move and to travel in order to engage with service users, and the car is central to how this is achieved. In recent years, I have discovered, through research interviews with practitioners and the many experienced professionals who have eagerly volunteered car experiences to me, the crucial role the car plays in practice and, in particular, its importance as a space in which children talk about their deep concerns.

In a case of neglect of four children aged between 8 and 16, I shadowed their social worker on a home visit to them and interviewed the worker in the car on the way back to the office as part of the research approach. There was a long history of social work involvement and the children being on the edge of entering care. Both parents were addicted to alcohol and drugs and their mother had significant mental health prob-lems. There had been domestic violence by both parents to one another. The children's mother was in hospital, having attempted suicide. I began exploring with the social worker where she generally regarded the best place to see a child on their own, would she normally see them on a home visit? What happens?

SOCIAL WORKER: If they're out in the garden, you see them where they are,
I think. So if they are playing out in the garden, I'll talk to them out there,
if they're happy out there. I do try with the children I work with that are a
bit older, like these boys, to take them out somewhere, because they chat a
lot in the car; they never chat much on the actual outing but they chat
going along in the car, quite a lot.

HARRY FERGUSON: Why do you think that is then?

SOCIAL WORKER: Because you are not looking at them, not direct sort of face to
face, and it's the motion of going somewhere maybe taking their minds off
things, just like you're doing [giggles because I am interviewing her while
she is driving a moving car] and they can just look out and just, its not that
confrontational type. I mean I don't know, [the 14-year-old young person]
who we just met there [on the home visit], she chatted all the way to [the
hospital where her mother is] in the car and of course I can't take any notes
because I'm driving; she said some really quite profound things that day
going along in the car, more so than she has on any visits I've done really.

HARRY FERGUSON: Profound things about?

SOCIAL WORKER: About where her mum used to keep the [drugs] that she
used, the fact that she's worried about getting schizophrenia herself, that
her mum blames her for her mental health; about the fact that her mum
was blaming her saying her dad was having affairs, right, left and centre. All
sorts of quite profound stuff. I mean we were chatting about other things,
about clothes and that. Yeah, she said a lot in the car.

Unprompted, the social worker had introduced the car as a space for therapeutic practice in response to my question about where she thought the
best place to see a child was. The 14-year-old service user was sitting
in the front, there were just the two of them in the car. The conversation started with her saying she wants to learn to drive and the worker
telling her how she learned to drive when she was 17 and 'I said it's a
really good thing to do and it went from there really.' So the car itself
was a crucial vehicle, so to speak, in opening up a discussion that
led to 'profound' disclosures, information the worker's experience suggested would not have come from working with her elsewhere, such as
in the home. The car was crucial to therapeutic depth being reached
and assisting in building a meaningful relationship, which the social
worker felt she had with the children. Implicit in the worker's comments
is a recognition that, at its most basic, the car is a safe place to talk
because the child cannot be overheard, unlike the problems that can
happen when children are interviewed in their bedrooms or other parts
of the home, which were discussed in Chapter 6. The dialogue is truly
private.

This worker also shows just how sociologically smart practitioners can be and the intuitive understanding that experience gives them of the importance of the car in day-to-day child protection work. As the worker perceptively notes, the car is an effective space for practice because of the forward motion, the seating arrangements and how the young person can fiddle with the radio/CD player, gaze out of the window or at least avoid face-to-face, 'confrontational' engagement, observe passing objects and places, all the while talking about what is important to them.

This has deep resonances with how Clare Winnicott, pioneering social worker and academic who I quoted at the start of this chapter, conceptualized the car as a 'third thing', which provides for 'shared experiences' and helps to facilitate communication with children:

> When adapting our casework techniques to work with children, one of the first things we discover is the value of an indirect approach in making contact with them, and that in the majority of cases it helps to have something between us and the child, a third thing going on which at any moment can become a focal point to relieve tension. In this connection car rides can be important, or it may be drawing, or playing, or walking round the garden, or even the presence of the cat or dog or whatever. (Winnicott, 1963, p. 50)

Many practitioners intuitively understand how the car acts as a 'third thing' not just during moves occasioned by traumatic placement changes, but in day-to-day casework and taking young people for rides to try and stimulate a breakthrough in communication with them. As another social worker from the same research project put it:

> I quite often take [young] people in my car...Well, sometimes they won't engage, so if you can pick them up from school and maybe drop them home, they might be more likely to. It's kind of a way of getting in, isn't it? It can be quite a good time to talk things through as well.

Writing in 1972 in a rare academic analysis of social work in cars, Juliet Berry makes a number of perceptive observations:

> Workers vary in whether they consider a car a suitable setting for casework: some feel they should simply concentrate on their driving. I think a car journey is a good time for communication because people often talk more freely when sitting side by side than face to face; also it may be easier to talk about the two places at each end of the journey when one is travelling

between them, and thirdly the client may easily change the subject if he wishes by pointing out some object of interest. (Berry, 1972, p. 58)

Like the social worker in the first case example above, Berry recognizes the significance of seating arrangements – how bodies are not positioned face to face – in the dynamics of communication and intimacy in cars. The social worker/driver's gaze focused straight ahead permits the service user to make or avoid eye contact, which helps to free them up to disclose intimate information. This is borne out by Laurier et al.'s (2008) study of communication on ordinary car journeys, which concluded that intimate conversation was also made possible by the 'pause-fullness' and slowness of conversation on journeys, in how cars have to stop and start. This pause-fullness and slowness of conversation is, of course, similar to what happens in the reflective nature of professional interviews with service users.

The rhythm of a journey is also important to what and how things are disclosed. A powerful pattern to emerge from the car stories I have gathered from current practitioners is exemplified by a social worker who observed how, in one case that involved a weekly 45-minute trip, the worries and concerns expressed by the child would become more and more serious and meaningful the closer they got to their destination. Children pace their disclosures according to where they are on the journey, as not only the positioning of the body but the timing and spacing of intimate talk on journeys is evidently significant.

What should not be overlooked is the effect that doing this kind of work in the car has on the worker. In the same interview in the car with the worker from the first case study above, the social worker was asked: 'How able are you to talk back, you know, to engage when you are driving?' She replied:

> Quite good. I've got two kids of my own so I'm quite used to not concentrating on what I am doing [laughs] . . . I'm used to doing five things at once.

The worker relates her ability to engage attentively while driving to her capacity as a mother to multitask and how her concentration is split between the driving and attention on her children. It is precisely this apparent inattention to focused interviewing that works to the benefit of the service user and worker. Evidence from approaches to psychoanalysis that use traditional methods of having the client out of view 'on the couch' shows that significant numbers of therapists experience the non-face-to-face approach, made possible by the client being behind or to the side of them, as a liberation (Goldberg, 1990; Giacomantonio, 2003). In mobile social work, the requirement that the worker look at the road ahead and not the service user acts as a 'third thing' for the worker – in Winnicott's words, as 'a focal point to relieve tension' – and provides for them a similar kind of freeing up of their psyches and creativity. This is further assisted by being freed from the demands of administration ('I can't take any notes because I'm driving'). The demands and distractions of driving paradoxically help social workers to be attentive and focus in 'pause-full', reflective ways on what their service users need.

This wise practitioner also recognizes with a giggle that I am doing to her what she did with this young person, using the car as a third thing to extract quality information by interviewing her while she is driving it, on the move. This is precisely why such mobile research methods are now being used to try to produce this kind of rich data (Ferguson, 2011). Floresch's (2002) detailed participant observation study of the practices of social workers who work with people with mental health problems is exceptional for showing aspects of how time in the car is used and given meaning in social work. The car was experienced as a source of freedom and security for workers, physically in separating them from dangerous service users on home visits and economically in terms of mileage allowances. But the car was also seen by workers on occasions as a place of danger and invasion of personal space because it placed them and their service user so close together in an enclosed space. Those who had neglected themselves and had body odour caused workers discomfort and to want to avoid touching their knee when changing gears. However, the car was valued as space for casework, both in the opportunities for therapeutic dialogue that went on in it and in practical ways, such as when workers got service users to fill out forms while they drove them to appointments (Floresch, 2002).

Written accounts of practice in the car today are rare. Their meanings and therapeutic possibilities are exemplified in a wonderful account by Andy Cook of the central role of her car in the work she did with Tandara, who she removed from her family into care due to child abuse when she was five years old:

> The journey to the emergency foster placement was the first of many journeys Tandara and I took together. Our relationship greatly benefited from

the necessity of travelling to hospital appointments, interviews [by video regarding possible criminal proceedings] and new placements. Going on car journeys together gave us a reason to spend time together. Initially, conversation did not flow freely and it was my responsibility to judge how best to use the time and at what pace and intensity to attempt communication. I used the first journey to talk to Tandara about what a foster carer is and what a social worker is and also spent periods with little being said. My main aim was to keep Tandara fully informed about what was happening, as her experience had taught her that the world was a potentially dangerous place and I wanted to alleviate any worries she might have. On subsequent journeys, as we grew to know each other more, Tandara played a more active role in directing the conversation and she proved to be a delightful companion. Journeys together gave us the opportunity to have serious conversations but also the opportunity to sing at the top of our voices, to play I-spy and to have fun with words such as changing each other's names (I was obviously Andy Pandy). Car journeys provided continual distractions in the form of changing landscapes; they allowed for avoidance of eye contact when eye contact was too daunting and were, for us, a perfect forum for getting to know each other. (Cook, 2008, p. 218)

This wonderfully perceptive account of creative, skilful practice exemplifies the potential there is for the car to be used as a space for serious communication and playful, soulful practice in ways which benefit children and other service users.

Theorizing the car and therapeutic spaces and relationships

I now want to take further the analysis of what it is about the car that makes it such a productive therapeutic space for practice and what this tells us about the nature of child protection practice and therapeutic relationships more broadly. I am going to do this by focusing not just on contemporary practice but on the brilliant insights provided by the first generations of social workers and academics who used the car in practice. A remarkable feature of accounts of social work practice with children in the 1950s and 60s is the prominence given to driving and experiences in cars, and the compelling accounts that were offered of therapeutic social work with children and families being done in cars, which were theorized as crucial spaces within which to do such work. This may have been because cars were still novel for this generation of workers, but it was also because of how imaginatively they applied the psychodynamic theory that was emerging at this time to make sense of practice.

Olive Stevenson, writing in 1963, gives a wonderful account of practice that went on in a car with a 10-year-old girl, Anne. Her foster placement, where she had lived for seven years, had broken down and the social worker was taking her to a residential care placement. Stevenson quotes at length from the case record of the social worker – who at this time was known as a childcare officer (see Chapter 2) – which begins from the start of the journey:

> She [Anne] leaned out of the car waving to Miss N [the foster mother] as we went off and then sat down, saying nothing. I was having difficulty in negotiating heavy traffic and could not get even a look at her for a while. When I was able to I could see that tears were pouring down her face though she was very quiet about it and turning her head away from me. I drew the car to the side of the road and said that I expect she was feeling a bit sad. She nodded and did not protest when I put my arm around her and cuddled her. (Stevenson, 1963, p. 92)

Anne began to cry again and wrapped herself in the worker's travel rug, which she – Anne – referred to as her 'magic rug'. Safely wrapped in the rug and skilfully facilitated by the social worker to open up, the child talked about her mixed feelings towards her foster family, her grief, anger, fears about the move, and her fantasies about going to a lovely new family home with nice children and adults. At lunch, the social worker talked to her about what the children's home looked like, the names of the people there and the children who would be in her group. With the travel rug wrapped around her shoulders and clutching a teddy bear, the practitioner wrote that Anne then 'pretended to go to sleep, but obviously didn't and while she had her eyes shut managed to arrange herself across the seat so that her head was on my lap'. During the deep discussion about her feelings, Anne eventually sat up and 'asked if she could have a jelly baby and took one out of the box on the car shelf' (p. 93). The worker explained that she would be taking Anne back to visit the foster family in eight weeks' time, following which 'Anne finally fell asleep, and then when she woke appeared to be very depressed, saying that eight weeks was a terribly long time and I might forget' (p. 94). The worker reassured her:

> I said I knew it was hard and I knew she hated it and it made her feel all funny inside, but I would be there and I would see her quite often and

I would help her all I could. She cried a little, saying, 'Please take me back now', but became a little calmer and finally settled down in the seat as close as she could get to me with her hand on my arm. I talked about her brother and said that he was terribly excited about seeing her and Anne began to show slight interest in this. She finally began to talk about seeing him in a pleased way and continued so to the end of the journey. (Stevenson, 1963, p. 94)

This demonstrates clearly the process children went through – and continue to go through – in making such life-changing journeys and how workers have consciously facilitated them to express the emotion, the 'funny feeling inside'. It is a vivid and moving – in every sense – account of intimate practice in how the worker uses professional touch to calm the child by cuddling her and subsequently the child snuggles up to the worker and places her hand on her arm. This is professional touch at its best, as defined in Chapter 7, generous, humane and comforting. Commenting on the social worker's practice, Stevenson (1963, p. 95) observes that she

> comforts the child but recognizes the need to keep the feeling open and flowing; her experience and knowledge will have shown her that if the feeling is damned up, the child's pain, anger, resentment may effectively block the later adjustment, in this case to the children's home and to the foster home to which she was to return for holidays.

Teddy bears, sweets and travel rugs were strategically kept in cars for the purposes of helping children to settle on the journey and for facilitating direct therapeutic work on the changes that were occurring through the journey (see also Berry, 1972, p. 55). This is another example of the importance of the creative use of objects and everyday 'material culture' in effective child protection.

The academic attention that was given to the nature of relationships with service users and psychodynamic practice in the 1960s went on in a context where social work was under attack for allegedly making what were regarded as grandiose claims for how it could change people's psyche's and behaviour. Barbara Wooton (1959) famously claimed that social workers were foolishly and ineptly attempting to be 'miniature psychoanalysts'. Olive Stevenson responded to Wooton's criticisms, and refers to the case study of 10-year-old Anne outlined above:

> It is very clear in this record that the child care officer is not a 'miniature psychoanalyst' for her concern is not to explore deeply unconscious

fantasy – which she is neither trained nor employed to do – but rather to recognize, as it were, the little pieces of the iceberg which show above the surface in order to help the child handle better the realities of the situation. On this long car journey, the child care officer is deliberately bridging the gap between the past and the future by the purposive references to both. The child care officer knows that in children who move from one place to another the images of people and places are often blurred and disturbed by the feelings – of anger, of fear, of sadness, which surround them, and that these are often intense. The task is therefore to try to keep the reality of the situation alive and relatively unclouded by fantasies. In order to do this, the child care officer must be alive to the significance of casual remarks or significant stories, such as Anne could tell when encouraged by the magic rug and the child care officer's interest. (Stevenson, 1963, p. 95)

This attentiveness to the child's life experiences and 'keeping the reality of the situation alive' is precisely what the wise practitioners profiled in this book achieve. What practitioner/academics like Olive Stevenson, Juliet Berry and Clare Winnicott brilliantly understood was that effective social work was only concerned in selective ways with the unconscious, fantasy life of the service user and, crucially, this always needed to be in the context of their relationship to external reality, that is, real events in their lives.

It is experiences such as being taken for a medical examination due to suspected abuse, a hospital visit to a parent who has attempted suicide, talking to your social worker about your sadness and worries while on a standard journey undertaken as part of casework, being taken into care, or a move to a new placement that bring external reality into sharp focus for children, while also having a deep impact on their internal emotional life. Stevenson's emphasis on 'keeping the feelings open and flowing' reflects the influence of theories which held that a key task of social work was to have relationships with children that enable them to process their experience and integrate thought and feeling by 'holding' or 'containing' them.

Bion's (1962) concept of 'containment' was developed at the time when these social work scholars were writing and Stevenson drew explicitly on it. Containment refers to how the infant's dependence on their mother/parents for food and survival creates anxiety, which they project onto their carer. The parent takes in the infant's anxious projections and gives them back in a nurturing form the child can tolerate, through active listening, using responsive comforting touch, kisses, smiles and the provision of food, quality physical care and warmth. This allows the child to feel secure, think more clearly about themselves and the external world and to trust. Donald Winnicott, Clare's husband and an eminent paediatrician and child psychotherapist, likened the professional–client relationship to the kind of 'holding' that goes on in a healthy parent/mother–infant relationship. By this he meant both physical holding and touch, and also the emotional holding that comes from having feelings contained. The parent provides what Donald Winnicott (1953, 1957) called a 'facilitating environment' for the child to develop. Both the Winnicotts were influenced by Melanie Klein and the 'object relations' school of psychoanalysis (Hinshelwood, 1991). Klein was actually Clare's analyst (Kanter, 2004). Perhaps Donald Winnicott's most celebrated concept is the 'transitional object' (Winnicott, 1953), which describes how children become attached to objects like blankets and cling to them at times of transition, such as going to bed, or on journeys.

In forming a relationship, the social worker becomes a deeply meaningful 'object' to the child. It happens with parents too. However, Joel Kanter (2004) suggests that social workers are more than 'transitional objects'. In his important book on the work of Clare Winnicott, Kanter argues that applying such terminology to social work is misguided, because it doesn't do justice to the creativity the worker brings to the encounter and implies that the professional is a passive recipient of the child's experiences and projections. Social workers are active *participants* in the lives of those who use their services. They can help them to articulate their wishes and needs, their fears and hurts, deal with trauma and enhance their emotional development and interpersonal relationships. They are also in contact with significant persons and experiences in the child's life and can help the child to maintain contact with positive life experiences. Kanter argues that the social worker is best understood as a 'transitional participant', who gives children continuity throughout the investigations, assessments and changes to which they are subjected and a sense of someone able 'to gather together the separate threads of the child's life' (Kanter, 2004, p. 75).

There can be no guarantee, of course, that children will open up and freely disclose, but workers need to be ready for it and skilfully use the transitional space of journeys to try to create the kind of dialogue that might help children to 'move on'. Even though there can be a planned, anticipated basis to it, there is an important dimension to this that can be characterized as what Ward (2008, p. 181) calls 'opportunity-led work with children'. The case examples in this chapter have shown that the practitioners were ready and prepared to take the opportunity to communicate and do therapeutic work in the car when the young people presented it. The journey itself, if associated with the trauma of past and current experiences, constitutes a risk to the child and their development if not handled skilfully, but also brings therapeutic opportunities (Jacobucci, 1958).

The social and therapeutic possibilities of this kind of containing and opportunity-led experience are further enhanced in how the car provides a context where it seems to enable greater equality between worker and service user, for the duration of the journey at least. Laurier et al. (2008) analysed interactions during ordinary car journeys and argue that the nature of the seating arrangements and the kinds of conversations that car journeys give rise to influence the dynamics of power and disclosure. Applied to social work, it appears that some of the freedom to disclose while on the move arises from the car being a place where some of the power imbalances of face-to-face social work in home visits, offices and other interview settings – what the worker above called 'that confrontational type' – are levelled out and given greater parity in the car. While the social worker/driver is in control of the car, the passenger has more power and scope to engage or disengage, and maintains the greater freedom to move, gesticulate, avoid looking straight at the worker and so on. The service user acquires a greater sense of control over the relationship while both they and the worker are moving forward together, heading in the same direction. As the worker in the first case example above rightly commented: 'it's the motion of going somewhere'.

This is not to say that good practice requires the practitioner to relinquish their power. The exercise of good authority depends on the worker's knowledgeable and sensitive use of self and maintenance of boundaries, while having a deep and continual awareness of their 'role and tasks and the previous experiences of them both, in particular the child's experience of loss, uncertainty, insecurity of attachment, powerlessness, trauma and abuse, [which] can inhibit, interrupt, even derail intended communications' (Lefevre, 2008, p. 35). The vulnerable, relatively powerless service user's sense of freedom is experienced in a context where the professional remains in control of the car and the direction of the journey, while using good authority in a manner that is crucial to enabling the service user to feel emotionally safe and contained, and to trust. It is the child's feeling of relative freedom within a contained environment that is central to the therapeutic dynamics of car journeys.

Conclusion

This chapter has developed further the argument of this book that greater attention needs to be given to where social work and child protection goes on and the implications of particular contexts for how skilful work can be done. Revealing the importance of the car in child protection creates the possibility that it can be consciously mobilized and used to promote the welfare of service users and, indeed, practitioners. Agencies need to increase their awareness of how practitioners use such spaces creatively in their work and support staff in doing so – in a material sense in terms of adequate mileage allowances, and with permission from managers to travel whatever distances are necessary. I have encountered a social work department where, due to financial cutbacks, limits had been placed on the amount of travel staff could undertake and social workers felt it was seriously affecting the quality of their practice. Attention to the mobile, experiential and therapeutic dimensions of social work during car journeys has been largely expunged from academic writing and case recording systems today, because of a narrowing of the range of what is counted as 'practice' and more minimalist, computer data case recording approaches (Parton, 2008). Case recording, case discussion in agencies and academic accounts of practice need to (re)include the car journey and 'moving stories' that are so central to professional and service user experiences and to effective child protection practice in the skilful creation of therapeutic journeys.

9
Practice in hospitals, offices and other public spaces

Meetings should also take place away from the home, preferably in a quiet setting with suitable facilities. Sessions away from the home not only provide an opportunity for the family and workers to undertake planned work with distractions but also test the family's motivation to attend.

(DH, 1988, p. 2)

Work to identify, assess and stop child abuse does not just go on in the home but in other spaces, such as hospitals, health clinics and social work offices. The dynamics of how the work is done differs according to context. As I have been arguing, the home has some particular features that set it apart from other places where child protection goes on. Houses contain distinct atmospheres born of those who reside in them and afford opportunities for concealment of abuse, people and family secrets that are not as possible elsewhere. Practising in someone's home is not the same as working with children and parents in a hospital or the social work office. The obvious difference is that in the latter two areas service users are required to enter the professionals' space. If having control over the physical settings where practice goes on is a key form of power and influence in shaping encounters, this would seem to hand the initiative to the professionals.

While broadly true, how this manifests in practice is far from straight-forward. To begin with, families don't simply leave the ways they behave and interact at home in private behind them but bring them with them into public spaces and have a capacity to use these public buildings and rooms to act and reveal or conceal aspects of their lives. Second, the organizations that parents and children step into are not neutral spaces or in any sense 'empty' of atmosphere and emotion. Just as I have argued that the home is characterized by atmospheres that arise from the lived experiences, systems and emotional worlds of those who live in them, so too is the feel and behaviour of organizations shaped by the people, emotions and relationships that go on in them. The atmosphere or 'culture' of the organization is crucial to the nature of the practice that goes on. What constitutes social work and child protection is always a product of the interaction between lives and buildings, people and organizational settings.

This chapter will develop this perspective by focusing on child protection in hospitals and social work offices. It will argue that at the heart of making sense of the effectiveness or otherwise of such practices must be attention to the emotions. The dominant response to disclosures of the deaths of children in child protection cases has been concerted attempts to change organizations, by developing the law, procedures and case recording practices, and micromanaging the practices of child protection staff. In the process, the psychological and emotional aspects of doing social work and child protection have been largely ignored and squeezed out. This chapter seeks to illuminate the nature and complexities of child protection practice by reintroducing the emotions and exploring their dynamics in public places like hospitals and offices.

The office interview

Social workers recognize that office interviews potentially give them greater control over the session and this comes into play particularly when working with anger or hostility:

> You learn about positioning yourself between the service user and the door but in reality it's so difficult to make that happen. You can make it happen in the office, but when you're going into somebody's house you just sit in whatever seat is offered to you.

Practitioners should always try to avoid passive acceptance and just sitting in whatever seat is offered and instead respectfully seek to influence where they sit (or stand, or walk) so as to be at their most effective.

The case of Kimberley Carlile, who at the age of four and a half was murdered by her stepfather Nigel Hall, despite the involvement of several professionals, provides compelling evidence of problems that arise in office interviews (London Borough of Greenwich, 1987). There was high suspicion that Kimberley had been non-accidentally injured in the past and there was a history of a difficult relationship between Mr Hall, who resented and resisted social work involvement, and the social worker Martin Ruddock. At a time when suspicions of abuse to Kimberley had been running high after several home visits, Mr Hall, Mrs Carlile and the four children arrived unexpectedly at the social work office one morning:

> The only space available for interviewing clients were two rooms at the end of a short passage.

> To say that the room where the Carliles talked to Mr Ruddock was incommodious would be to overstate its suitability. Those who sat on chairs at opposite sides of the room virtually knocked knees. There was just enough space for the adults to sit down, with [child] Z on Mrs Carlile's lap. Kimberley was close to her mother with her arm over Kimberley. So confined was the space that the other children could run about only in the corridor. Nothing could be less suitable for watching and listening to interaction between members of the family.

> . . .

> Partly because of these wholly inadequate conditions, Mr Ruddock misread the signs. Whatever antennae Mr Ruddock possessed for picking up the messages of suspected child abuse, they were desensitised by the physical environment. Doubtless, Kimberley was wearing clothing that covered up most of the body which might have revealed the signs of physical abuse; there was no possibility for any examination beyond the most cursory and anatomically limited. Clearly, he did not see bruises or marks on Kimberley's hands or face. (London Borough of Greenwich, 1987, pp. 109–10)

The social worker did note, however, that Kimberley was 'withdrawn, sallow, pasty and still', but that she did brighten up as the interview wore on. The social worker told the inquiry into the case that he was impressed by the initiative the parents had taken in coming to him, instead of waiting for a home visit by him. The report remarks:

> The irony of that observation, then and now, is that in fact the Carliles were coming to him, and not him to them, in order to conceal, rather than to reveal. The social worker began to shift his assessment of the situation from probable child abuse to behavioural problems, but he commendably kept the issue of medical examination on the agenda, subsequently writing to the family to explain that he had written to the health visitor requesting that she 'considers arranging a medical examination'. (p. 110)

The inquiry report concludes that: 'Whatever favourable signs came out of the meeting, there could be no excuse, at least, for not having seen the child undressed' (p. 111).

The social worker told the inquiry of how he had walked the family to the door of the building and watched the parents holding the children's hands as they all seemed to happily walk to the car. This reassured him that he was witnessing 'a happy family scene'. The report concludes that: 'Far from being reassured, Mr Ruddock should have been alive to the risk of being manipulated. Plainly, he had been deceived – to some extent, self-induced' (p. 112):

> Our conclusion is that Mr Ruddock was in part handicapped by the circumstances of the venue for the meeting, and in part by his inability to isolate Kimberley from the other children, and thus to focus on her. But his reading of the family situation left much to be desired in terms of good social work practice. (p. 112)

This is a compelling argument about the negative influence of the physical environment on child protection practice, with regard to the office and cramped interview room. The report is so vivid that it even provides a photograph of the interview room and a profile drawing of the front section of the building where the interview rooms were situated. A clear implication of this is that effective child protection practice requires space. Workers need enough room to be able to protect their personal space – rubbing knees with interviewees is the antithesis of this – and to be able to be creative, to move or whatever feels right. The space should be large enough to allow the family to do the same, to be able to interact in a mobile way as well as when seated. Much can be learned from observing how parents respond to young children, for example as they move around the room, seek or avoid attention and so on. As I have already argued in this book, performing child protection effectively requires workers to act purposefully by moving towards children, and in organizational spaces this can only be done properly if there is adequate room to do it in. All social work offices should have spacious, well-stocked play/interview rooms, with toys and other communication aids routinely at hand for workers to use with children (Brandon et al., 1998, pp. 74–5; Lefevre, 2010; Koprowska, 2010, pp. 102–3). When, as is often the case, these are not available due to shortages of space, at the very least social workers need access to other spaces, in places like family centres, to carry out this vital work.

Offices provide other opportunities and resources, notably the option of calling for reinforcements who are available in the building. This is not simply to deal with threatening people, but can be perfectly benign.

An example of this from my research was when a social worker was interviewing a father who had come to the office to seek help with his debts, homelessness and the fact that he had hit his child, bringing his three-year-old son with him. The father became 'very emotional at this point so I returned to the office and [name of social worker] came out with me, the aim was to take [child] out of the room so he didn't hear or see his dad getting upset, however [child] would not leave his dad'.

Much less convincing in the above extracts from the Carlile report is the certainty with which it argues that this was poor social work practice and the reasons other than limited physical space given for why it happened. The interpretation that the family's visit to the social work office was, in fact, a tactic to conceal abuse rather than to be more open is a helpful one, and the emphasis on the vital importance of it being a priority in such circumstances of concern for a professional to 'see the child undressed' is spot on. The stress on the importance of workers ensuring that particular children are 'isolated' from others so as to ensure a focus on them is also an important insight. What is problematic is the tone and underlying assumptions about what determines how and whether such challenging things are done, which is also revealed in the ease with which it is stated that when deception by parents occurs, it should be unearthed. Of course it should, in the sense that we all want such effective practice to happen for the sake of the child. We need other ways to try and account for what it would take to be truly 'alive to the risk of being manipulated', and why social workers become closed to this and other difficult aspects of performing child protection.

Hospitals

Let us now explore alternative ways of thinking about these challenges by looking at hospitals. I shall focus particularly on an analysis of the case of eight-year-old Victoria Climbié who died a horrific death from child abuse in February 2000 despite the attention of social services, health and housing professionals and the police. This shows that the focus needs to be broadened out so that the face-to-face dynamics of interactions with children and parents/carers are placed within a wider analysis of the properties of organizations and offices that promote or block effective child protection.

Victoria Climbié died with 128 separate injuries to her body after suffering months of torture and abuse by her great aunt Marie Therese

Kouao and Kouao's lover, Carl Manning, who are serving life sentences for her murder. She was brought to London by Kouao from the Ivory Coast less than a year before she died. Her parents hoped this would give her the opportunity of a better education and life, yet Kouao never ever enrolled Victoria in a school. Victoria was starved, beaten and left in a freezing bathroom trussed up in a bin bag strapped into a bath, existing in her urine and faeces. A public inquiry into the circumstances that led to Victoria's death, chaired by Lord Herbert Laming and published in January 2003, argues that a massive system failure occurred, with an estimated 12 poorly handled occasions when Victoria could have been protected. While the report itself gives little or no analytic attention as such to emotional and psychodynamic processes, the narratives of the workers and managers involved, which are presented with great precision, can be used to illuminate neglected areas of organizational and emotional experience. The Laming Report undoubtedly explains a lot, as the source of the failures to protect Victoria are put down to a combination of events and 'woefully incompetent practices'. There was evidence of profound organizational malaise and an absence of leadership, as exemplified by senior managers' apparent indifference to children's services, which were underfunded and neglected. Local child protection procedures were way out of date and this was compounded by major staffing problems and low morale among staff who were invariably overworked and 'burning out'. Frontline workers were given little support or quality supervision and were uncertain about their role in child protection. Extremely poor administrative systems existed for tracking referrals and case information. There was poor or non-existent interagency communication and a consistent failure to engage with the child in any meaningful shape or form as a service user or to assess the child's needs, coupled with a focus throughout on Kouao, Victoria's carer, as the client in the case (Laming, 2003).

Much of this was already familiar from the many other high-profile inquiry cases and child death reviews that have gone on (Reder et al., 1993; Brandon et al., 2008). What is distinctive about Victoria's case is that she was not a child who was hidden away. She was actually admitted to hospital on two separate occasions with suspicious injuries, on one of which she was diagnosed by a consultant paediatrician as having scabies. While the inquiry adjudged this to have been an accurate diagnosis, the opinions of other doctors who suspected non-accidental injury were not given the same prominence as the scabies, especially by social services.

Injuries were also misinterpreted as marks from where Victoria scratched the infected area. Some staff wrongly attributed these marks to being 'normal' for a child brought up in an African culture, an assumption that was racist.

Despite casting its net wide in terms of examining key issues and events, the Laming Report ultimately exemplifies the limitations of such texts in how the primary emphasis in seeking to improve child protection is on the need for better management and accountability. The underlying premise on which the recommendations for change are based is naive in the extreme, as one of the central messages of the report is the idea that the way forward is 'doing the simple things properly' (Laming, 2003, p. 105), and 'Doing the basic things well saves lives' (p. 69). What the report is alluding to are so-called 'simple' tasks such as speaking to other professionals about concerns, writing up case notes, reading faxes, files, or even reading the child protection guidelines, never mind following them, engaging with the child and challenging her suspected abusers, and doing regular home visits – none of which were done.

But why is it that the simple things so often are not simple? Why aren't the basic things done well? A consistent finding of all such child death inquiry reports is that what looked like straightforward tasks just weren't done. This requires us to, in many ways, explain the unexplainable and to focus on the neglected psychological and emotional features of child protection work, as performed in particular places (Cooper, 2005). Time and time again in such cases, we see well-intentioned, often experienced professionals from all disciplines who simply can't explain their inaction in the face of evidence of marks and injuries on Victoria and clear suspicions of non-accidental injury and, on one occasion, sexual abuse. Things do not appear to be much simpler than writing up an observation in case notes. Yet during one of Victoria's stays in hospital in July 1999, for example, Laming writes that:

> Numerous witnesses from the hospital came before me and gave disturbing accounts of the injuries they saw on Victoria's body. I heard a variety of nurses say that they thought Victoria had been bitten, branded and beaten with a belt buckle. (Laming, 2003, p. 272)

On one occasion as many as five nurses observed Victoria's injuries while she was taking a bath. On another, nurse Pereira, who was bathing Victoria, was so disturbed by what she saw that she called in nurse Quinn to observe the marks 'which she thought may have been caused by a belt buckle. She also noticed that Victoria's arm was bruised and swollen' (p. 266). Laming concludes from this:

> I have found it very difficult to understand why important observations of this nature were not recorded in the notes. Both Nurse Pereira and Nurse Quinn were aware that Victoria was a child about whom there were child protection concerns, and Nurse Pereira had seen fit the previous evening to make a note in the critical incident log concerning the master–servant relationship between Kouao and Victoria. Nurse Pereira was frank enough to accept that she should have made a note of her observation that night. Nurse Quinn simply told me that she could not account for why she chose not to do so. (Laming, 2003, p. 266)

Similar examples could be given for social workers, the police and housing officials in the Climbié case. The case reveals what Stan Cohen (2001, p. 295) calls 'the complex obstacles between information and action'. It is one thing to know about something, quite another to act on that knowledge. These professionals were caught in the midst of what Cohen calls 'the dynamics of knowing and not knowing'. They became bystanders before an appalling atrocity. They knew but they didn't know what was happening to Victoria and did nothing. Cohen refers to 'the essence of denial and bystanding' as 'an active looking away, a sense of a situation so utterly hopeless and incomprehensible that we cannot bear to think about it' (p. 194). This is another example of the avoidant behaviour professionals engage in when faced with intolerable feelings stirred up by having to think the unthinkable about what may have been done to a child. In further considering what leads professionals to this kind of paralysis – in public spaces like hospitals as well as in the office and on home visits – particular attention needs to be given to the impact of having to work with resistant and manipulative service users and the underlying psychological and emotional dynamics that appear to have been present in these organizations and workers' experiences.

Office politics and organizational dynamics

When considered in terms of the emotional dynamics between workers and service users and their impact on workers and professional systems, it becomes possible to see some of the deeper emotional and psychological processes that may have been at work in these cases. Although in Victoria's case, Kouao never overtly threatened violence against any professional, there are many descriptions in the report of her being aggressive and menacing in her manner – 'difficult', 'forceful', 'manipulative' (Laming, 2003). Of crucial importance in terms of the impact Kouao had on people was what professionals observed of her relationship with Victoria, especially in terms of a so-called 'master–slave relationship', and how Victoria would jump to attention and often wet herself in Kouao's presence.

Not only was Kouao 'master' to Victoria in a disastrous manner, she and Manning dominated professionals, who, in an important sense, behaved like their 'slaves'. We now know that she and Manning stage-managed the pre-announced home visits that social workers made to the flat and that the professionals did not challenge them. Systems theory and psychodynamic theory can help us to understand these dynamics in terms of how professional systems and family systems have a tendency to become enmeshed and reflect one another. Professional relationships come to mirror the distorted and abusive relationships within families (Reder et al., 1993). Unconsciously, workers mirrored Victoria's feelings of terror and took up the 'servant' position they observed Victoria taking. The sense of helplessness, fear and discomfort workers felt was partly their own but also, crucially, Victoria's. The painful nature of these unbearable feelings and an unconscious desire to repress them goes some way, I believe, to explaining the inaction of the nurses when faced with disturbing evidence of injuries to Victoria's naked body in the bath, as well as the social workers' paralysis in the case. This does not happen in isolation, however, and the risks of it occurring are much greater in organizations that do not actively work to acknowledge and support workers in dealing with their intolerable feelings (Cooper and Lousada, 2005).

Thus lack of attention to these processes in Victoria's case was compounded by various aspects of organizational culture. The social workers were overworked and underappreciated. The Laming Report does detail the excessive caseloads of the social worker Lisa Arthurworrey and others and a further tragic dimension of this case for the workers was that they worked so hard. Lisa Authurworrey, the social worker who had most contact with Victoria, had actually accumulated 52 days off in lieu. However, the Laming Report does not expressly assess the wider meanings of professionals' workloads. Thus we know nothing about the kinds of experiences these nurses, social workers and police officers had immediately before they dealt with Victoria's case, be it an hour, day, week or months preceding it. This again speaks volumes for the limitations of the focus of the inquiry process on individual cases to the exclusion of a wider analysis of practitioners' lived experiences. What can be said is that workers' judgement and capacities to confront the possible reality of abuse and to tolerate more anxiety will have been deeply affected by the wider experiences they brought into their dealings with Victoria's case.

The social workers did not just have to deal with menacing and manipulative clients, but similar kinds of colleagues, including managers. The social work team acted out distorted and abusive patterns with *one another*. The report's descriptions of the internal politics of the social work team demonstrate that there was little comfort or release there for the workers. One social worker recalled that

> the team was very divided, and there were a lot of deep conflicts. At times the working environment felt hostile, and it was not a comfortable place to work comfortably in. (p. 192)

There were allegedly 'two camps', with 'insiders and outsiders within the office'. Similar distorted relationships and communication extended to relationships between agencies: social workers were afraid to challenge doctors' opinions, while at least one team of social workers had it in for the police. The very dynamics that professionals had to routinely confront in families were also embedded in the workplace. Lisa Arthurworrey actually referred to her team manager as 'the headmistress. I was a child who was seen but not heard, and had seen what had happened to those who challenged [manager]' (p. 192). As I have already suggested, these kinds of dynamics are not a coincidence, but from within psychodynamic and systems theory can be understood as an expression of how chaotically and pathologically enmeshed workers and service users were.

These destructive dynamics were compounded by a one-dimensional performance management culture in the social work office. One social worker referred to the office being characterized by 'conveyer belt social work' and how

> the ethos seemed to be particularly about getting the cases through the system and meeting the targets, meeting the statistics, getting them through the system rather than doing the work that needed to be done. (p. 112)

Others spoke of the 'bombardment factor' of the relentless work that came into the office. Cases were just 'plonked on social workers desks', with no attention to the worker's needs, feelings, worries, or the degree to which the level of difficulty in the case reflected their experience or competence. As Lisa Arthurworrey, Victoria's social worker from the north Tottenham office, told the inquiry: 'we always worked at a fairly cracking pace in north Tottenham' (Laming, 2003, p. 184). The dominance of performance management cultures creates a demand that the work be done more and more quickly within the terms of what it is possible to measure at an organizational level. Little is known about the nature of the hospital and nurses' experience of their organization, but it is not unreasonable to assume that it was characterized by similar issues.

In total, there was a complete lack of attention to workers' feelings, no space for reflection, for slowing things down, as the social work office itself was not a safe or nurturing space. Pressure to get cases 'through the system' also creates a situation where attention, time and resources are diverted from doing in-depth, needs-driven work with children and families in ways which can promote child safety, welfare and healing. Such tragedies are, in part, a consequence of how the soul has been squeezed out of the work, pulling workers' and the entire system's attention away from understanding and developing the kinds of deep relationships with the self, children and carers that are required to do meaningful child protection practice.

Child protection practice is never simple

It is against this background that doing even the simple things seems to become enormously elusive and difficult. So you don't read the case file or write up notes because you might have to confront yet more trauma; you don't make that crucial call to another professional, follow those guidelines or even read the procedures that are sitting on your desk. You don't engage in a necessarily intimate way with the child in hospital even when their injuries are staring you in the face, or ask the awkward challenging questions of parents or carers. You know about the abuse, but you don't know. You don't visit the child or make any attempt to get close to them because, unconsciously, you fear contamination by their diseased, unkempt bodies and their pain. Indeed, these feelings threaten to overwhelm you. You are just too busy trying to survive, defending yourself against the anxiety and perhaps overidentification with the perpetrator. Becoming aware of these stresses, strains and dynamics is vital to enable professionals to be fully 'alive to the risk of being manipulated', as the Carlile report put it, and, in the face of all the challenges, staying focused on the child.

The health of an organization is also deeply influenced by the stability and continuity of its staff and the strength of teamwork. The more retention and recruitment problems social work organizations face, the harder it is to build teams with the necessary coherent knowledge base, emotional honesty, resilience and strength. Retention and recruitment problems have resulted in an increased reliance on agency staff on short-term contracts who tend to come from other countries. While the global movement of social workers enriches practice and the profession, this brings new challenges in achieving continuity of practice wisdom, professional development and maintaining good practice grounded in local knowledge. For example, in at least one deprived London borough (Brent) in the mid-2000s, there wasn't a single social worker in its duty teams who had trained in the UK (Laming, 2003; Munro, 2005, p. 380). The absence of local knowledge and wisdom derived from experienced colleagues who know families as well as the 'lie of the land' intimately has significant implications for skilful child protection work. All these examples are illustrative of how organizations are characterized by what Sheller and Urry (2006) refer to as 'dwelling in mobility'.

Conclusion

I have tried in this chapter to explain the unexplainable in terms of how abuse can be known about and not known about, how this occurs in different public settings as well as on home visits, and how workers and professional systems become paralysed because of the psychological and emotional nature of workers' experiences and the positive and negative influence of organizations on what does and does not get done. The extent to which organizational settings enable or constrain the identification of child abuse and effective longer term work with it depends on having good enough resources and surroundings, such as decent sized rooms that are well stocked with toys and other aides to effective communication. The availability of video recorders and two-way mirrors has a huge amount to offer for the promotion of thoughtful, reflective practice. But the analysis has tried to go further by showing how significant the emotional life and atmosphere of the organization and the relationships between staff are to the nature of the practice that goes on. The importance of offices and other organizational environments, such as hospitals, clinics and family centres, being experienced by workers as supportive, nurturing spaces simply cannot be exaggerated.

10
Working with mothers

When I started to work with the social worker I just cried. The social worker told me that is exactly what she wanted me to do. To get it out no matter, whatever it was. And I got to trust her then and that's how I started to work out of it. I'd do the talking and they'd do the lilstening. It's good to talk.

(a 28-year-old mother of two in a neglect case)

This chapter focuses on working with mothers. Unlike evidence of work with fathers, which will be covered in Chapter 11, this is huge subject. Mothers, it can be said, *are* child protection. Throughout its history, there has always been one corollary to the aim of keeping children safe: improving how women mother their children. As Jonathan Scourfield (2003a) has shown, applied in an uncritical way, such instrumentality leads to mother blaming. This means women being expected to carry on with caring adequately for their children irrespective of the hardships they endure and how men treat them. Over the past 30 years, the women's movement and feminist theory have critically analysed practice and clarified the components of what effective ethical work with mothers has to involve. This chapter considers how mothers can be worked with in ways that ensure their responsibilities to provide safety and adequate care for their children are met, while making notions of fairness and justice meaningful.

This chapter and the two that follow it are thematically linked in addressing the work that needs to be done with parents and other adult carers to help them develop their caring abilities and be made safe. These chapters cover the full range of stages in the child protection process, from how to engage mothers and fathers, assess them, and work with them in long-term supportive and therapeutic relationships. As parenting must always be seen in the context of relationships with children, further attention will also be given to how to promote children's safety and wellbeing.

Assessing mothering

How mothers should be worked with obviously depends on what the child protection issues are. The mother who is a non-abusing parent in a case of child sexual abuse requires help to come to terms with the discovery that their child has been abused and support to believe and support their child. Mothers can experience grief-like reactions of disbelief and workers need to help them move through this, while ensuring that, as far as possible, the child's needs are being met (Hooper, 1992). Working with a woman who has been found to physically harm her child requires a thorough and immediate assessment of the severity of the harm done and whether it is safe to leave the child with their mother. Quick decisions must be made about the actions needed to ensure that the child is safe, based on a detailed assessment of every aspect of the child's life, the mother's parenting capacity and motivation to change (Morrison, 2010). Similar challenges arise in cases of child neglect, depending on how serious it is. A key issue here is that cases very often do not present with a single problem. A crucial pattern to emerge from research is that high-risk cases predominantly involve mothers who are parenting alone, misusing alcohol or drugs and who have experienced abuse in their own childhoods and were either in the past or currently are the victims of domestic abuse. A shadowy man is often in or around the family. Most live in poverty in disadvantaged and sometimes hostile environments and some also have to deal with serious child behaviour and control problems, such as with challenging adolescents. The suffering and vulnerability of these women and their children therefore emanate from several sources and are often severe. In one study, 67% of the children who entered care were from these backgrounds (Ferguson and O'Reilly, 2001).

Garrett (2003, 2004b) has argued that, in general, social work with mothers has not changed even in recent decades when feminism challenged the traditional ways gender roles have been thought about and performed. Social work, he argues, continues to overlook women's poverty and responds to them in oppressive ways. He claims that 'research still points to social work's continuing reinforcement of maternalism, even in the so-called "post-traditional order"' (Garrett, 2003, p. 388).

Maternalism refers to a belief that mothers must be made to mother because this is what women are biologically determined to do. It is their 'natural' role. I agree that social work still tends to focus on mothers and not enough on fathers and a pattern of intervention is evident where women are sometimes held too responsible for problems to the neglect of men. Yet social work today is categorically not simply about the 'reinforcement of maternalism' (see also Houston, 2004). Important evidence for this is to be found in the pattern of service user mothers recognizing that they have problems and that they need help. In the aforementioned child protection study (Ferguson and O'Reilly, 2001), by far the most significant referral source was mothers, who raised initial concern in 27% of cases. In 11%, children brought the concern to light, either by directly reporting it or, much more often, by telling someone who then reported it. Some 61% of these self-referring mothers had histories of social work involvement and were therefore re-referring themselves in a context of already having received a social work service. Why would these women behave in this way if all they were getting was some kind of crude 'reinforcement of maternalism'?

Having interviewed a sample of these women (and their children), as well as the professionals who worked them, the stereotype of social workers indiscriminately oppressing such women just doesn't reflect the sheer complexity of what is going on. These women, and some children too, were choosing to report problems such as sexual and emotional abuse and domestic violence that remained hidden within the traditional family. In so doing, they were engaging social workers in historically new ways in helping them to plan their lives. Such women were enabled to make crucial decisions, such as: Do I want to stay in this relationship? If I do, then what kind of relationship do I want? How can I have better relationships with my children? And what kind of life do I want for myself and my children? This reflects how new opportunities are available today for people to (re)shape and plan their lives and especially those aspects connected with emotional distress, violence and trauma.

To speak of 'life planning' in these terms is not meant in the sense of a total life transformation, which suggests people are able to lift themselves out of poverty or other forms of disadvantage. It refers rather to how service users have opportunities to gain insight into the choices they do have, their rights, behaviour, emotional life; how they need to be challenged to take responsibility for violent, abusive or neglectful behaviour, or helped to challenge powerful others to cease violence; and be accountable, to learn about who they are as children, siblings, parents, lovers and, where needed, gain some healing. It is because of their suffering and the risk that pervades their lives that vulnerable disadvantaged people have something to gain from interventions that assist them with their life planning.

Working with mothers in practice

I want to take these issues and debates further and show how mothers and children can be effectively worked with by focusing on a case study, one that contains the key components of intimate child protection practice: the skilful use of empathy, authority, touch and other communication skills in working with parents and in direct work with children. It also demonstrates good interagency communication, understanding of roles and actual working with family members, individually and together. The case involves substantiated emotional abuse and neglect in relation to four children. The eldest, here called Joanne, was aged 10 at the time of the referral and the three boys were 7, 5 and 2 years old. The family first had social work involvement three years previously due to allegations of physical abuse and neglect by the parents, here called Mr and Mrs Smith. Prior to the referral that set in motion the practice featured in this chapter, the case had been closed. The case study is based on interviews with Mr and Mrs Smith (separately), Joanne, the social worker, family support worker and the school principal, as well as data from the case file.

The referral to the social work department that led to the case being reopened was made by a school and centred on Joanne, whose behaviour there was alleged to be extremely 'disruptive and aggressive'. The principal asked to meet with Mrs Smith to discuss these concerns and suggested that the school seek further help, with her consent. He reported the matter to the social work department and also sought psychological support for Joanne: 'It was not just a problem for [the girl], it was a family problem.' The social worker investigated the case and felt there was some evidence of neglect and emotional abuse. There were also concerns about home conditions, possible domestic violence and the parents' general capacity to cope. The children were deemed to be at 'high risk' at the time of the referral. During the 12-month research follow-up period, the case was re-referred, alleging the mother hit Joanne. A case conference took place and the social worker was the lead professional and she and a family support worker delivered the child protection plan in the home. A child psychologist was introduced to develop a behaviour modification programme with Joanne at school and she was assessed as 'depressive and suicidal'. Respite care was also provided for Joanne and her eldest brother. Two review case conferences occurred within a six-month period, at the last of which the case was closed for child protection concerns but left open for childcare concerns. By then, Joanne was deemed to be doing well and was due to be re-assessed by a psychologist.

The process of engagement

It was noted in the case file prior to this intervention that the mother 'does not like social workers'. Initially, both Mr and Mrs Smith were adamant that they didn't want social work or any other kind of intervention. They felt this way, in part, because of past experience with a social worker, who, as Mrs Smith put it, 'never gave me a chance to explain myself. If I tried to say something, she thought I was hiding things and if I didn't say enough, I was still hiding things.' For Mr Smith, 'She was coming down asking questions, questions, but there was nothing coming back.' They felt that the social worker imposed things without exploring with the family what she could do to help them to resolve some of the difficulties they were experiencing. Things got worse when one of the children was allegedly examined for sexual abuse while undergoing a medical examination. Not feeling able to trust social workers meant that Mrs Smith could not actively engage with any formal support system, despite recognizing the need for some help: 'I knew my little girl needed a psychologist. I couldn't come in here and say I think she might need someone to talk to. I thought if I do, they'll say I'm not looking after her and then bring me into a social worker.' While the gain for the parents of this approach was that it protected them from undue interference from an oppressive form of social work practice, the downside was that it left them isolated and bereft of the kind of support they and the children needed.

The social worker recognized that Mrs Smith was 'quite hostile you know, a lot of the time. With the mother very frightened of social work involvement and not trusting, the issues had to be explored very sensitively.' The family support worker found Mrs Smith 'extremely hostile and she used foul language. She did not want to know about social workers.' When the social worker made her first home visit, by her own account, even though she was expected because of the negotiations with the school, Mrs Smith started 'crying' and asked, 'What did I do now?' The social worker did not push the issue too far and arranged to call again the following day. Facilitating this process meant, in the social worker's words, 'trying to understand where the mother is coming from, and the issues she has gone through. You can actually work when you know where it's all coming from, you're going from what their issue is as well.' This skilled, empathetic approach by the social worker worked well to win over the confidence of the mother, who was adamant that: 'You need someone that is going to sit down, listen to you and not judge you, if you have a problem.'

Even to get to the stage of addressing parenting issues, the family support worker worked hard to build a rapport with Mrs Smith, which took some time:

> Maybe two visits a week for about a month until I drank her coffee, smoked her fags and she was quite comfortable with that. She gave me a load of personal stuff which was not really relevant to our work but it gave a bigger insight on her as a woman and as a mother and partner to the father and that was the way we worked it to try and help the mother help the children.

What was impressively empathetic about this intervention was how the mother and father's lack of engagement with professionals was viewed within a context that took their feelings about their past experience with social workers into account and enabled them to express their fears and unhappiness and feel heard. This cleared the air and the development of a more democratic professional–service user relationship had begun. This is quite different to an approach that would view the parents' struggle to focus on the problems at hand as an unwillingness to engage with social workers and simple proof of their incapacity to parent, which could then lead to a judgemental, unethical approach.

Keeping Mrs Smith focused on the problems at hand required an ongoing skilled approach by the social worker:

> When you go in to address an issue, she will try and dismiss it or keep talking about something else, then if you say something the wrong way with her you can get the door. I know her now and know how to say something. She's getting there, you know. Before she used to see me and she was so petrified that her mind was racing. She might hear the first sentence and that was it.

At first Mrs Smith found it easier to talk to the family support worker rather than the social worker. Both professionals were aware of this and used it skilfully and strategically to their advantage. As the social worker recounted: 'Sometimes it can be easier for the mother to hear things reinforced from the family support worker. She's less of a threat, so in the beginning she was able to focus in with the mother regarding parenting and stuff.' The mother was, however, aware of these tactics: 'I was lucky, because the social worker really did work with me, but she sent in the family support worker first and she softened me up, to be honest.'

Improving parenting skills and the practice of intimacy

A main focus of the work was to promote Mrs Smith's self-esteem, knowledge and emotional health as part of improving her parenting skills. As the social worker said:

> Their parenting is so disastrous that they really don't know how to start or what good parenting is. So it has to be done at a very slow level. It may take up to a year to discuss issues, even the most important issues. One step at a time.

Developing this mother's capacity to help the children and helping her in her own right also meant focusing on Mrs Smith to make her feel better about herself. 'I felt she needed to like herself more, because she did not like herself' (family support worker). Building Mrs Smith's self-esteem was done by encouraging her to take care of her appearance. As the family support worker observed: 'She did little things like get her hair cut. She had no teeth and then she went and had her teeth done. She began to look after herself a little more ... it was much more positive stuff.' In this way, the practice reached into and developed Mrs Smith's self-worth and helped her to value and love herself more.

The family support worker used small sections of a parenting book as part of her approach to developing the mother's skills. She also actively modelled how to physically care for a child, feeling that the mother 'was not really aware of the emotional stuff her children needed. She found it difficult to touch her daughter ... I could talk till I was blue in the face about nurturing and until the mother saw me nurturing it was no good until I left her to think about it.' The family support worker would give the daughter a 'hug' when she met her, in the presence of the mother. Here we see the value of professional touch being practised in an ethical, comforting way with a child, in the manner discussed in Chapter 8. Another example of 'modelling' intimate parenting arises from the school principal's observation: 'There'd be very little affection shown to the daughter by the mother, you know even how her hair looked.' The family support worker agreed: 'Her mother was not taking care of the daughter's hair and it took maybe a month and then I went in one day and did the hair', and then she told Mrs Smith to 'Go down to the pound shop and get a bottle of oil and treat her hair and you can use half of it yourself.' This was, the family support worker said, 'turning a negative into a positive in a very simple example'. Another such example she gave as: 'The mother would focus on the daughter's "got seven spellings wrong out of ten" and I'd say, "Brilliant, you got three right, get four right next week".'

Relationship-based practice with the child

A crucial feature of the creative intimate practice in this case was the direct work the social worker did with the child. She met with Joanne every week for five months, and after that every two weeks. Joanne was allowed to set the agenda about where she would meet the social worker and what they would talk about. Strategically, the child's mother and father were not made aware of what the social worker and their daughter talked about, unless it was a child protection concern that demanded limited confidentiality. In common with other children (Butler and Williamson, 1994), Joanne really appreciated this. As she expressed it in the research interview: 'I knew that what I said there was no way it was going to get out . . . that helped me express my feelings more.' Part of the social worker's aim was to improve parental competences – or, more accurately, most often *maternal* competences – by learning what was needed from the child's viewpoint. Joanne, for instance, told the social worker she was embarrassed because her mother was 'always roaring and shouting at her in front of her friends'. The social worker discussed this with the mother and daughter and 'a compromise was come to. Mum wouldn't do it, but she expected something from the daughter, that she would respond to the mother, fairly reasonably rather than ignoring her.'

A key task for the social worker was to help Joanne get her message across to her mother. As Joanne said in her research interview: 'She said she was a social worker to help me and things I couldn't say to my mam, she'd help me to say them to her.' Prior to working with the social worker, Joanne said she herself 'was a really grouchy person and angry always, annoying my ma and just getting in the way. The social worker has just taught me better ways to deal with my problems and that made me feel better. If I was going home, I'd feel happier.' Joanne conceded that she also 'exploded' against her mother and that the social worker helped her overcome this 'problem':

> She told me, it just wasn't worth it, put your foot down and say, 'you're not going to explode' and just keep your head and think what you're saying even if she's exploding. I'm [now] able to keep control. I'm not as bossy as I used to be.

This is intervention work at its best, showing how, through the therapeutic process, the child not only gets support to deal with the impact of the trauma she has experienced from being poorly parented and is rendered safer, but herself is helped to learn anger management and emotional literacy. This kind of work equips abused children to grow into adults who are able to provide care to their own loved ones and practise intimacy in a respectful, healthy way. Research shows that this kind of therapeutic work with children and young people is a key factor in enabling people who were abused as children to grow into being non-abusing parents and breaking the intergenerational cycle of abuse (Egeland, 2009). In addition to Joanne being helped with her immediate problems, the longer term child welfare agenda was secured through this work. As the family support worker notices: 'The daughter has been empowered and if something does happen or she is very unhappy, she, as a child, knows where to go [to get help].'

Working with a mother's trauma, anger and loss

The social worker felt that it was Mrs Smith's 'behaviour that causes the problems and if the kids are to remain at home, it's her behaviour that has to change'. Mrs Smith had the same perception: 'The issue was me and my moods and my temper and how that was affecting the kids and how it was affecting my daughter in school.' Intervention was also focused then on how Mrs Smith could control her 'temper', as she explains:

> The family support worker was there to help me with losing my temper and how to cope with what if my daughter came in with a problem. Rather than say, 'Go away and leave me alone', I'd try dealing with it and if I couldn't, rather than shout at her, I'd say, 'Listen, give me five, I'll have a cup of

coffee.' Whereas before if she came in, I would have said, 'If you don't go away, I'm going to murder you.' I would have slapped her. I would've lost my head.

Mrs Smith also recognized how the family support worker worked to increase her self-esteem while teaching anger management skills, by 'Just words of encouragement, you know, [for example], nobody's perfect. I always thought everything was my fault, I was stupid and silly, the family support worker showed me that I'm a person for myself.' Joanne spoke of how her mother has changed because of this type of work: 'If she was going to say something, she stops. In her mind I'd say she says, "No, I'm not going to shout, the family support worker told me not to do it" and she'd walk out of the room before she'd explode.'

The legacy of abuse and trauma from the past was present in Mrs Smith's life. At the age of 17 she was raped and became pregnant with Joanne. She did not tell anyone at the time, including her partner, who until recently did not know who was the biological father of Joanne. The mother carried around this 'secret' for over 10 years and considers it to be part of the reason why she acted abusively:

> The father didn't know I'd been raped. He didn't know what was making me carry on like this. It was breaking me up, so I contacted the social worker, explained the whole lot to her and said 'Will you work on it with me, yourself and the family support worker?' That took so much off my head. I was able [then] to work on other issues that I needed to sort out.

For the mother, the social worker's totally non-judgemental approach when she told her about the rape made all the difference and 'that made everything seem as if, God, why hadn't I been able to meet this woman 10 years ago and tell her this and then it wouldn't have been so bad'. For the social worker: 'Because the daughter is a product of rape, that is underlying a lot of how the mother sees her daughter. Because the mother can love the boys so easily. So as those issues are addressed, that relationship will improve.' The social worker and family support worker gave a lot of support to the parents on this issue, over a period of three months from start to finish: 'He finding out the first time who the daughter's father was and coping with that and moving on to the daughter, to tell the daughter.' In order to facilitate the father in coming to terms with the issues, the social worker and family support worker would call at the house later in the evening when he came in from work, something he very much appreciated. However, the man's role was still minimized because he was seen as a supplementary parent to the mother (Daniel and Taylor, 1999; Featherstone, 2009). The intervention could have gone further in focusing on how he could assume greater responsibility for the childcare and be a greater resource to his children and partner. Yet, it must be stressed that the view within the family, as well as the professionals' view, was that it was Mrs Smith who was most in need of help. And she got it. This constituted a tremendous gain for her. If there was a cost to her, it was that she was left to carry too much parental responsibility (Scourfield, 2003b). The cost for Mr Smith was that he did not have the same opportunity to benefit emotionally as well as practically from the intervention, as a parent and for himself.

Helping an abusive mother

The work done in this case effectively balanced authoritative, negotiated child protection, family support work and informed risk taking. A year after the initial referral included in this study, Joanne called on the social worker and made a self-report to the effect that her mother hit her and showed the social worker her bruises: 'There was quite serious bruising. This is what she alleged, so I could have gone to the doctor with her and she could have been out of the home.' The social worker did not take this approach: 'I think you just take a risk, I know it's not good enough for the kid to have that sort of beating. Mum spoke about what she did and we all sat down together and the mother apologized and there was hugs and kisses.' While this involved taking a risk, in that the social worker made a decision to deal with this without calling a case conference, crucially, she did not hide the allegation of abuse or quietly collude with the family. She did discuss the matter with her manager and referred it to the police, as she was procedurally obliged to do, asking them to hold off their investigation because she and the family support worker were working 'intensively' with the family.

The social worker took into account that the family was experiencing huge financial problems and possible eviction. To help relieve the stress, it was after this abusive incident that respite care was provided for 10 days for Joanne and her six-year-old brother. The social worker situates her analysis of abuse by women in a context that takes account of the difficulties of mothering in patriarchal conditions where little support is given to women to parent – especially in poverty – while holding them responsible (and not fathers) if things go wrong. This is a social worker

who clearly constantly engaged in critical reflection and shaped her practice accordingly to try and promote safety and democratic relationships
in families. We see how she has internalized the influence of a theoretical
framework based on feminist theory and an understanding of gender and
motherhood as social constructs and how this interacts with individuals'
identities and emotional lives: 'She has the main responsibility with the
kids all day, so that's why it makes it more understandable.'

However, the social worker is also clear that parental culpability rests
with the mother because it was she who hit the child, which means that
the fact that 'the kids are with her all day' is also a social work concern. The social worker made it clear to her that 'the issue is you can't
hit your children' and explained to Mrs Smith that in the event of further abuse, she would not hesitate to take the matter all the way. Thus,
despite – or perhaps more accurately, because of – the openness and
trust in the relationship, the social worker was not afraid to take risks
and to use good authority to confront the consequences of child abuse.
This is the kind of truthfulness in practice that is essential for promoting
child safety, and shows how authoritative child protection can honestly
be done in the context of empathy, support and therapeutic work (also see
Chapter 12).

By the end of the intervention, Mrs Smith was clear about why she
found it hard to care for her children: 'I couldn't help my daughter
because I needed help first.' Being able to shed the burden of the rape
felt 'great . . . things got better with the kids, because it was all off my
mind, I can talk to them now, before I shouted at them, because I didn't
trust myself. I had all those emotional problems for 10 years back.' The
way in which this process of recovery from the trauma of sexual violence
that Mrs Smith had begun with the support of family support and therapeutic intervention is similar to other women's experiences, as shown by
feminist research and commentary (Herman, 1992). Mr Smith saw how
his partner 'is a lot better in herself, because a lot of the pressure that
was on her, over that [rape], was taken off'. Increasing her level of confidence and modelling tactile caring and loving enabled Mrs Smith to
become more intimate with her daughter, to whom the social worker sees
her as being much more tactile, as she is towards her sons, and 'there'd
be a lot more laughs and fun'. The intimate practice of the professionals
is reflected back to them in the increased intimacy in the parent–child
relationship. According to Mrs Smith, this transformation in her extends
to the practicalities of everyday living: 'We go shopping as a family now.
I can . . . do the shopping without screaming.'

It is in the interests of good child protection for professionals to help women to develop their own sense of self outside the life of their children (Featherstone, 1999). The theory and practice of 'containment' (Bion, 1962) in therapeutic work with children was outlined in Chapter 8. Here we see its value in how the workers acted as a container for all the family members' anxieties, fears, hate and trauma. Through the skilful use of relationship, the workers enabled the mother, Joanne and, to some extent, the father to process their destructive feelings, begin repairing painful experiences and strengthen their internal resources and capacities to cope and love well (see also Trevithick, 2003; Keeping, 2008). As this case typifies it, this often places the worker in an ambiguous and uncomfortable position of being what Winnicott (1957) called 'a reliable hate object'. Having been angrily rejected by the service user one day, workers return on the next visit to a warm welcome, a sign that their role as a container is working. Like good enough parents, Mrs Smith's workers had the wisdom to understand that the anger and rejection that was fired at them from time to time was a mark of how much this parent had come to trust and value their work. The mother couldn't have been more grateful for the help and support she received, which, she insisted, prevented the children from going into statutory care: 'Without the family support worker's help, I wouldn't be here.'

Conclusion

I chose this case to focus on because it is typical of the multiple and enduring difficulties that characterize the lives of mothers in child protection cases (Morris et al., 2008). It was also chosen because it provides many insights into how mothers and their loved ones can be effectively worked with. The workers shaped a form of creative intervention that was 'intimate' and tailored to the specific needs and life plans of the mother, daughter and, to some extent, the father: from the careful way in which the referral was negotiated by the school with the social worker and the mother, the sensitive way in which the process of engagement with the resistant parents was managed, to the authoritative and supportive therapeutic work that helped the child and parents to confront their difficulties, trauma and emotional lives, all leading to some resolution of their difficulties.

Of course, some cases do not always end so well. Some children need to be removed into care for their protection, often against the wishes of one or both parents. In some cases, family members will agree that the children should not be taken into care, or the family can be divided in their views on its merits. One 12-year-old girl in my research (Ferguson and O'Reilly, 2001) was clearly unhappy about being in care and saw little value in social work intervention, while her 16-year-old sister, who had been sexually assaulted by some 20 different men over the years and suffered parental neglect and who reported the abuse through the school, experienced it as life saving and life affirming. The parents were (literally) divided in their perspectives on events: mother left father, the marriage ended and each made accusations against the other about domestic violence. Some mothers in the same study deeply resented social workers because of what they had done to them, while their children welcomed the intervention. One such mother of seven children who initiated contact with social services 12 years previously to get help with her second child, spoke of how 'I regret it now' and all her trust in social work was gone because her eldest two children were taken into care. Her 13-year-old daughter was now choosing to stay in care and alleged physical and sexual abuse by her father and that her siblings were at risk from him also. According to this 13-year-old, the risk of violence and misuse of drugs was such that: 'I'd be dead by now if I was still living at home. I would be dead.' This typifies how social work intervention promotes contradictory experiences and outcomes for family members: this young person regards her placement in care as an opportunity to both literally have a life and live a life of her own, while her mother feels that her life has been ruined and taken from her by oppressive social workers. The fact that often there is no outcome that satisfies everyone and that some people feel destroyed by what social workers have to do is a painful truth that is at the heart of the ethical complexity that it is necessary for professionals to come to terms with in working with mothers and children in effectively performing child protection practice.

11
Working with fathers

Is this all going downhill, am I failing at this? God, I'm a man you know.
I don't go crying looking for help.
(44-year-old father in a child protection case)

Of the many gaps in practice that have been identified in child protection, few loom larger than working with fathers. As several of the cases
already featured in this book have shown, huge challenges surround men
perpetrating abuse and how professionals engage with them to identify
it and stop it. Brid Featherstone's important conceptual work on fatherhood shows that service user fathers can be categorized in three ways: as
resources; as vulnerable; and as risks (Featherstone, 2004, 2009). It is
difficult to achieve positive outcomes for children and women without
engaging fathers because it means that men are not held accountable
for their abuse. Women and children are also disadvantaged when men's
resourcefulness as carers is left undeveloped. Men themselves lose out
because they miss the opportunity to develop their parenting abilities
and relationships with their children, and their own vulnerability, trauma
and suffering risks going unaided. This chapter considers how workers can effectively engage with fathers, assess their safety and, where
appropriate, work with them to develop their capacity to be safe, loving
carers.

Finding and engaging fathers

It seems that as they go about their day-to-day work and approach the
homes of service users, one of the things that most fills practitioners
with anxiety and even dread is that there may be a man behind the
door. In many practitioners' minds, fathers and houses don't seem to
fit well together. The gendered assumption that the home is a woman's

responsibility and domain runs deep in the DNA of social work and child protection. This holds that the home is where mothering goes on. A father's relationship to home is, in comparison, uncertain and problematic. From the beginnings of child protection traced in Chapter 1, social workers have visited homes to see the mother not the father. He was supposed to be at work. Home was a place where he replenished himself, getting ready to go out and do more work, so as to be a good breadwinner, which is what child protection workers expected of him. Historically, there was no expectation that the father would do anything with his children or contribute to housework. For social work to change this professional state of mind would require a sea change in attitude and approach.

The term 'father' is being used here in a general way to include not only biological fathers but men who are resident with the children's mother who are father figures. The fact that social workers and other child protection professionals tend not to engage with fathers is now widely recognized (O'Hagan, 1997; Daniel and Taylor, 2001, 2005; Scourfield, 2001, 2003a; Featherstone, 2003, 2004, 2009; Featherstone et al., 2007; Brown et al., 2009). This is confirmed by social workers' experiences, of which the following comment is typical:

> In my experience, yes, it's quite common that it's mums. That even if mum and dad are separated and the kids live with mum, that's usually the norm. Or else fathers...they'll deliberately stay out of the way, or they'll stay upstairs, it's quite common that much of our interaction will be with the mum, and not dad. It's great though whenever you can go out and visit and actually mum and dad are there and willingly engage and actually give you...it gives you a whole different perspective on the whole situation if you can speak to both parents rather than meet with one parent. But no, it's quite often that it's just mum that we will engage with.

Men in child and family work tend to be, in Brown et al.'s (2009) evocative phrase, manufactured as 'ghost fathers'. When they are present in families that are known to services, so often they are absent from the work that goes on. This is not only a consequence of how men are ignored, avoided or actively kept out of child and family work by professionals, but how men absent themselves, or are kept out by other family members. Research evidence supports the involvement of fathers as being good for children in general (Lamb, 1997, 2001; Lamb and Tamis-Lemonda, 2004; Lamb and Lewis, 2004), and for abused and neglected children

(Dubowitz et al., 2000; Lamb, 2001), and this is broadly the position adopted in recent UK government policy (DfES, 2004; see also the resources at www.fatherhoodinstitute.org). In the main, children desire to have actively involved, positive fathers, while some children and young people are grateful to have been protected from abusive fathers. Some fathers constitute a risk to children and intimate partners. The exclusion of known violent men from families is legitimate in order to promote women's safety, the safety of children and to promote their mother's parenting strengths (Sinclair and Bullock, 2002; Featherstone and Evans, 2004). Attempts at engagement and making him accountable for his violence need to be pursued through the criminal justice system and resources such as an offenders re-education programme utilized (Shepard and Pence, 1999). The same can be said about work with known sex offenders.

The first imperative of child protection practice with fathers or father figures is to find out about them. This is often difficult due to the fluid, mobile nature of practice, where the presence of men in homes and families is often unclear, sometimes deliberately so. In order to counter this, it is important to understand the reasons why men avoid professionals and why women assist in hiding men. A powerful reason arises from the impact of poverty and marginality. A couple can gain more money to try and ensure family survival if they claim social security as single people. The couple have a strong incentive for the man not to be seen by state officials and in order to try and be as convincing as possible, the story will be stretched out to say that the man does not have any involvement with the children at all. For similar reasons, the names of many marginalized unmarried fathers are deliberately kept off their children's birth certificates, which then means that the man does not have formal parental responsibility within the law and this jeopardizes his right to inclusion in formal decision-making, case conferences and legal proceedings. Poverty-stricken families who exist like this are terrified of being caught and have good reason to fear being inspected by social security officials. This is how, in their minds, all state officials meld into one great big threat – 'Big Brother'. Social workers have work to do in trying to reassure mothers that, as professionals, they have a legitimate interest in the impact of levels of income on children's welfare, but it is not about the source of that income. Their reason for being there and needing to see the man is to inquire into parenting and child protection issues rather than seeking to become involved with their financial arrangements.

We live in times when relationships are more chosen and when they do not bring satisfaction, they can be ended (Ferguson, 2001, 2008). Families change, new partners come onto the scene. It is not uncommon for there to be multiple fathers to children in some families, and workers need to engage with them all, unless there are compelling reasons not to. Assessments and ongoing work need to take account of the toxic effect that men who are abusive have on mothers and children. In the case of Khyra Ishaq, who died as a result of child neglect, which included starvation and malnutrition, the inquiry into her death found that Khyra's mother was basically cooperative and coping well with social services support until her new partner moved in. He had mental health problems and his psychosis resulted in strange ideas about food deprivation and deep suspicion of outsiders. Khyra's mother became progressively less and less cooperative with the authorities to the point where she withdrew the children from school, saying they were being home educated (they were not, as it turned out), and refused all access to the home and Khyra and her siblings were not protected (Birmingham Safeguarding Board, 2010). Every time a new man comes into the lives of children who are known to be at risk, he needs to be assessed and his relationship with all the children carefully monitored and worked with. This does not mean that mothers are never harmful to children or never the source of toxic relationships in the family. But a key difference is that mothers are always the focus for interventions and invariably are worked with, while men so often are not. And it is often that women are worked with even when it is the man who is the problem (Scourfield, 2003a).

Working with men and masculinities

However, research and high-profile cases have shown that some fathers are avoided by professionals and/or excluded from having responsibility and caring for their children because they are suspected of being dangerous when in fact they are not (Ferguson and Hogan, 2004). In the Baby Peter case in London, Peter's mother Tracey Connelly always led the authorities to understand that she was a lone parent. Peter's biological father had left the family home some time ago and apparently did have some contact with him from time to time. When it was known that Peter had been non-accidentally injured and he was the subject of a child protection plan, following which there was further concern about injuries to him, his biological father was not assessed as a potential alternative carer for Peter due to the mother's unsubstantiated claims that he had hit the child in the past. It seems from what is known that this man had something potentially positive to offer in caring for Peter. As the case shows, at the extremes, the consequences of non-engagement with fathers can be lethal. In reality, Tracey Connelly had a cohabitee, whose brother also resided in the home and these men were involved in abusing and killing Peter (Haringey, 2009). These two men were not known about, let alone engaged with, or the home inspected to see who lived there.

The complexity of this for professionals is that their fears, frustrations and concerns about having to deal with men are invariably based on some real experiences of difficult and abusive men and what mothers tell professionals about them is often painfully true. But the assessment of a father should always be based on social workers establishing for themselves the risks and resources that the man represents by engaging directly with him.

While professional orientations are crucial to shaping interventions, what service user men themselves bring to the encounter is also influential. Some fathers are able to identify the impact of constructions of masculinity on how they have not been prepared to be seen as vulnerable and needing 'help':

> Because you lose control of your own manliness, your own masculinity, if you go looking for help, you know. The old cliché: the man is the bread-winner, the man is the hunter-gatherer, you know, the man is the one that does everything. But if he looks for help, he loses a bit of that masculinity or manliness, he becomes a bit more feminine, to ask for help. So you don't do that. (38-year-old father of three)

This shows how, traditionally, male identity has been constituted in terms of the opposition between the masculine and the feminine. Within this ideology, to be male means boys and men having to repudiate any signs of what is regarded as feminine about them. Being vulnerable and seeking help are viewed as signs of weakness and the kinds of 'sissy stuff' women get up to, and regarded as a failure of what real men are meant to be (Kimmel, 1994; Connell, 2005). One strategy professionals can use is to let the man know they are aware of this inhibition and to acknowledge the feelings of failure that some men have on becoming the subject of social work intervention (Ferguson and Hogan, 2004). I return below to these dynamics of helping men redefine their masculinity as part of becoming a safe, loving father.

A powerful reason why men are avoided is that they are perceived as dangerous, unreachable and/or useless. Some fathers are judged harshly on the basis of their appearance, such as having tattoos, a 'hard man' persona, lifestyle, doing hard physical work or violence-prone work, like being a bouncer. 'George', a 37-year-old lone-parent father of three children, aged 15, 13 and 11, was a former boxing champion and he worked as a bouncer in the night-time economy because of the flexible hours and time it gave him to be there for the children during the day. His 13-year-old daughter ended up in hospital due to mental health problems and a hospital social worker wanted to take the three children into care simply on the basis of his appearance. However, the community-based social worker was prepared to see beyond the man's appearance and fully assessed him not as a risk, but as a resource to his children. As she explained:

> Dad wasn't in the picture. Mum had given a very bad account of dad and said that he was very abusive to her, that he had been violent towards her and really he wouldn't be any fit parent for the girls. I spoke to a social worker in the hospital who was very much against dad. Like the way he looks, you know, he has the tattoos, the shaved head and I think she just felt on presentation alone that we won't even go there.

This father felt judged by social workers and the police because of his appearance. In transcending this in her assessment, the social worker did excellent work in engaging with the children as well as the man himself to establish their perspectives on this father and family life. His 15-year-old son explained in his research interview how he saw his father:

> Dad's kind of a mix of things, like he's very good, like. Like he looks like the hard man and when you talk to him he's fierce quiet. He cares and like he's working as a bouncer, so lots of people think that bouncers are the hard men, you know, but he's not as hard. He thinks he's hard, that he can take a lot mentally but he's not as hard as he thinks he is because he gets sick, like . . . All the stress and worry and stuff, I think that's what drew it out of him and when my mam left it really came bad.

A crucial factor in whether or not professionals engage with men is whether they are able to see what this man's son could: that there are multiple sides to men and masculinity and there is a need to directly engage with every man about his fatherhood role and caring, no matter how 'hard' looking or unlikely he seems to have the capacity to nurture and be a caring father. The social construction of the 'hard', 'dangerous' father that is evident here and which the social worker managed to overcome drew on beliefs about gender and social class, which assume that men, especially 'rough', working-class men, are unable to be caring. Similar dynamics occur with fathers from black and minority ethnic backgrounds. Scourfield (2001, 2003a) found similar negative assumptions about 'feckless' and dangerous men among child protection social workers in his participant observation study of a social work team in Wales (see also Peckover, 2002a, 2002b, on health visiting).

In assessing men's parenting and safety, their needs and risks, they should be approached in broadly the same way as women. Another negative assumption about masculinity is that men do not have a capacity to talk about their feelings, relationships and intimate subjects. But in my experience of conducting several research studies into men, even the most apparently unreachable men are able to talk about their relationships, love for their children, their trauma and vulnerability and their abusiveness. I don't wish to overstate this: men can be hard work. How they are conditioned from boyhood to be 'real' men knocks a lot of their capacity to be expressive out of them and undermines their self-esteem and belief in their ability to talk intimately about their lives. But men themselves have often swallowed the 'big boys don't cry' cliché and are surprised to find that when interview conditions of safety and confidentiality are established not only do they cry, but they are well able to talk about it and their feelings (see also Robb, 2004). But given the legacy of the messages they receive about gender, men need help in feeling good about this. The social worker for George, discussed above, gives a wonderful example:

> As I was coming away, [George] said, 'Jesus', he said, 'I'm sorry for being so weak', and I said to him, 'George, you know tears aren't a sign of weakness, you know as far as I'm concerned that's a sign of strength.' And I told him, I think he's wasted, I think he should be in there telling other fathers and other men that it's OK to cry and it's OK to be and it's OK to make mistakes and it's OK to do, you know just to be.

Engagements with fathers throw up fateful moments like these that practitioners can use creatively to help the man rethink his masculinity and achieve positive developmental outcomes for himself as a father. George had been crying because of his relief that the attempts by the hospital social worker to take the children into care had been foiled by the statutory social worker. She not only gave him a chance, but through the sensitive management of such moments actively built up his self-esteem, parenting capacity and helped him to develop a different view of himself as a man and a father. In this manner, interventions help men to engage in life-planning work (Ferguson, 2001) by identifying the choices they have about what kinds of fathers and men they want to be. This kind of work with people's self-identities, emotional lives and vulnerability constitutes another dimension to the 'intimacy' that this book is seeking to capture in speaking of intimate child protection practice (Giddens, 1992).

Making fathers safe

I will now develop the arguments by focusing on a case study that helps to show further how fathers can be worked with to make them safe. 'Ben' is 44 and has always worked and provided for his family. He was married for 20 years and has been separated for four. He has four children, aged between 15 and 8. There was a history of extreme marital strife and the family had been known to statutory social workers for several years. The house was regularly wrecked as a result of violence by the children, in part, it was thought, as a reaction to the disharmony between their parents. Matters became so bad that the statutory services considered taking the children into care, but instead they were placed on a supervision order. The current social worker described it as 'an incredibly difficult case . . . really antagonistic – the case from hell . . . it was the most time-consuming case ever. They'd both be on the phone to you for hours, we had loads of professional meetings and no one knew what to do with the family.' For the family centre worker, the complexity was such that 'it's the most unbelievable case ever'.

The mother had a pattern of seeking help from a number of agencies without the others knowing. When the social worker took over the case:

> the mother was making huge allegations about the dad having just been incredibly emotionally abusive to her, having a loaded shotgun by the bed and bullets, leaving bullets on her pillow and, you know, hitting her. But that wasn't the main thing, it was more emotional stuff. He just allegedly had no interest in the kids. She did absolutely everything and, you know, he kept kind of the purse strings and all that kind of stuff.

By the time the social worker included in the research took over the case, the couple had been split up for about a year, with the father having moved out of the family home into a flat, leaving the children with their mother. Her team manager had a similar negative view of the father. Ben's use of guns was never actually substantiated and when confronted by the social worker, he always denied abusing his wife or the children. Ben was rarely seen by this social worker quite simply due to fear:

> I was quite frightened of him because I believed the stories. It was a given that they were true. So I phoned the odd time but he really unnerved me, because, you know, his manner. But if you have all these stories behind that manner, then you think there's something kind of weird. Whereas he's just got sort of a gentle soft-spoken manner, maybe now. I'm not convinced, you know, I'm not, I just don't know. He had, like, everyone, the whole family had everyone stumped, all the professionals just stumped.

The social worker initially saw her role as supporting the mother, who repeatedly called her throughout the day and she feared would 'crack up because there was always a crisis'. The father was seen as unsafe for the children and disinterested, even, according to the social worker, being 'all on' for some of the children going into care.

The (male) family centre worker was instrumental in facilitating a shift in perspective by openly challenging the other professionals' view of the father. According to this worker, at one of the many case conferences, both parents were present and the professionals took the mother's side, while the father was 'annihilated': 'The man did not get a chance ... I mean I sat in the meeting and saw that happen and I just thought "No! This is inappropriate".' The family centre worker had no doubt that the man could be abusive but he 'fought for' him to be given a chance; at the same time, he was acutely aware of the risk involved in what he was advocating and of being manipulated by the father. Although there remained significant doubts about how safe the father was, following an incident of substantiated non-accidental injury by the mother on one of the children, he was fully assessed and allowed to have care of the children. This was managed in a phased, planned way and one condition was that he attend a parenting course. He responded positively and this changed the social worker's impression of him:

> Each week we'd give him a chapter [of the parenting workbook] to work on and he'd give very obviously clear examples of when he'd used it and how it'd worked and all that. So, I thought, he is trying, and I was really pleased. So then I sort of warmed to him more. He never caused any trouble or anything. He was always cooperative with everything.

Ben himself felt strongly that the social work intervention had made him safer and developed his capacities to care for his children, but it did not come without a struggle:

> I've dealt with, I'd say, about 10 different social workers because of their job and their rate of turnover in the job every few weeks you'd go down there ... and a different social worker would be dealing with the case. And you had to go over the whole rigmarole again and that could be very 'here we go again', you know. And you have to relate the whole thing over and over again. And there are a lot of frustrations involved in it.

What ultimately sealed the constructive relationship between the father and social worker was that the latter agreed to sit in on a parenting course with him. This was a condition placed on the social worker by the family centre and the multi-agency child protection plan. As Ben explained:

> I felt that there was, there was some back-up coming there. The first thing that entered my head when I was asked to do a parenting course was 'for God's sake, how can you do a course to be a parent', you know. I was thinking of washing and ironing and, you know, the mundane jobs a parent does. I wasn't thinking of parenting skills. But when I started doing the course, I could see the advantages of it straightaway. And I think the fact that she [social worker] actually sat in on the course, it was actually a colleague of [family centre worker] done the course with us, the fact that [social worker] sat in and, you know, she was quite interested in it and we got a good rapport going between the three of us, I found it very, very helpful.

The social worker also felt that the 'rapport' and accompanying the father to the parenting course was a positive experience in developing a relationship with him. The degree of commitment on everyone's part is clear from the fact that the meetings took place in the family centre at eight o'clock in the morning. Once again we see that while there are significant systemic pressures that often prevent social workers from devoting the time and energy to doing the kind of supportive and therapeutic intervention work they would like, some make it possible to choose to do genuinely creative work – if not with every case, then at least some.

The practical, skills-based work and therapeutic basis to the intervention helped this father:

> [It worked] because I think she [the social worker] gave me confidence in myself. When it was first decided to take the boys out of the family home, I started to panic because I didn't actually think I'd be able to look after them and keep working. And I think [social worker] was very, very supportive. And she got this parenting skills course together for me as well. She actually sat in on the course which I found very, very helpful. And she actually said for herself that she found an enormous help from it. But she, I think she gave me a lot of confidence. As I say, a lot of the time I can be a very, very insecure person, you know, if things are looking me straight in the eye, I'll think to myself, 'my God, I'm not going to be able to', I usually manage to get through them, but the thought of it, you know. But I did get very, very good support from her.

Not only is he able to care for his children, he has had a great deal of positive feedback from them and the relationships have developed as a result. Through it, his entire attitude to seeking help, masculinity and his view of himself as a man have changed. At the height of the family problems, he says: 'No. I would have been afraid to ask for help at that stage. I was a man. And that's honest to God. I would have been afraid to go to somebody and say "look, I can't handle my wife".'

Ben also had counselling that helped him to recognize the legacy of past traumatic events on how he is in relationships in the present. In effect, he learned emotional self-awareness and communication skills and how to recognize his feelings, take responsibility for them and express them, and in a manner which did not blame or harm his children. Experiencing a meaningful relationship through continuity of social care professionals was also important to him, and he realized this, having not previously had it before because of the high turnover of staff. Ben placed a premium on informality, or an absence of overt 'officiousness', as a key way to develop helping relationships:

> I've got different responses from different social workers. I mean they're all individuals, but some can be very officious and I think the officious side of it, it instantly sends you the message that they don't see the real problem here, they're looking for something they can write down on paper, you know. I think you pick up on that straightaway.

Fathers, just like mothers, respond better to feeling 'talked with' than 'talked at' or 'to'. It is not simply *what* is asked, but *how* it is posed and the entire tone of how the worker conducts the encounter that matters. What astonished and pleased this father was how the social worker worked so constructively alongside him. The kind of confidence-building he articulated is a basic, but crucial part of practice with men and typically takes the form of professionals building on positive signs by sharing with the father available evidence of the capacity he has to care well for his children. As Turnell and Edwards (1999) formulated it in their classic study, workers need to adopt solution-focused, strengths-based approaches that look for and build on 'signs of safety' as opposed to focusing in counterproductive ways on deficits in parenting. A strengths-based approach does not, however, mean ignoring or minimizing the parenting deficits and dangers for the children that are apparent. Hard questions must be asked and challenging things done to ensure that all evidence of protection is measured in terms of levels of child wellbeing and safety. Interventions are effective when they help men to change by revising their relationship with toxic parts of their life connected to feelings of worthlessness and depression, alcohol misuse or other addictions, the shame of being abusive, and to heal the effects of hurt and trauma from childhood (Leigh and Farmer, 2008).

As the case study also shows, a range of services and approaches, either on their own or in combination, can be effective: authoritative one-to-one casework; parenting classes; support and therapeutic work in family or children's centres; family therapy; family group conferences; and in-depth psychotherapy. It is crucial for work to be done on the relationships between fathers and their children, from developing nappy-changing skills to learning about how to appropriately respond to teenagers. Enabling men to change has to involve supporting mothers – to recover from any abuse and feel safe in the man's presence, and, generally, in understanding what he is learning and still has to learn about being a safe nurturing father. Mothers are often mentors to fathers and help them to develop, as long as the man has the humility and commitment to equality to allow it. This kind of work illustrates again how intimate child protection must be *critical* practice by, in this instance, helping young people, women and men to understand and change the effects of gender inequalities and power on relationships.

Conclusion

This chapter has tried to show how we are coming to understand more about the ways in which social workers and other professionals either ignore men or miss their presence in the home. A question that has to be at the heart of child protection practice is: Who do these children live with and who has regular contact with them in the home and outside it? If answers are not forthcoming from mothers or elsewhere and there are grounds for suspicion, the worker must look around the home to find out. Three factors interrelate in determining the extent to which agencies and practitioners identify and work with fathers:

- The culture and norms of the agency and the extent to which father-centred practice is on their policy and practice agendas

- Individual practitioner's and manager's life experiences and the assumptions they make about gender roles and what fathers should be expected to do in parenting

- Professional training.

Father-inclusive practice requires institutional support and needs to be an explicit policy and part of the culture of agencies. Whether fathers are seen as resources or risks, social workers and other professionals must be motivated to engage with them and go beyond mothers, who are given too much responsibility and blamed for family problems (Scourfield, 2006; Featherstone, 2009; Brown et al., 2009). This also constitutes a challenge to professionals' personal beliefs and values. Education and training need to provide opportunities for workers to critically reflect on their assumptions and attitudes towards men, women and gender roles and their own experiences of being fathered, so that learning can occur about how these influence their understanding of masculinity and practice. Professionals need to practise in reflective ways, which can ensure that men are purposefully worked with so that children can benefit from being cared for by safe, nurturing, loving fathers.

12

Using good authority: working with resistance and involuntary clients

'Authority' is not a dirty word. Indeed, it must be brought officially from behind the arras of social work training onto the public stage, not just of child care law but also into the practice of all social workers. We regard it as an essential ingredient in any work designed to protect abused children.

(London Borough of Brent, 1985, p. 295)

Broadly speaking, there are two kinds of service users in social work and child protection: those who go to professionals for help because they have a problem; and those to whom professionals go with help because they pose problems for others or themselves – *voluntary* and *involuntary* clients. Although this puts the matter rather simplistically, it does have the virtue of distinguishing between cooperative and uncooperative service users. Social work literature has been quite poor at making this distinction. Most is written as if the service user is voluntary and stresses the importance of respect for them and their rights and 'empowerment'. In the childcare literature, this is frequently expressed in terms of the goal of 'working in partnership' with parents and families. As Ruth Pearson (2009) has shown, this has resulted in limited analytical attention being given to the complexity of the work when risk is high and the parents do not want a service and try to avoid and deceive workers. One effect of such resistance is the constant worry and threat of intimidation and sometimes actual violence that practitioners have to deal with (Littlechild, 2005).

Values of empowerment and partnership working are inevitably compromised by the constraints placed on service users and practitioners by the statutory role, when risk is such that involvement must be insisted upon. The limits to straightforward empowerment models immediately become evident if we ask: How do you empower someone who only wants to see the back of you, or who does not regard themselves as having a problem? How, or can, the worker remain true to social work values – like self-determination – and use power and authority in directive ways? This chapter will seek to answer such questions by examining the dynamics of practice where parents and/or children do not want a service, the forms of resistance involved and how these can be overcome. The seriousness of the issues makes it imperative that detailed attention is given to making the dynamics of resistance and deception explicit, so that workers can become aware of them and their emotional impact and seek to avoid or overcome them and act to protect the child. The second half of the chapter sets out a model of authoritative negotiated child protection, which identifies the processes, steps and dimensions of good practice that can be used to engage involuntary service users and keep their children safe.

Physical blockages and resistance to reaching the child

There is nothing new about the presence of hostile and deceptive adults in child protection, as some of the case studies in this book going back over 100 years have demonstrated. However, the issue is now gaining at least some prominence in the literature (Ivanoff et al., 1994; Trotter, 2006; Calder 2008c) and its presence in high-profile cases has driven it onto the policy agenda. A recent national review of child protection/safeguarding in England, prompted by the Baby Peter case, refers to the need to develop skills for working with 'parents who, in some cases, may be intentionally deceptive or manipulative', and that social workers need to learn how to 'understand signs of non-compliance' (Laming, 2009, p. 51). Detecting and understanding signs of non-compliance depends on knowing what resistance is and the forms it takes, understanding why resistance occurs, and being attuned to the dynamics of resistance in relations with service users.

The risks of being prevented from performing child protection effectively are most obvious where social workers have to contend with high levels of physical resistance, intimidation and actual violence from family members who do not want a service (Stanley and Goddard, 2002; Littlechild, 2005). Such resistance pervades child protection cases where children die (Brandon et al., 2008). The tactics used by parents and carers to actively hide the child and/or the perpetrator or the signs of the harm perpetrated on the child include:

- Mobile families: going on the move and changing addresses, registering with different GPs, taking children to different A&E departments with non-accidental injuries – all to avoid detection.

- Blocking the worker's way into the home.

- Once in the home, parents/carers 'stage-manage' visits by restricting workers' sight of and contact with the child.

- Using the physical space of the home and objects in rooms – tables, televisions, dogs and other pets – to control where workers and children sit, obscuring views of the child and distracting the worker and stopping them from moving.

- Using clothing and substances (such as chocolate) to hide injuries.

- Coaching children to suggest all is well.

- Dirt and smell used to disgust workers and prevent them from moving towards and touching the child.

- Using part of the home to hide abusers – classically when men hide in bedrooms – and children. At the extremes, children are confined to rooms that are constructed as fortresses to hide them from the remainder of the family and the world and in which they are sexually and physically abused, as shown in the Austrian case of Joseph Fritzl (Marsh and Pancevski, 2009).

As this book has already shown, the dynamics of concealment and disclosure in child protection depend to a significant extent on where the practice goes on. The case of Baby Peter illustrates the scope for concealment on home visits. The social worker asked for the chocolate on the child's face to be cleaned off, so a family friend, on the instruction of the mother, took him away to clean him, but never brought him back and the social worker did not follow through on it. The use of chocolate to conceal bruises on the child's face and removal of him from the room were tactics used by the mother to conceal the abuse, one of many deceptions she engaged in. Others included hiding, from visiting professionals, the presence in the home of the violent men who were abusing the child.

Violence and intimidation are painful realities of social work practice and have demonstrable toxic effects on workers. Stanley and Goddard's (2002) Australian study of 50 cases of child abuse, where children had been the subjects of a legal protection order, although all were living at home at the time of their study, recorded the amount of violence to which the workers had been subjected during the previous six months. Serious incidents were common and psychological violence appeared to be all-pervasive in everyday practice. The assaults included pushing and shoving, punching, hair pulling, hitting with a chair, coffee table and ashtray, and an attempted strangulation – all in six months. Many workers were keen to relate previous episodes of serious violence and threat. Also worrying was the fact that workers were not entirely open about their experience: 85% censored information they told their families about their own safety, most in order to prevent families worrying about them (Stanley and Goddard, 2002, p. 103).

Stanley and Goddard argue that if not properly acknowledged and dealt with in organizations and through supervision, abusive and intimidating clients grind workers down psychologically, causing them to act in ways similar to hostages held in captivity. Feelings of fear and helplessness in the face of indiscriminate violence, as well as fear of death, define the hostage experience. Hostages – classically in the Stockholm syndrome – adjust to their helplessness by attempting to please and meet the needs of their captors. Submission to your violent captor works, it enhances your chances of survival. The key implication for child protection concerns the danger that social workers and other professionals are at risk not only of real harm and trauma from being assaulted, but also that, psychologically, they become 'captives' to their violent clients. This should not be taken literally, as obviously workers are free to leave encounters in the sense of walking away. But they are not necessarily free to leave the *relationship*, at least until the children are safe and abusive parents and carers have changed their behaviour. The capacity of workers to protect children is then seriously diminished as they do not, in any meaningful sense, have a relationship with the children because the abusers are controlling and orchestrating what happens. An illusion of the safe child then takes hold in the worker's mind (Munro, 1999).

Everyone involved in this kind of work knows these feelings. That sense in which you are so preoccupied with your own safety and survival that the child's becomes an afterthought, where just getting out of the house alive or relatively unscathed becomes the defining criteria of a good intervention – but of course this is never made explicit. Or when not getting to see the child becomes not a source of concern, but a relief. In fact, you have written to the family to pre-announce your visit not as a strategy to ensure they are there, but (un)consciously to sabotage the visit by giving them a chance to be out, or hiding in the house when you call. And when you knock on the door and there's no reply, you skip back down the path and suddenly the world seems like a better place again, all because you don't have to struggle through yet another torturous session with angry, resentful people. Yet through it all, you keep going back as you feel drawn into a profoundly ambivalent relationship with the aggressive carer. Implicitly in such cases, workers define a successful intervention superficially as, for instance, giving a child in hospital a bath and taking care of their physical needs but not doing anything about their apparent injuries – as occurred in the Victoria Climbié case (see Chapter 9) – or getting into the home, having a reasonable conversation with the parents and getting out in one piece.

Pathological communication: when resistance is non-physical

When there is no overt hostility and stage-management and manipulation of the worker going on, the resistances are much less tangible, they are in the air, the atmosphere. They are communicated and become enacted through the encounter and expressed in the relationship. There is often something in the atmosphere of homes where child maltreatment goes on, and the emotions and relationships they embody, which stops professionals from feeling able to talk, move and act more freely in them. The notion of 'passive-aggressive' responses has been used to account for such situations where overt rejection or hostility is not shown: the family are out when you call even though you were expected; they are in when you visit but hide inside; family members say they will do something and don't (Dale et al., 1987). Some parents and carers even seem cooperative, but it turns out to be 'disguised compliance' (Reder et al., 1993) and a front for concealing child abuse. These tactics are much gentler than overt aggression and hostility but have a similar effect of keeping professionals at a distance from the child (Calder, 2008d).

Passive aggression undoubtedly goes on but neither it nor hostage theory are sufficient as concepts to account for how non-physical resistance paralyses workers. Instead, I suggest the concept of 'pathological communication' in child protection because it does better justice to the 'active' component of the non-physical resistance at work between service user and professional. This concept relies on insights from psychoanalysis and an understanding of how, through the dynamics of relationships, workers are affected by unconscious processes (Froggett, 2002). Parents project the hostile, rejecting part of themselves, which lies behind their neglectful and abusive behaviour, onto the worker. This results in the latter not merely losing focus on the child but embodying behaviours that are typical of the parents' lack of care. When professionals get caught up like this in the emotional world of service users, they are likely to be experiencing what psychoanalyst Melanie Klein called 'projective identification'. This refers to how the recipient of projections is left with the feelings of the person who projected them. These feelings are then felt by the recipient to be their own and they begin to identify with them and act them out (Casement, 1997).

Such projection can be aimed at controlling the professional's mind and body. Think again about why the social worker in the Jasmine Beckford case did not carry out what the inquiry report describes as the elementary task of walking across the room to engage directly with Jasmine and get her to move even a little so that her broken leg would have become evident. Or why the nurses in the Victoria Climbié case did not report or even properly record the serious injuries they saw on her body when she was in the bath. Or why the social worker in the Baby Peter case did not follow through on seeing him with the chocolate cleaned off his face or insist on looking around the home to check for any men who might have been living there. Or why neither the social worker nor doctors even touched Peter during the last few days of his life, despite him previously having injuries and being in front of them, in what the GP referred to as 'a sorry state'. I am arguing that, in such instances, unconscious communication occurred where the messages 'don't move' and 'don't ask' to see, listen to, walk with, or touch the child were projected onto the worker by abusive and/or fearful carers. At an unconscious level, the worker re-enacts the hate and neglect towards the child that the abusive carers have projected onto them. The worker becomes a neglectful bystander to the abuse of the child, doesn't move towards them and engage them directly to check for injuries or relate to them in ways that could reveal abuse; doesn't challenge mothers, inquire about men, or use authority to see around the home, or achieve anything else.

In Chapter 7, I argued that one reason why professionals do not touch children is because of how they become an object of disgust and I tried to show how this occurred in the Baby Peter case. The concept of pathological communication provides another vital piece of the jig-saw in explaining how such detachment from children occurs. Tracey Connelly, Peter's mother, had experienced significant trauma from abuse and neglect in her own childhood. There appear to have been few if any protective factors or compensatory experiences that built up her resilience and softened the impact of the harm done to her. Her attachment pattern appears to have been 'disorganized', characterized by an inability to trust and form any secure attachments (Howe, 2005). Tracey Connelly appears to have been shown a lot of compassion by workers, but they did not adequately take into account the impact on her of the abuse she suffered in her own childhood and its effect on her capacity to parent, or how this influenced how she related to the workers themselves and manipulated and deceived them (Haringey, 2009). Up to 80% of children who are abused have a 'disorganized attachment' and when they become parents themselves, their interactions with their children are characterized by hostility, unpredictability, low levels of reciprocity, engagement and synchrony (Barlow and Schrader-McMillan, 2010). Peter's mother, then, was likely to have been filled with feelings of rage and helplessness and overwhelmed by her sense of inadequacy as a parent, not only by the legacy of abuse she carried from the past but due to the abuse her children (and possibly herself) were experiencing at the hands of the men she hid from professionals. All the conditions for pathological communication were present and the workers internalized the mother's feelings of rage and disgust she felt towards herself and Peter. Without good supervision or help to recognize the pattern, the workers became neglectful bystanders to the child's suffering and did not act proactively to stop it. The digust and detachment from Peter the workers acted out was, in some measure, his mother's.

Good authority

A vital feature of the concept and approach to child protection developed in this book is the use of good authority. As Roger Smith (2008) has shown, despite its centrality to child protection and social work, especially with involuntary service users, remarkably little has been written about the constructive use of authority. Some authors are clear about how authority must be used to keep children safe (Turnell and Essex, 2006; Calder, 2008c), but the literature tends to emphasize the need to avoid the misuse and abuse of professional power by being anti-oppressive. Explicit attention to a concept of good authority is largely absent. By this I mean theorizing and practising child protection in a way that is ethical because it uses authority in a skilful, empathic yet forthright manner, which is not only in accordance with standards of justice, but essential to keeping children safe.

Understanding and using good authority requires three things:

- a model/conceptual framework that clarifies its nature, role, ethical dimensions, appropriateness and methods of application

- an analysis of the relations of authority within the organization and their impact on how frontline staff feel about and exercise authority

- an understanding of one's own personal relationship to authority.

In terms of conceptualizing the nature of authority, all social workers have authority that derives from their statutory role. This is what Smith (2008), following sociologist Max Weber, calls 'legal-rational' authority in social work. Social workers also have 'reputational authority', in the sense of the reputation and standing of their profession (Hoggett et al., 2006). This seems to have declined in recent decades due to criticism of social workers for failing to protect children in high-profile cases, which has resulted in governments and social work employers having less trust in workers' capacities to make skilled judgements about risks to children, with increased proceduralization of practice as a result. In addition, human rights legislation has given service users more rights to make formal complaints about workers, which agencies take very seriously. This is entirely appropriate, of course, if there is suspicion/evidence of malpractice. However, the cumulative impact of these various regulatory processes can create systems and organizational cultures that corrode frontline workers' sense of their own authority, voice and skill. This, in turn, undermines the extent to which these workers feel able to exercise authority in the organization and with service users (Munro, 2004, 2010; Broadbent et al., 2010a).

But in recognizing how organizational systems can dehumanize workers, the capacity of the professional to think and act creatively in how authority is exercised is crucial to how they perform their role. This is relevant to a third form of authority, 'personal authority'. As shown earlier in the book with respect to touch, how authority is used depends in part on the worker's personal characteristics and their own experiences of authority, what Hoggett et al. (2006, p. 231) call the 'internalised authoritative voice'. In a fascinating study of community development workers, they show how significant professionals' life experiences are in shaping their values and experiences of being 'an authority' and using authority. This points to the importance of practitioners learning about how comfortable they are with having and using authority by gaining insight into the impact on them of the experiences of authority they have had in their lives and coming to understand their own 'internalised authoritative voice'. As Hoggett et al. suggest, for those workers who have histories of having been exploited and abused, feeling comfortable with authority can take many years and needs to be assisted by them gaining insight and self-understanding through personal development work.

All three dimensions of authority come into play in every intervention social workers make. Practitioners' legal-rational authority gives them the right to be present with children and parents in their home, but if they avoid asking to see children on their own in that moment, this constitutes an omission of personal authority. But it may also be a symptom of the relations of authority they experience in their organization, especially if they are managed in controlling and disrespectful ways. This disempowers them and corrodes the sense of authority they have and how they take it into their practice.

Working with involuntary clients/service users

I will now look in more detail at how good authority and other knowledge and skills can be used to work with resistance. As Bower (2005b) puts it, workers and interprofessional groups need strategies for 'working with families who see help as the problem'. I shall outline a model for working with involuntary service users that I call 'authoritative negotiated child protection'. In a neglected contribution, Barber (1991) identifies three broad practice options in work with 'involuntary clients'. 'Casework by concession' involves workers persisting against all odds in their quest to affirm and show warmth towards the service user. This arises from their feelings of discomfort and being apologetic about their authority and the constraints involved. The statutory dimension of the work is buried by the worker and conflict and confrontation are avoided. Concessions can be made on particular (bad) days by workers who don't usually make them. An example is the worker in Chapter 5 who avoided asking to look around the bedrooms and kitchen because on that day she couldn't face confronting the parent with her task. But much more worrying are those workers for whom making concessions is a regular pattern. They fail to understand the scope for authority to be used in a constructive way to promote change, and/or they are ideologically opposed to it being central to the child protection role. A child protection practitioner who is unprepared (in every sense) to use authority should not be doing the work. Rooney (1992) observes that there is not only the 'involuntary client' but the 'involuntary social worker', who is reluctantly involved with service users they do not like or wish to be with.

A second practice option identified by Barber is 'casework by oppression'. This involves a thoroughgoing acceptance of the authoritative role to the extent that confrontation and conflict are embraced. Such workers fight to ensure that what they believe should happen and should be in the safety plan must be complied with and have no compunction about browbeating the service user into accepting their view of what must be done. There may even be talk of 'partnership working' and 'partnership agreements', but this is just rhetoric that conceals practice that is essentially coercive, in the worst sense (Morris, 2010).

Forrester et al.'s study (2008b) of how social workers communicate with parents in childcare cases points to elements of casework that borders on, or is, oppressive being common. The study was based on an analysis of taped interviews between social workers and an actor playing a parent (a 'simulated client'). Social workers asked many closed questions and often raised concerns, but they used few reflections and rarely identified positives. They performed well at achieving clarity about issues of concern, but tended to demonstrate low levels of empathy. Empathic social workers created less resistance in the encounter and increased the amount of information disclosed, while still identifying and discussing concerns. The researchers argue therefore for the centrality of empathy to good social work communication in child protection situations and that the use of this skill while raising child protection concerns needs to be developed.

Forrester et al.'s work points to the third option in working with involuntary service users, which is what Barber (1991) characterizes as an attempt to reconcile the first two positions by adopting the role of 'negotiator'. This is the model or approach I call authoritative negotiated child protection, to which there are eight dimensions or steps.

1 Recognize authority and assume conflict not cooperation

It begins with recognition that the interaction between worker and the involuntary service user is defined through relations of authority and is based as much and often more on conflict as cooperation. Adapting Barber's (1991) work, the negotiated element of authoritative negotiated child protection involves identifying opportunities for maximizing the service user's influence over the child protection plan, their self-determination, within the constraints under which the work is conducted.

2 Encourage openness and honest expression of feelings

At the outset, the resistant parent(s) or carers should be given the opportunity to express, as openly as they can, their feelings about professional involvement. This must be done after stating a ground rule that while differences in perspective between them and professionals can and should be openly acknowledged, intimidating and abusive behaviour towards the worker is not acceptable and mutual respect in communication is essential. The more they feel enabled to express their anger and disappointments about past and current involvement, the more they will get the message that the worker wants to hear about their feelings and fears, which may clear the way for them to engage and contemplate trust. An excellent example of how this can be done well is how the parents in the Joanne Smith case in Chapter 10 started out vehemently opposed to and fearful of cooperating with the worker because of the bad experience they had had of a previous social worker. The new social worker facilitated engagement by, in her own words, 'trying to understand where the mother is coming from, and the issues she has gone through. You can actually work when you know where it's all coming from, you're going from what their issue is as well.' We saw how the social worker and family support worker skilfully allowed the mother to express her dislikes and fears and moved at her pace, while not compromising in setting out what was needed to ensure the safety of the children. Engagement worked, in part, because the parents were permitted to adopt what Turnell and Edwards (1999) call a 'position' with respect to their views on their children, problems and social work involvement. Their position was, at the outset at least, in opposition to that of the workers who not only listened to it and respected it but encouraged these resistant service users to articulate it, thereby giving the message that their views and feelings are taken seriously.

3   Identify what the resistance is really about and what is working well

The obvious thing that causes service users to resist is the threat of losing their children and, more generally, restrictions to their freedom. But there is often more under the surface that needs to explored and brought out. It is important for the worker to gain a clear understanding of the range of reasons why service users resist intervention, of which at least three broad areas can be identified. A common one, already covered above, is that parents do not like the system, worker or the approach on offer. Another reason for resistance is due to social circumstances where family members fear being criminalized by the intervention and that this will be used to build a case towards them losing their children. As was shown in Chapter 11, a common example is where the presence of fathers in families is hidden because the couple are claiming as single people to acquire an income that can support the family. The existence of the man in the children's lives is then systematically hidden. The family need to get the message that any concerns they have about the lawfulness of their income arrangements are of no importance to workers as compared to their sole concern for the safety of their children, which requires knowing who is living with and having regular access to them.

A further reason for resistance concerns the service user's personal characteristics and how psychological and emotional problems block them from forming healthy relationships and attachments, with professionals as much as with their children (Howe et al., 1999; Ferguson, 2003a). As has already been discussed with respect to pathological communication, a crucial factor here is the impact of trauma and childhood abuse, which interferes with the parent's capacity to trust and sustain relationships. The risk of the kinds of rejecting and ambivalent relationships that parents experienced with their own parents and carers being reproduced within their relationships with professionals needs to be openly acknowledged. This is a difficult form of resistance to deal openly with when, as is so often the case, it is expressed unconsciously and in avoidant behaviours. As the work and relationships progress in the case, the worker needs to take (or make) opportunities to reflect back to the parent(s) the dynamics of what is happening between them and the effects of such avoidant behaviour on the children's safety.

Once again, the key thing in the process of engaging resistant service users is for them to feel that they are being heard and empathized with, through statements such as: 'It must be very hard for you to accept me being involved with you, given that you don't like it.' This opens the way for the worker to provide the parent/carer with an objective: 'How can we work together in a way that is going to make it so productive that I do not need to be involved with you any more?' The worker should be open about the difficulty and discomfort that hostility and resistance create for them and what they, as workers, have to gain from the child protection plan working. Turnell and Edwards (1999) and Turnell and Essex (2006) show how working through resistance is helped by the use of questions, which give the parent an opportunity to talk about their strengths, what they feel is working well, and what they like about their child.

4   Identify the dangers to the children

Identified strengths must always be located within a risk assessment framework. Following Turnell and Essex (2006, p. 118), the level of risk and child abuse dangers that the child protection plan is being created to address must be clearly identified. This should include statements about who it is that constitutes the risk to the children and the behaviours, attitudes and nature of relationships that are causing harm.

5   Identify what is not negotiable

The actions that must be taken to address those dangers that are non-negotiable must be identified. This involves engaging the parents in identifying what needs to change and how. The worker needs to be directive in including the issues that service users do not mention. When age and understanding allows it, the child's experience and views on their safety and the kinds of interventions needed should be gathered and taken fully into account. This must include identifying a 'safety support network' of people the child trusts and cares about who can be brought into the plan (Turnell and Essex, 2006). In my experience of talking to practitioners and covering this material when teaching students, what precisely is negotiable and non-negotiable is open to debate.

For instance, some regard whether visits are announced or unannounced and whether or not bedrooms are checked as being negotiable. In accordance with the arguments of this book, my list of what the worker should hold to be non-negotiable includes: rules that set out the frequency with which the children must be seen and by whom; the need to make unannounced visits; the need to regularly see the bedrooms, kitchen and know about all people who live with the children and/or have significant contact with them; misuse of drugs and alcohol must stop or be brought under control and treatment complied with; specify who must never be allowed to be alone with the child; the preschool child must attend a daycare service, and so on. Issues that are inevitably contentious need to be grappled with and insisted upon, such as: the use of professional touch with children by the social worker on home visits; the need to see all exposed areas of the child's body clean and free of dirt and other concealments; as well as speaking to the children, on every visit the child will be seen interacting with their parents and other carers and experienced by the worker in active mode, be it crawling, walking or playing. The plan is a multi-agency one and this planning work will be formalized at a case conference. The roles and responsibilities of all professionals should be set out, for example how often the infant will be seen by the health visitor for developmental check-ups, or examined by the paediatrician; how the police will respond to a man who is a domestic abuser, and the requirement that he attend an education programme for offenders.

6 Identify what is negotiable

Some aspects of the child protection plan will be negotiable and the worker should encourage the parents to think as broadly as possible about the areas where they can exercise choice. Much will depend, of course, on what the worker regards as non-negotiable. My list of negotiable areas would include possible choice about: where the children are seen on *some* occasions; children of appropriate age and understanding have to have a say in identifying where they regard as being the safest place for them to be seen and given the opportunity to talk openly about their experience. Ivanoff et al. (1994) suggest that parents can have some choices about selecting an intervention to promote their adherence to the plans. This can include the style and method of approach and what support and therapeutic services they feel comfortable taking up.

7 Formulate a child protection plan

The child protection plan should include a clear statement about the dangers and all the non-negotiable and negotiable areas. The plan should set out how the risks will be worked with by different professionals and the role of the 'safety support network' in promoting child safety. The time frame within which change is needed should be clearly stated.

8 Be clear about criteria for progress

This involves social workers in collaboration with other professionals specifying what will count as evidence of children's safety and well-being and what the carer has to do to be regarded as a safe parent. Generally stated aspirations by professionals about parents needing to improve their care are not enough. Goals must be set to address how specific behaviours must change if specific dangers are to be regarded as having changed for the better. Identification of service users' strengths must be backed up by concrete examples of how they are demonstrating improved care and protection of their children. The focus needs to be 'on the enactment of the good intentions in clear demonstrations of protection, over time' (Turnell and Essex, 2006, p. 116). Change – when it happens – can be uneven in its progress and relapses can happen. Calder (2008d) provides a 'cycle of change' model for working with involuntary clients, which practitioners can use to help them understand the stage that parents are at in recognizing their problems, contemplating change, and being motivated and helped to achieve it. Direct evidence of the child's physical and emotional wellbeing and experience must be at the centre of all assessments of progress.

Conclusion

These dimensions to authoritative negotiated child protection constitute the rudiments of what working at protecting children has to involve and the areas that need to be covered in assessment, planning and implementation. It is through such a process of authoritative, empathic engagement that 'care' and 'control' can be discharged to make it more likely that service users' resistance can be recognized and worked through to increase the prospects of positive change for children and parents. Such work needs to go on within a clear understanding of the nature and use of good authority in child protection practice. The chapter has also sought to show how worker protection and child protection are inherently linked. The impact of violence, fear, threats to and manipulation of professionals is not inevitable. Much depends on how individuals adapt to it, the openness there is in teams and organizations to confronting it, dealing with feelings and the quality of supervision and support. What is clearly needed are supportive systems that are emotionally aware. This is particularly important if the complex dynamics of pathological communication are to be brought to the surface and combated. Workers' sense of safety or danger must be seen as a key measure of child safety. Organizations, managers and case supervisors need to give considered attention to all the emotional dynamics and relations of authority outlined here. Workers' feelings need to be at the centre of this, not simply so that their concerns for their own wellbeing can be addressed, but because their emotional experience provides crucial data about what children are feeling and experiencing. If workers don't feel authoritative and safe, the strong likelihood is that the child is not safe either.

13
Multi-agency working and relationship-based practice

The social worker is the anchorman, or more usually the anchorwoman, in the long-term treatment of child abuse...When dealing with child abuse, the social worker needs others to work with her.

(Kempe and Kempe, 1978, p. 96)

Child protection is a multi-agency endeavour. Its effectiveness depends on information about children at risk and their families being clearly communicated between professionals. At every stage in the child protection process, the roles and responsibilities of all the agencies and professionals involved in a case must be well coordinated and planned. To achieve this, strategy meetings between involved professionals at the point of referral and case conferences at the point when initial investigations and assessments have been completed must be a routine part of good practice. The coordinated multi-agency child protection plan agreed at the conference must then be implemented by each professional performing their designated role. Regular formal case review meetings must happen (usually every three months) and good quality interprofessional communication maintained on a day-by-day, week-by-week basis until the identified goals have (or have not) been achieved. This chapter considers the nature and dynamics of multi-agency working at the level of day-to-day practice. It does so by analysing the complex nature of relationships between workers and families and between different professionals, and exploring what relationship-based practice with children and parents means in the context of increased multi-agency working and authoritative practice. Bion's concept of 'containment' will be used to theorize some of the key components of therapeutic relationships between workers and service users. Kanter's (2004) notion of the social worker as a 'transitional participant' will also be used to make sense of the deeper meanings of their coordinating role in children's and families' lives.

Problems in multi-agency working and communication

As discussed in Chapter 2 and referred to elsewhere in the book, ever since inquiries into child abuse deaths began in the 1970s, breakdowns in communication between professionals have been given huge significance in the reasons why children were not protected. The types of problems that have been revealed can be summarized as follows:

- Professionals were working in isolation, in their own 'silos' and not relating to other involved professionals.

- Information that was known by one professional about children was not passed on to others, which prevented those workers taking it into account in their dealings with the child and family. This manifests in several ways:
  - Communication was never made because the professional (wrongly) did not see it as their role to pass on information or felt that ethically they could not do so because of needing to honour their patient's/service user's confidentiality.
  - The communication was intended and even attempted but it didn't get through because the fax wasn't legible, the email didn't send, didn't arrive, or it did and wasn't read.
  - The communication was read but the message of serious concern that was intended was not interpreted in that way by the recipient, who saw the risk as being lower; or the high level of risk was interpreted correctly but the professional who received it either misunderstood or failed to discharge their responsibility and what was expected of them and did not act.

- There was no central coordination of concern, which meant that the totality of information and concern about the child was never brought together and the high level of risk understood and acted upon.

- Role confusion existed, with a lack of clarity and planning about which professional was meant to be doing what and when.

- The dynamics of interagency relationships and/or meetings prevented full communication of information and the effective use of professional judgement and planning. These destructive dynamics include hidden agendas where power plays are at work fuelled by interprofessional conflicts about status. Classic examples are where a health visitor or social worker do not feel they have the status to challenge a consultant paediatrician. As the work of Brandon et al. (2008) shows, the lack of challenge means that statements about children and risk that are mistaken or misleading are allowed to stand. These dynamics are compounded by gender issues – a male police superintendent may talk down or disregard the views of a female social worker because of implicit sexism; and because men are generally known to speak more at public meetings, women may not feel entitled or confident enough to challenge and insist on their views being taken as seriously as others' views.

- And then there is the impact of stereotyping on professional communication and decision-making – a good example of which I have just been guilty of by making the police superintendent a grumpy (no doubt older) man and the social worker a timid (no doubt younger) woman.

Significant attempts have been made over the years to provide training and develop structures and processes to aid interprofessional communication and decision-making. Some jurisdictions have introduced 'whole system approaches' with statutorily governed, integrated working between organizations, as in England where social care and education are joined up. Other initiatives include having independent, and therefore neutral, case conference chairpersons who are not involved with the case and not implicated in interprofessional status rivalries or other negative dynamics.

Authoritative practice and the complexities of interprofessional working

Good multi-agency working is not just a matter of trying to get professionals to work together and communicate better in a mechanical sense. As Reder et al. (1993, p. 62) point out, 'communication is much more than the structured handling of information and its mechanical transfer from one person to another'. Professionals bring all their human frailties as well as strengths to these practices. They not only communicate through the head but the heart. As with all aspects of child protection, multi-agency working does not bypass the emotions but goes on through them. The complexity is such that the emotions professionals bring to their relationships with one another are not only their own, but those of the families with whom they are working. As I showed in Chapter 9, systems theory and psychodynamic theory enable us to understand these dynamics in terms of how professional systems and family systems have a tendency to reflect one another. For instance, tensions or an actual row at a case conference between our (older) male police superintendent and (younger) female social worker may, at some level, be a reflection of the abusive relationship between the father and a teenage daughter in the case under consideration. This is an example of how 'pathological communication' (see Chapter 12) goes on between professionals and how multi-agency relationships come to mirror distorted and abusive relationships within families (Reder et al., 1993). If professionals can be helped (by the chairperson or afterwards in supervision) to become aware of these dynamics, the ways in which they relate to one another can be used as the basis for reaching a deeper understanding of what is happening in the case. A case example will help to bring these complex processes to life.

The case covers a 15-month period of work in a high-risk child protection case, which involved physical abuse and domestic violence in relation to a Traveller family of eight children, aged between 15 and 2 years at the time of the referral. There had been long-standing social work involvement, which included five other children with disabilities being looked after by the state for non-child protection reasons. Mr 'Gates' was known to have abused his wife, who explained in the research interview how, following one incident alone, her husband's violence caused her to have 48 stitches to her face. The case was re-referred twice within a year by the school who were concerned about hygiene and care of the six-year-old child. Five child protection case conferences were held within the 15-month study period. The children were also the subjects of a statutory supervision order, which gave social workers the right to visit and see them.

To have any chance of protecting the children and an abused woman, this case required the full force of the law. It was unambiguously centred on the use of good authority to try and achieve safety for the children. A key to whatever success occurred was that the father was mandated by the courts via a supervision order to see a counsellor, who was employed by the social work department, to work on his violence. According to the father, this was also part of a probation order that arose because 'I lost my temper, over a [policeman].' Crucially, the case conference planning agreed a coordinated approach involving the police, the judiciary, social work, health visiting, the schools, counselling and family support. The integrated approach taken by the police, the judiciary and social work was crucial in addressing the man's violent behaviour. In taking this systemic approach, the practice went well beyond isolated professionals simply 'challenging' a violent man about his behaviour, which can increase levels of danger for workers and women and children (Milner, 2004). Research suggests that this kind of work is best carried out as part of a sanction that makes the man accountable to the state for his violence (Dobash and Dobash, 1992). There is no guarantee that offenders will be motivated to change – some turn up for sessions but don't meaningfully engage in the intervention work. What it does mean is that if he doesn't engage with the programme, he can be brought back to court and sanctioned. Group programmes show the best outcomes (Shepard and Pence, 1999), but because none were available in the locality in question, creative multi-agency work had to suffice. Intervention into domestic abuse is often thought of as needing to be about anger management. But research and practice evidence show that anger management is not sufficient on its own and needs to be done in tandem with a concerted strategic attempt to challenge the offender's sexist belief system and abuse of power and control, which are at the heart of his violence against women and children (Mullender, 1996; Hearn, 1998).

Part of the social worker's approach to protecting the children was to see them regularly on their own and always away from the intimidating environment of the father and the caravan. This she did while taking the family's Traveller culture into account, but not engaging in 'cultural relativism', the view that no culture has a right to judge another's lifestyle and child-rearing practices and tolerating abusive practices on the assumption that they are 'normal' within particular cultures (Dingwall et al., 1983). Traveller people are among the most oppressed ethnic minority groups in the western world and have long held that status, experiencing high infant mortality rates, much shorter life expectancy than the settled community, and persistent, extreme racism (O'Connell, 2002). The workers faced a difficult challenge of taking into account issues of class and ethnicity and respecting the family's culture, while needing to be authoritative in seeking to protect the children (Connelly et al., 2005). For instance, some of the recommendations from the case conferences were focused on trying to ascertain a suitable caravan halting site for the family to live on. More adequate housing was a legitimate focus for intervention, not least because the parents themselves wanted it, rather than it being imposed by professionals on the basis of their cultural assumptions. According to the social worker: 'How can you clean the kids when you don't have anywhere to wash them . . . and parenting at that level was difficult [to address] until they are based in a place where they do have facilities.' The social worker and family support worker also worked hard to try to support Mrs Gates to leave her husband, including getting her another caravan. She did not take it up and, although frustrated and concerned about her diminished capacity to care adequately for the children, they understood the cultural and other pressures and fears that led her to this decision.

Taking the remaining eight children into care was not regarded as a simple solution either, as account was taken of their cultural background. As the social worker put it: 'We're talking about a whole new culture of people and houses. The son, if in care, would run away. There's no way you could ever move him.' Implied here was a recognition that if accommodated in care, the children would require a transracial placement due to the absence of carers from their own community, which some argue harms the identities of children from minority groups (Small, 1986).

Homes and domestic spaces where child protection practice is done do not come any smaller and tighter than a caravan. The spatial dimensions of practice were even more challenging, given that the father also acted in a threatening manner towards professionals, which meant they had to adopt strategies that ensured both their own personal safety and access to the mother and children. When visiting the caravan, the family support worker employed the tactic of: 'If he is really angry, I will physically remove myself towards the door and I will say, "Will we have a [cigarette]?", and my lighter is in the car. I won't go back where I was sitting, I will stand at the door or sit nearer the door.' For the (female) social worker: 'On two occasions I was accompanied by two male social workers. He can be quite verbally aggressive, quite threatening, [saying], "Have you ever been hit?", and things like that.' In being accompanied on the visits and getting good supervision and peer support at the office, the worker received the kind of physical protection and emotional support that was needed.

The case shows how the use of power, authority and coordinated interventions can have unintended effects. The father was suspected of continuing to hit the children and his wife. Visible marks were evident on one child that could have been consistent with marks left by blows by a ring worn on a hand. The father denied abusing the child and as there was not enough medical evidence to prove it, the case conference decided that the social worker should increase the number of visits to the caravan. The family responded by moving their caravan to try and avoid the authorities because, as the father explained in the research interview: 'She [the social worker] was telling me she'd put the kids in care ... I didn't really like it. I moved away. I thought I was going to get rid of them [the social workers], but they still kept coming round off me.' This shows the contradictory consequences that can occur when, in balancing the care and control aspects of the work towards greater control, the family regarded this as coercive and retaliated by pulling back from intervention, thus heightening the risk to the children.

This is a compelling example of how the professional system and family system can be seen to influence one another. When the family did not comply with the supervision order by permitting access to the home, the social worker adopted a more controlling stance and brought in male colleagues to support her in confronting the father. Pressure from the professional system caused 'closure' in the family system and the family took flight in an attempt to completely shut the professionals out. Shutting out professionals is a way of attempting to regain control. It involves creating an emotional and physical distance between themselves and professionals as a way to control the relationship (Reder et al., 1993, p. 102). Any evidence of such closure in high-risk cases should be taken very seriously indeed. It has been present in many cases where children have been killed by their parents and carers, a tragic phenomenon that Reder et al. call 'terminal closure'. This arises from how when the family turn inwards, stress levels increase and destructive patterns within the family are triggered further.

Even by moving, the family did not manage to escape the clutches of the social worker and other professionals. What defused the tension in the case was the father's assurance that he would cooperate and go to counselling, and that social workers could see the children when they wanted to. One year on, the father was becoming resigned to social work intervention: '[Social workers] will probably see me for another three or four years, but I don't mind, that's their job, like.' Over time, the social worker felt the father was gaining more control over his violent behaviour. For instance, he chose to follow due process of law as opposed to fighting with a man who destroyed his caravan: 'He actually responded by not going down and killing [the man], which he probably would have done previously. He seems to be dealing with his anger a bit better outside the home.' The professionals worked authoritatively and in a coordinated way with an abusive man, whose violence would not otherwise have lessened and almost certainly would have worsened. And they developed relationships with the mother and achieved sufficient safety for the children to the extent that they could remain – for the time being at least – within their own community.

Case management and relationship-based practice

This kind of case exemplifies the challenges involved in doing child protection, both as an individual practitioner and as part of a multi-agency system. As already discussed in the Introduction and Chapter 2, critiques of current practice suggest that workers no longer have time to do proper therapeutic work with children and families because of the increased demands of case recording, with their performance being managed and audited and having to act as case managers. There is certainly truth in this but I want to suggest that there is an important dimension to multi-agency working and case management that can be understood in terms of the more positive virtues of relationship-based practice.

This trend of an increased case management role for social work became apparent to me in the late 1990s through a research study that examined 286 childcare referrals made to three social work teams over a three-month period. The cases were tracked over the next 12 months to see what kinds of problems the children and families had and what services were offered. In 40% of the substantiated cases where the children were considered to be either at risk or in acute need, social workers performed a case management role only, doing no direct casework themselves. Casework was undertaken by a range of other services, especially psychological and family support services. In 60%, the social workers did some ongoing work and this was usually alongside other agencies and support or 'care' staff (Ferguson and O'Reilly, 2001). The kind of configuration that typified this arrangement was for the social worker to act as case manager while various family support and/or other 'therapeutic' professionals did the intensive work. This narrowing of social work to assessment and then 'signposting' of services rather than the direct delivery of a service is now common. Since the mid-2000s, such multi-agency working has become more and more embedded in the system as part of the statutory duties of integrated teams, reflecting the shift to a 'whole systems approach' that is at the heart of the UK government policy *Every Child Matters* (Luckock, 2008a).

While bureaucracy and the obligations on professionals to comply with coordinated working through whole systems approaches have increased, it is important not to underplay the emotional meanings and relationships that remain within practice, including in multi-agency practice. The notion of the practitioner acting as a 'container' and as a 'transitional participant' for children and families was used in Chapter 8, and I shall draw on them again here to make sense of the increasingly significant role of the social worker as case manager within multi-agency systems. A case example will help to illustrate the argument. I shadowed a social worker on a visit to a single-parent mother of two children, who had been referred to social work three months earlier due to concerns about her drug use and the children's welfare. 'Julie' had given up drugs soon after the social worker first visited and had now been off them for 12 weeks, having been using them for two decades. Her children, aged 13 and 5, were missing a lot of school and were often late and there was concern about possible neglect. During the visit, the social worker gave Julie assistance with sorting out some housing and benefit issues and they discussed how she was coping. Julie presented the social worker with a drawing that her 5-year-old daughter (who was at school) had done specially for the social worker, who was delighted by this. The social worker, Julie and I then travelled together to the school attended by her 13-year-old son, 'James', for a meeting that also included a year teacher, year mentor and a drugs worker with links to the school. James joined the meeting after about 30 minutes. It was an excellent discussion. Plans were agreed between Julie, James and the school about homework, and setting boundaries regarding his sometimes disruptive behaviour in class. The school will ring Julie weekly with a report, which can include positive feedback too. The social worker agreed to keep seeing James on his own again (as she had done in the past), which he was happy to agree to. There had been a huge improvement in James's attendance, which was now 100% for the term. James was suspected of having been a young carer for his mother and sister. The spirit of the meeting was very positive and highly respectful to the young person and his mother, who had never before set foot in this school or ever spoken to a teacher there.

On the way back to the office in the car, the social worker commented in a self-critical tone: 'I haven't been able to do much in this case except be a case manager.' She meant by this the role she had played in communicating with and coordinating other services – school, addiction and housing. This typifies how workers themselves often seem unaware of the emotional significance of their role as case managers. This seems to have arisen from how case management work is lumped in with administrative tasks and regarded negatively because of the increased amount of time workers are said to have to spend on them. Activities other than direct contact with the child and family may now be undervalued. It is crucial to separate out the nature, meaning and value of different tasks. The social worker's judgement contrasted significantly with my own view, in that she clearly had a good relationship with Julie, who I could see liked and respected her, as did the children (note the five-year-old's gift of the drawing). She had developed and skilfully used the relationship with this mother to 'contain' her emotionally and build up her internal resources as she struggled to come off drugs. She was child focused, seeing the children on their own and doing similar kinds of containing work with them. She was clear about her role and the requirement to be authoritative, and during the initial assessment did the hard emotional graft of child protection by insisting that she needed to see around the house, including the children's bedrooms:

> Well, initially, it was just to do a welfare check, I guess, just to go in and make sure the children are okay, make sure the home conditions were okay. The children's bedroom was in quite a state and mum and [son's name] tidied it up within a week... on one of the beds there weren't any sheets, there was quite a lot of clutter everywhere, clothes, toys, just general mess everywhere, so it wouldn't have been a space that a child, I could imagine them wanting to spend any time in. They'd obviously worked really hard, so it looked good after a week.

The worker was fully aware of the poverty of the family and regarded the bedroom check as a way of reaching an understanding of the children's inner worlds and the degree of comfort they had in their lives. This was contextualized within the economic limitations this single-parent mother faced and how the worker was checking for signs that the mother's drug misuse had not adversely impacted on the level of care she provided. The social worker also dealt skilfully with the relationship of Julie and the children to their external world by enabling Julie to relate to the school (for the first time ever) and other services. The multi-agency work I observed at the meeting in the school was superb, and the social worker, educational support person, teachers and an addiction worker did a skilled piece of work. The improvement in the children's wellbeing clearly coincided with them becoming involved and working together in a coordinated way.

This kind of case example illustrates the importance of making sense of what individual professionals and their agencies contribute not only in terms of their own direct work with children and families but in the context of whole networks of services. Childcare work is no longer delivered by a single professional working in relative isolation and unaccountable to the wider system, which historically was the norm. It now goes on through networks and flows of practices between organizations and service users, carers, the office and the home (Ferguson, 2008). Within this, the role of the social worker as 'transitional participant' is pivotal. As was shown in Chapter 8, the concept of the transitional participant refers to how, in developing a relationship with children, the social worker provides continuity and security for them throughout the uncertainty and changes that child abuse investigations and longer term interventions often bring. In addition to the important one-to-one relationship with the child, Kanter (2004, p. 77) writes that, as a transitional participant:

> the social worker actively positions him or herself in the child's life, making direct contact with an array of significant others and informing all parties of this array of contacts. With the knowledge of this participation, the child is then able to internalize the social worker as an embodiment of this life experience.

This speaks very clearly to what the social worker in the above case example did, both in how she worked so closely with other professionals and in the direct relationships she developed with the children and their mother. The worker is able to hold together the separate threads of the child's life. This has emotional resonances for children and their carers because they know that the 'lead' professional/key worker is holding together different knowledge about them and the activities that affect them. The social worker as lead professional is relationally linked to the service user and coordinated services by holding the space within which care and control are delivered.

This argument is supported by other research. Ravi Kohli's (2007) study of social work responses to unaccompanied asylum-seeking children provides compelling evidence for how, even in highly regulated bureaucratic systems like the UK, practitioners who are emotionally attuned to the needs of the child, and include in this emotional engagement an understanding of the significance of their role in acting on the child's behalf with agencies, can make a huge difference to their lives. He conceptualizes the journey that effective social workers take children on as: creating safety, a sense of belonging and ultimately success. Writing about the needs of children in care, Barry Luckock (2008b, p. 2) suggests that good practice requires the worker to act as an emotional 'bridge' for children between past, present and future, rather than just being a care manager, or 'tour operator'. He argues that the 'tour operator' role has become more prominent, as the UK government has increasingly adopted the metaphor of 'travel' and viewed the role of social workers as being to help young service users to 'navigate' various services and help them through their care pathways. Luckock (2008b, p. 4) argues that both the emotional bridging and tour operator roles are important, but they must not be at the expense of a third dimension, a 'continuously engaged relationship' with the child. For this to occur, the social worker must commit to being 'the trusted ally' of young people in care. The same argument applies to children at risk living at home and the role of the social worker as transitional participant. This has to involve a combination of being a tour operator, coordinating child protection plans and helping children and families to navigate their ways around different services and agencies, while supporting a continuously involved emotional relationship with the child, young person and their parents or other carers.

Child protection in complex systems

While commentators and critics rightly worry over social work's apparent loss of identity and purpose in an age of increased management, bureaucracy and multi-agency working, the value and integrity of social work can no longer be seen just on its own terms but must be grounded in relation to the whole system of professional, service user and community practices. Ultimately, it is service users' experiences of the total system and what it delivers that really matters, central to which is the regularity, flows, rhythms, skill and humanity with which interventions are carried out.

Social work interventions on their own – even short-term ones – remain remarkably significant in terms of the skills and knowledge that must be brought to bear on the lives of children and families. But these actions and how, or if, they are performed today also need to be understood in a multi-agency and systemic context. As Eileen Munro (2005, p. 382) puts it, when arguing that child protection needs to be understood as a 'systems problem':

> Judgement and decision-making in child protection are best seen not as discrete acts performed by individuals in isolation but as part of a constant stream of activity, often spread across groups, and located within an organizational culture that limits their activities, sets up rewards and punishments, provides resources, and defines goals that are sometimes inconsistent.

We need a new language to capture the interaction between organizational culture, individual casework practices and the work that is done by and through multi-agency networks (see also Healy, 2005, Ch. 7). This chapter has outlined the difficulties that exist in multi-agency working when breakdowns in communication and cooperation between professionals occur. The complexity of these practices has also been shown in how authoritative coordinated interventions can lead to closure in the family system, which can increase the risk to children and prevent systems from protecting children. Once again, a key to recognizing these patterns and taking the necessary action to break them is reflective practice. Coordinated multi-agency working and case management involve significant emotional dimensions and meanings for children and parents, and the chapter has drawn on Kanter's concept of the 'transitional participant' to try and account for these. The social work role and whole systems approaches are in need of reform to ensure that social workers are able to spend as much quality time with children as is needed (Lonne et al., 2009). But whatever the future may hold, it is vital that the therapeutic impact that social workers currently can achieve is given full recognition, as it constitutes the ground upon which both individual and multi-agency relationship-based practice must develop.

14

Spaces for reflection and organizational support

It can make the unbearable bearable.
(social worker)

These words were spoken by a social worker who was referring to the support she receives from supervision and other frontline colleagues. In trying to evoke the lived experience of practice, this book has shown social work and child protection to be immensely challenging areas of work, which require courage as well as skill and knowledge. The demands of everyday practice routinely give rise to the adventure of the unknown and meaningful and satisfying encounters with children and parents who have been helped to live safer, better lives. But what I have called 'professional insecurities' are also ever present for workers. The emotional intelligence and resilience of practitioners are crucial to their capacity to deal with these insecurities and tune into children's experiences, read the signs of distress and intervene effectively (Howe, 2008). Also important is the intellectual understanding of the task, how it is conceptualized and whether professionals are supported to practise in the kinds of mobile, intimate, authoritative ways that are necessary to protect children. The focus of this chapter is on the kinds of supervision, support and organizational cultures that workers need if they are to perform effective child protection.

A crucial way to try and ensure that children are held in mind and not lost sight of is for staff to have available to them what Gillian Ruch (2007a) calls 'emotionally informed thinking spaces'. It is in such spaces that social workers and workers from all agencies engaged in protecting children need to have peer and supervisory relationships that are attentive to their emotional lives and the conflicting feelings that encounters with voluntary and involuntary service users and their homes routinely bring up. The office is the key place where such support is provided, but the car will also be analysed for the crucial role it plays for workers as a space for reflection and building their resilience and capacities to do the work.

The circularity of office-car-home visit experiences

The book has been organized around analysis of three broad sites of practice: the office, (car) journey, and home (visit) as distinct domains. In practice, they are deeply interrelated and connected. Experiences in one domain are carried into others in a circular fashion and reverberate around and through the system. For instance, social workers carry the emotional effects from one home visit into the next visit, and then take the effects of those visits back to the office. The office is a physical structure in which bureaucratic tasks are completed, but also a place full of emotions and relationships. The experience of the office and whether the feelings from home visits are dealt with in turn influences what workers take onto the road with them, and the car is another space where workers may process their feelings and thoughts, all while on the move. All of this is further influenced by what goes on in the professional's personal life, and how the experiences and meanings of social workers' own homes, intimate relationships, values and emotions come into play. Their home is a place that contributes to the emotional impact of the work being processed. Froggett (2002, pp. 137–8) gives an example of a social worker who, having visited a child during the day, only recognized the high degree of risk the child was at when she was in the bath that night. The bath provided a containing environment that enabled the worker to make the links between what she had really observed, experienced and felt.

Because of this circularity of experience and emotion, there is an important sense in which social work and child protection are ultimately not under anyone's true control. They are too multilayered across different domains, too joined up, too complex and elusive for that. While individual actions matter hugely, there is no linear model of cause and effect available where we can say one thing absolutely resulted in a failure to protect a child or the delivery of good practice. This circularity of experience and emotion makes it all the more vital that robust spaces for reflection are created. Speaking of how difficult it is to bring what goes on in complex mobile systems under control, John Urry (2007) speaks of the need to create 'moorings' in the midst of movement and complexity.

In social work and child protection, the office is – or needs to be – the key place for workers to find a secure mooring in the form of pleasant nurturing surroundings, supervision and support. But when social work is thought of in terms of movement and mobility, the car also emerges as an important mooring – albeit a fluid one – and I shall deal with it first.

The car as a secure base and space for reflection

Chapter 8 showed the importance of the car as a space for therapeutic practice with children. In many respects, the car carries similar emotional meanings and possibilities for workers. This is shown in Smith's (2003) research, in which he, quite unintentionally, discovered the significance of cars to welfare professionals. In a qualitative study of 60 social workers' and 12 counsellors' experiences of fear and distress, he found that many wanted to talk about the central role their cars and driving played in their personal and professional identities and emotional lives. Smith (2003, p. 157) writes:

> People 'humanise' their cars by giving them names, referring to them as human (usually female) and wooing and/or berating them accordingly. They displace strong feelings onto their cars. One participant in the research into fear said that having returned from a fear-provoking incident she washed her car. She went on to say that this is something that often afforded her satisfaction. She talked of this in a similar way to which people who have been assaulted will often describe wanting to shower or bathe themselves (Smith and Nursten, 1998). It seemed there was a sense in which the car was 'standing in' for her, being washed, on this occasion.

The car becomes a secure base to return to after a difficult, fearful encounter with a service user, and/or the means that would take them to the secure base of the office or their home. John Bowlby (1988) developed the psychoanalytic concept of the 'secure base' to account for how the infant needs to know that their mother – or any other attachment figure – will be reliably present as a base to move from and back to so as to feel safe enough to explore their world. Within the internal life of the professional, the presence of their car provides a sense of security that makes the emotionally challenging aspects of the work more doable.

Thus cars have deep meanings for staff as spaces where the self can be replenished and helped to build up the emotional resources needed to do effective social work. In addition to promoting personal safety through providing the means for a quick getaway from hostile people, cars seem to provide an emotional comfort zone for professionals, a haven from office politics as well as services users. It is a 'back-region' (Goffman, 1959), where the demeanour required to conduct professional interviews can be relaxed and one can be 'oneself' again. Of the many professionals' stories relating to this I have heard, a health visitor told me of how she used her car straight after home visits to vent her anger at the parents and the experience she had just been through by shouting, seeing the car as a space where she felt secure to do this and, crucially, enabling her not take these emotions home and dump them on her loved ones. Social workers have told of using their cars to meditate and reflect before and after difficult home visits and agency meetings. This kind of self-management is aided today by the fact that cars enable greater control of the mood through radio, music and telecommunications. Cars, in these respects, are important spaces to occupy *alone* and have privacy (Sheller, 2004).

Cars also provide enclosed confidential spaces in which supervision or debriefing and peer support go on between the worker and the manager/supervisor or another colleague who accompanied them to see the service user. This is an element of how the car is used as a transitory office. It is also used as a mobile office between visits to different service users and agencies, or between meetings, in which mobile phone calls are made and notes of visits and case reports worked on. Social workers have long used the car to do office work, often with the aid of other technology, such as the use of Dictaphones to record their notes to be typed up as case records and reports. With the advent of computerization, the use of the car as a mobile office is taking new forms, as the increasing deployment of laptop and palm-held computers permit direct inputting of information about service users into administrative systems, assessment forms and case records. In effect, one 'mobility system' (Urry, 2007) – the car – meets another mobility system – the computer/internet – and permits information gathered on the move to enter the administrative system, to be stored and flow around.

The office, emotional listening and organizational containment

Due to these changes, the meaning of 'the office' and the boundary between it and the worker's home life is changing. Increasing numbers of social care organizations are following the trend of creating call centres to take referrals (Coleman and Harris, 2008) and open-plan offices that house large numbers of the workforce. Often, in such spaces, social workers no longer have an allocated desk but take what is available on a given day, having placed their possessions in their locker or secure 'pod' overnight. The organizational rationale is to save money and is based on a concept of 'agile working', where workers are permitted to do some home working, such as report writing and case recording. While such flexible working may bring some benefits to staff, it is a source of concern because it appears to limit the scope there is for the workplace to be used for doing face-to-face work with service users. Such arrangements are in danger of promoting practice that is detached and literally distant from service users and lacking in intimacy. As this book has been arguing, practitioners need to have real choices about where they relate to children, and the office, well stocked with toys and other communication aides, should be preserved and developed as a site for doing direct work.

Similar concern surrounds the implications for practitioners of not having an allocated desk. As I have been arguing throughout this book, lived-in spaces have deep symbolic meanings and emotional resonances. Having a designated desk matters because it constitutes your own piece of territory, however small, that is adorned with the photographs and other objects that personalize it for you – what Danny Miller (2008) calls 'the comfort of things'. Security also arises from having a fixed location within a community of colleagues where you know from day to day who your neighbours are. These relationships are crucial to how workers gain the support they need on an hour-by-hour, day-by-day basis. At its best, the office should provide a 'secure base' for workers to go into in the morning and to return to after visits, where the relationships and support that are needed can be found.

A key challenge in enabling effective child protection practice is how to manage the atmospheres, anxiety and projections of anger, hate and love that workers have to endure as a central part of the work. The office provides a space for what Ruch (2007a) calls 'organisational containment'. As this book has already shown, this notion of containment was developed within psychoanalysis as a way of trying to account for the kind of love and support that enable the healthy management of anxiety (Froggett, 2002). As a normal part of child development, parents, usually mothers, are called upon to 'hold' and 'contain' their infant's primitive feelings of anxiety and confusion, for example depending on a parent to provide food gives rise to insecurity when that need is frustrated or not met, and routine anxiety that it may not be. Containment occurs in how the parent receives the infant's projections of anxiety and confusion, processes them and sends them back, making them available in a less threatening form, enabling the child to think more clearly about the parent and themselves. As earlier chapters have shown, effective practice regularly involves workers performing the role of containing parents' feelings with the aim of building up their internal resources and capacities to love and care for their children. We have also seen how helping children to integrate their external and internal experiences is at the core of the containment role with them. Bion (1962) argued that not being contained in this way causes the links between thought and feeling to split off from one another. Too much uncontained anxiety stops professionals from thinking straight. In child protection work, it leads to the child being lost sight of and not being 'held in mind'. Workers need containment of their own feelings and those projected onto them by service users (and also by other professional colleagues) if they are to think clearly and keep their focus on the child.

Central to organizational containment is the provision of supervision that gives workers the space to talk openly, think, be still, to process their feelings, and to enable them to *know* their experiences and make sense of what is reverberating within them. Supervision should allow busy practitioners to address those situations where they are perhaps dimly aware that they didn't engage sufficiently with that child and their surroundings. As one social worker expressed it:

> Sometimes I'm rushed for time, sometimes actually sitting down afterwards with hindsight to think, maybe I should have looked into that, maybe I should go back for that, and that's what good supervision is. And as I was telling you earlier, I'm very lucky that I do have fantastic, regular, good supervision and it makes a massive difference to my practice, because I am forced regularly to rethink some of those decisions in those cases and then go 'yeah, maybe I do need to find out a bit more about that', and then I go back and I do that, and that's safe practice.

I shadowed a social worker on a home visit to an investigation of an alleged assault on a child. The worker had to be very authoritative in seeking to see the child, around the home, and insist that the alleged perpetrator, who was mother's partner and stepfather to the child and who was in police custody, was not allowed back into the home until the assessment of risk was complete. On the way back to the office, I asked the social worker how she was feeling and what her experience is of the team and the kinds of supports she needs and gets in the office:

> People are really supportive. It's got a team spirit about it. You can go to people and say 'I need an extra body on this visit' and people try and help you out, they don't say 'I'm too busy, I've got too much on.' You can natter about each other's cases, get other people's opinions. [The team manager and senior practitioners] are very available and supportive, really knowledgeable. It feels like a safe team to work in where things are done properly and thoroughly. It's a two-way process. I feel really, really lucky because it makes such a difference. It can make the unbearable bearable. You are not just carrying stuff all on your own and not feeling like you're making decisions alone. You can have an offload on the team manager, where you can speak your mind. You can say those inappropriate things – 'ah fecking this and that'. You can just be open. I don't know if that really makes sense. It's nice to have an environment where you can speak your mind, even if that's not always the most appropriate thing. But that's accepted because it's a way of separating yourself from really serious kinds of [abusers] or whatever. It's a way of taking any emotion you feel out of it and simplifying it in a way, if you know what I mean. That's a black and white label, rather than you sitting there thinking about what he has done or anything like that. It lightens it in your head, not that it lightens the issues.

Management and managers have gained something of a bad name due to the rise of 'managerialism', where social work practice is much more regulated from above. But this worker helps us to understand what good management looks like and why it is essential. 'Making the unbearable bearable' perfectly captures the place of team support and quality supervision in enabling workers to keep on doing the job well. The ways in which this support is actually structured and delivered are crucial to its success. This worker's social work manager or senior practitioner was always there in the office and readily available for consultation, by phone or in person, on the worker's return. The assurance of knowing that such hands-on support is there and accessible is crucial to workers. They were open to hearing and containing 'those inappropriate things' that workers need to unburden themselves of. Having caring social work colleagues who will go out of their way to help also matters hugely. Then there is conventional weekly or fortnightly one-to-one supervision, giving the worker the opportunity to go through their cases. The supervisors for the above social worker, like all good supervisors, gave staff the right amounts of time and created the right kinds of spaces and conditions to enable these reflective processes to succeed. There has been a drift in recent years to supervision being provided from behind a computer screen, but this is not good practice. There may be a need to refer from time to time to electronic records and reports, but the body positions and lines of communication between supervisor and worker need to be face to face without obstruction. The supervisor must effectively create conditions that enable deep relationships between them and their staff – a supervisory version of intimate child protection. This relationship can then become a medium for exploration and learning, in the same way that practitioners can learn about their service users through reflection on their feelings. This is what is known as supervision being a 'parallel process' (Williams, 1997). In Chapter 12, it was argued that when they relate to children – or do not relate to them – workers can mirror and re-enact the neglectful and abusive dynamics that are present between the parent and their child. Similar mirroring can occur during supervision, as some of the tensions and conflicts in the worker–service user dynamic can surface and be re-enacted in the supervisor–worker relationship. Making sense of these dynamics requires understanding how the supervisory relationship is open to the same kinds of processes of transference and projection as go on between users and practitioners. Chapter 9 showed how controlling and non-reflective management styles can result in workplace relationships becoming destructive and even abusive, in a manner that mirrors the abusive relationships in the families workers are involved with.

The kinds of emotional support and containment referred to here should not be seen as some kind of esoteric preserve of psychoanalytically trained social work supervisors who delve deep into the unconscious of the worker. I do believe that some psychodynamic training, which elaborates on concepts like containment, projective identification, transference and the parallel process and how to apply them to practice, can only be of benefit to managers and practitioners. It is vital that this relational component is restored to social work and child protection education. However, good supervision and peer support that provide containment of the worker do not require exploration of the deeper reaches of the psyche and fantasy life. Workers can be helped to bring 'unthought' knowledge and feelings to awareness, which can occur through supervisors sensitively providing emotionally attuned listening and support.

This has to involve connecting with the complex relational dynamics that are part of the 'something' that can happen to workers which can stop even the best of them from carrying through on their intentions. Once again, we are involved here in developing theoretical resources and practical approaches that can enable the apparently unexplainable to be explained. Too often, accounts of social work and child protection, especially when failures to protect children occur, assume that practitioners know what they are doing most, if not all, of the time. Important aspects of our experiences are not consciously available to us or understood by us when we are in the midst of doing them. There is a great deal social workers can achieve in developing the knowledge and skills to be able to reflect on what they are experiencing while in the presence of children and parents, in homes, offices, family centres and clinics, that is, 'reflecting in action'. The supervisory role is crucially important in providing workers with the opportunity to critically reflect on the experiences they have had – promoting 'reflection on action' (Schön, 1983). This can enable them to become aware of their feelings, what has been projected onto them, and any collusions and pathological communication they are unconsciously acting out, which are preventing the child from being kept in mind and protected.

Another method of organizational containment outlined by Ruch (2007b) is case discussions, where the worker is facilitated by their social work team to talk about their experience of the case and the child and family. This requires what Ruch (2007b) calls 'emotional listening' from colleagues, where the emphasis is on encouraging reflection on the 'being' aspects of involvement as well as the 'doing' part of the job, which relates to the practical and administrative tasks that need to be completed. The aim should be to allow expression of the complexity of practice and the relationships and feelings involved, halting the search for simple 'doing' solutions (such as more procedures), which leave the emotional, relational components out and prevent true understanding of the worker's experience, the child's life and what needs to be done (see also Keeping, 2008). All these kinds of supports need to be provided within a context where workers and managers have a well-developed and articulated approach to safety planning and practice, based on research evidence and tried-and-tested clinical experience (Turnell and Essex, 2006).

Embodied listening and a child protection skin

Effective child protection can only be performed in the first place if all the dimensions involved in performing it are firmly on the agenda. As has been argued throughout this book, the work needs a strong intellectual and conceptual base. This means workers, supervisors and organizations having a deep understanding of the requirement to move around rooms and houses to engage directly with children, engage in professional touch and take into account what blocks and enables such protective movements. In advancing this agenda, organizations need to learn from the wisdom and accomplished performances that are enacted by team members in child protection day in, day out. For genuinely supportive learning organizations to exist, this is not just a matter for frontline staff and operational managers.

Psychodynamic and mobility awareness is required by senior management and right through to policy makers. Clear procedures, role definition and good resource management are crucial to containing workers, helping them to deal with the uncertainty that pervades this work. Managers at all levels also need to understand how organizational containment includes the need for them to listen and respond to issues such as workers' concerns about excessive administration and how time spent at the computer can deprive them of quality time to give to children and families. It is vital that practice is allowed to be determined by workers' professional judgement about the amount of time that needs to be spent with the child and family to fully understand and assess their lives, develop relationships and do the therapeutic and support work that is needed to effect the necessary change. The manager's role in organizational containment also has to involve creating the right relations of authority. Chapter 12 showed the influence that relations of authority have on workers' self-confidence, sense of efficacy and ability to exercise good authority with service users to protect children, especially with respect to workers' sense of authority derived from their own and the profession's reputation. To enhance this, managers need to treat staff in respectful ways that fully acknowledge their expertise. This should include a career structure that enables experienced practitioners who wish to remain in frontline practice to do so and to be well paid and rewarded for it.

I want to add to Ruch's (2007b) suggestion about the need for emotional listening by arguing that forms of *embodied* telling and listening are also needed. This means workers being encouraged to talk about how they felt in their bodies when in the home or elsewhere with the child or parents. This is not just about the professional's internal emotional life but the tactile realities, the smells, and the generally physical nature of practice. Supervision and peer support must be fundamentally concerned with whether the actions taken were sufficiently mobile to ensure the child's safety, or whether movement was blocked. Encouraging workers to talk about their bodily experiences gives them permission to speak the truth about their feelings, including, and especially, awkward ones such as fear and disgust. Encouraging embodied storytelling provides an invitation to speak about the atmospheres in which the work is being done and what is reverberating in the body, mind and intuition of the worker. The embodied listening by the supervisor enables workers to soak up and contain those reverberations and atmospheres, so that they might see, move towards, touch and hear the child afresh, ensuring that, as far as is humanly possible, they are protected.

To do this kind of work effectively, practitioners need to develop a 'child protection skin'. Social workers and other child protection professionals are, of course, not alone in having to ask difficult questions of people. As a way of helping psychotherapists to move beyond their resistance to discussing sexual matters with their clients in couples counselling, Kahr (2009, p. 19) speaks of therapists needing the 'ability to possess a sexual skin', which can enable them to engage openly and without embarrassment with clients about sexuality. Applied to social work, possessing a 'child protection skin' would involve:

- Insisting on getting into the home without feeling shame or that one is being overintrusive.

- Requesting to see children without undue anxiety about being intrusive and being able to negotiate seeing them on their own in the home or in another safe space.

- Undertaking a full history of children's and parents' experiences and relationships, including traumatic experiences, past and present.

- Establishing who is resident in the home/in contact with the children, by asking mothers and any other adults, or looking for oneself.

- Facilitating discussion of relationships and other intimate matters without feeling or being intrusive or excited and without shame or undue anxiety.

- A capacity to use authority without feeling guilt or shame, while being fully attuned to its impact on service users.

- Asking to see around the home, including the bedrooms, bathroom and kitchen, and doing it without shame, with manageable levels of anxiety and without feeling intrusive.

- A capacity to listen to and absorb parents' and children's anger, disappointments and pain, and to respond in empathic, authoritative, humane ways, which promote learning, change, safety and wellbeing.

Acquiring a child protection skin begins with initial professional education and training, further support as a newly qualified social worker and should continue to develop throughout workers' careers. Supervision, complemented by training and continuous professional development, is a crucial arena where practitioners can be helped to acquire and refine such a child protection skin. In order for this to happen, managers themselves need to have a clear concept of best intimate practice and feel comfortable in their own child protection skin.

Conclusion

The complex processes and emotional dynamics I have highlighted in this chapter and the book happen in child protection because professionals are in a relation of care with someone, where issues of vulnerability, need, dependence, power and control are present. While this goes on wherever such relationships happen, this book has given particular attention to what goes on when the worker leaves their desk and the office. In the service user's home, there are extra layers of atmosphere and reverberations, and challenges to enact movement and/or become immobile that may not be present in other places. Home visiting is the most fundamental act or step that child protection workers have always taken, yet it is the least well understood aspect of its practices. Practitioners need to be helped to understand their embodied experiences and to integrate thought and feeling so as to be able to keep the child in mind and move fluently and directly to engage with them.

We need a conception of child protection practice through home visiting, where social workers are understood to be carrying the organization and their role and intentions with them, of that flowing with and through them. But while the organization, at one level, holds them in a particular professional and emotional space, at the same time, they are separate from the organization when they cross the doorstep and step into the home, on their own, stripped bare to the essentials of a human being.

When face to face with children and parents, what goes on is fundamentally human not organizational, as the visit's organizational aims are mediated by the worker's experiences, emotions and the atmospheres in the home. Workers have to be able to contain themselves as best they can when on the spot, and feel 'held', in the sense of knowing that they will be organizationally and emotionally held when they return to the office through a genuinely attentive relation of care with their managers and colleagues. High-quality, emotionally informed support in the office (and car) enables containment of the emotions and bodily sensations experienced when relating to service users, in the home and elsewhere. As Ruch (2007a, p. 377) argues: ' "Emotional listening" transforms experiences of fear, anxiety, anger and frustration into "a resource for practice rather than a reason for disengagement".'

The extent to which social workers are able to delve into the depths to protect children and explore the deeper reaches and inner lives of service users – the degree to which they feel able to get up and walk across the room to directly engage with, touch and be active with the child or follow through on seeing kitchens and bedrooms – is directly related to how secure and contained they feel in separating from the office/car. They can only really take risks if they feel they will be emotionally held and supported on returning to the office, that their feelings and struggles will be listened to. Workers' state of mind and the quality of attention they can give to children is directly related to the quality of support, care and attention they themselves receive from supervisors, managers and peers.

15
Intimate child protection practice

It is cases like this one that makes the job worth doing. Cases like that where you see a real difference that you think, although that has all come from mum, because ultimately it has to come from her, but I've been part of that process. I've been like a cog in the works. So cases like that make this job worth doing.

(a social worker on work that prevented children coming into care)

An intimate journey: retracing our steps

This book has sought to account for the nature of child protection practice and social work by grounding it in an analysis of the everyday practices and movements of child protection. It has tried to understand why it is that abused children are not protected when professionals are face to face with them. The aim has been to provide systematic knowledge about how practitioners need to perform actual child protection practices while face to face with children and parents in their homes and other places. This book has set out the form that child protection takes from the moment practitioners leave their desks and offices, and the skills, knowledge and organizational support, as well as the courage and resilience that are needed if practitioners are to carry through on child protection in the intimate way that is required.

I have argued that a new concept of intimate child protection practice is needed. This concept of 'intimate practice' has been developed to try and bring into much sharper focus the places where the work goes on and their influence, and the centrality of the emotions and the body and mind of the worker and service user in doing and experiencing the work. This has involved us going on a journey, following practitioners along the streets, through housing estates, at doorsteps, entering the child's home, facing the dilemma of how to get to see children on their own, and ascertaining the best place for such contact to take place. As has been shown, even getting to the doorstep of the home where the child is often involves taking significant risks and makes huge demands on practitioners' personal resources. And workers carry the emotional effects of those journeys and adventures into the encounters they have with families and their homes, where the impact of still deeper atmospheres and visceral and emotional experiences have to be dealt with.

I have argued for the importance of professionals achieving intimate depth by using touch as part of keeping children safe and working with them therapeutically. This book has analysed how such practice can be performed in other spaces, especially the car, which is usually ignored in analyses of practice. One aim has been to rehabilitate – or better still, recondition – the car as a space for contemporary practice. The work that goes on in offices and hospitals, as well as schools and family centres has also been analysed and its emotional and practical complexities revealed. A core argument of the book has been that effective child protection practice requires intimate depth through the worker being prepared and able to move within rooms and other spaces in order to relate directly to children, and to go deeply into all the rooms in the family's home and their private selves and lives. Twenty-first century intimate child protection practice needs to achieve this in ethical ways by taking the scope that there is for empathy and negotiation with family members to their maximum. This is not a manifesto for 'walking all over' people's houses and rights, in the abusive sense usually implied in that kind of complaint. Yet it has to be insisted that effective child protection practice cannot be done without having a clear concept of 'good authority' and being prepared to exercise it in the name of seeking to keep children safe.

Because so much emphasis in recent years has been placed on the failures of the interprofessional system to communicate and share vital information about children at risk and entire new bureaucratic systems built up around it, insufficient attention has been given to the actual practices that are required to protect children, and we have lost touch with the lived experience of doing the work and how it needs to be done and theorized. The vision of intimate child protection practice that has been developed in this book has been fashioned from several sources of evidence and ideas. I have tried to rethink the nature of social work and child protection through the sociology of walking, touch and other movements, on the streets, in clinics and in the homes of service users. This, it is hoped, provides a much deeper feel for, and appreciation of, the state of mind and body of the practitioner when engaged in the work, and what influences their capacity to remain actively child-centred. If we are to properly understand modern child protection practices, it is crucial that we conceive of them as they are practised – on the move. Mobility is the air that social work breathes, the background noise, the mood music to all its performances. I have tried to open up new understandings of the mobile experience of doing child protection practice, in terms of the need to negotiate one's way around neighbourhoods, across doorsteps, to see children alone, to assess parenting, to do meaningful therapeutic work, most often while in the child and family's intimate space. This has led to consideration of how child protection is shaped by material culture and the environments – houses, rooms, offices – within which it goes on and objects such as homes, cars, teddy bears and computers.

Psychodynamic theory has been used to help identify the influence of the emotions and make sense of the complicated things that happen when practitioners relate to children and their carers and the generally complex nature of relationships in child protection. It is the fact that the goals of child protection have to be achieved well beyond the comfort of the office, while on one's feet and in the state of flux it is necessary to enter if children are to be seen in their homes, which account for a great deal of the creative, unpredictable and irrational aspects of social work practice. Kesserling (2006) defines 'mobility' as 'an actor's competence to realize specific projects and plans while being on the move'. This means that the entire project of social work and child protection is unthinkable and unrealizable without mobility and regular displays of skill, creativity and courage while on the move.

I am aware that some of the arguments in this book are contentious. I have taken up a clear position on several issues, such as the need for children to be seen on their own but only in what, to them, constitutes a safe space, to use professional touch with children, and to inspect homes. However, I have tried to do justice to the moral as well as the practical complexities these dilemmas give rise to and the differing viewpoints that exist. Good practice is going on and I have been fortunate to be able to draw upon some of it in this book. However, because recent decades have brought a loss of clarity as to how some of child protection's core practices should be carried out, and some new dimensions to how these practices should be performed are only becoming apparent, considerable confusion exists about what constitutes good practice and, in general, practice needs to become more deeply relational and intimate, in the manner I have outlined in this book.

In trying to provide such a vision, the book has also attempted to advance a shift away from an overemphasis on responses to risk and knowledge based on reorganizing office-based work and professional systems to promoting an analysis and understanding of the day-to-day 'practice risks' that pervade social work and child protection. The notions of adventure, atmosphere, movement, blocked movement (immobilization), flow and flux, which have been elaborated on in the book, are, on one level, useful as metaphors for capturing the 'liquid', unpredictable nature of practice and risk in child protection. On the other hand, their meanings and the substance of these practices go well beyond metaphor and reflect the real experiences and actions that take place and the challenges and tensions that exist in the everyday world of practice. I have also developed concepts for practice – good authority, avoidance, professional insecurity, pathological communication, containment, embodied listening – which are intended to enable better understanding of the lived experience of doing the work and more grounded ways of expressing what it is like to perform child protection and what impacts on it. The evidence from this book supports the argument of scholars, such as Eileen Munro (2010), Bob Lonne and colleagues (Lonne et al., 2009), Nigel Parton (2006, 2008) and Sue White, Karen Broadhurst and colleagues (Broadhurst et al., 2010a, 2010b), that overdemanding computerized record-keeping systems and performance management targets, which require social workers to spend too much time in the office, are dangerous. They create the conditions within which errors at the front line of practice can occur by squeezing the amount of time practitioners have to spend with children and families and to reflect on their work. However, this book has argued that the centrality of the emotions to child protection means that the increased bureaucratization of practice is itself, in part, a reaction to the heightened awareness that exists today of the kinds of risks, dangers and hazards experienced at the front line. As Sebastian Kramer (2009) has observed, 'the front line' originated as a military metaphor, which refers to how frontline troops are sent on operations to risk their lives and get killed (see also Beckett, 2003). The risky kinds of things social workers have to do on the streets and in the homes of difficult service users can make the office and even the most demanding computerized case recording systems seem very attractive indeed.

In effect, elaborate bureaucratic routines and the need to spend time in the office are manifestations of not only how individuals but organizations create defences against anxiety and intolerable feelings (Cooper and Lousada, 2005). A retreat to the secure base of the office is a way of managing the emotions that arise from having to work with children's suffering and the risk that they may die, as well as the physical and emotional risks to workers themselves in having to do such challenging work. High-quality emotional support is of vital importance to creating safe, enabling interventions by promoting professional wellbeing, creating opportunities for stillness, to slow things down and provide moments for reflection on the entire experience. As has been shown, this can happen in the office through formal supervision, peer support, spending time alone in quiet contemplation, or in cars, while in transit, grounding oneself, creating stillness and a mooring while on the move.

Analysts of walking and mobilities distinguish 'way finding' from 'map reading' (Ingold, 2000; Urry, 2007). Map reading involves moving across a surface as imagined from above and written down, while way finding is to move around *within* a world in a process of constant engagement and readjustment in relation to the environment. Social work, especially through home visiting, is 'way finding' par excellence, having to move within the family's world, their space, without pre-existing maps or well-trodden paths to guide one. Maps of sorts are formulated in child protection plans, but even then, 'pathways' in social work must be imaginatively created and trodden through repetition and wisdom borne out of countless steps taken over years of 'walking the walk' on the streets, garden paths, stairwells and in the homes of service users. This is why history and hearing the stories of practitioners today are so important, so that we might learn how to follow in the footsteps of those wise professionals who have already shown the way and a tradition of best practice identified that we can be proud of. Attending to these practices and experiences through research and by drawing out and documenting the accumulated wisdom of practitioners are crucial to how learning needs to occur at all levels of practice and management about how social workers can best protect and help vulnerable children by walking the walk, engaging in sensitive touch and doing the kinds of thinking on their feet that is at the heart of intimate child protection practice.

The intimate child protection practitioner at work

There will always be risks of child protection workers and systems not managing to keep children safe. Complete guarantees that children will be protected can never be given because of the scope for abusers to use the home and other tactics to deceive professionals, for workers to avoid facing up to the painful emotional truth of an abused child's life, or for information about children not being effectively communicated between professionals. The shadow of many tragically killed children has hung over this book, none more so than Baby Peter. While no guarantees can be given, I want to draw the book to a close by pulling together the various strands of the concept of intimate child protection practice by examining what such practice would look like in circumstances such as those we have examined where harm to children was missed. I do not mean by this to examine such scenes in a simplistic manner after the event using the benefit of hindsight, but exploring the practice as it unfolds and would be done in the here and now.

So let us imagine our practitioner of intimate practice turning up for a pre-announced home visit to a 17-month-old child, who is on the child protection register and a child protection plan is in place due to non-accidental injury, and his three older siblings, who are on a plan due to neglect. This little boy is in his buggy, his face is dirty, his scalp is covered with a substance and his mother tells the worker that he has marks on his arm, which she fears will be suspected to be grab marks, and that she has an appointment for him to be seen by the GP. The practitioner of intimate practice would want to see the child out of the buggy and witness him interacting with his mother and siblings. They would be respectful to the mother, asking her how things have been and how she and the children are. They would use the relationship they have with the little boy to try to ensure they themselves directly relate to the child, by going down to his level, playing with him and taking his hand and moving around the room with him. They would directly intervene to have his face cleaned, engaging his mother in the need for this to be done right here, right now, or seeking her consent to do it themselves. They would be clear about the need to use professional touch, understand its ethical basis, reflect hard on their feelings about doing it, and become aware of and overcome any resistance within themselves to it – due to difficult previous experiences, disgust, fear of allegations, or fear of the mother or father. They would also insist on the parent showing them the grab marks on the child's body and ensure that the appointment with the GP is real and carried out, and, if there are grounds for it, that he is seen by a paediatrician. While this visit was pre-announced, she would make sure that the next two or three are not, so as to adhere to what is in the child protection plan about needing to discover how the family live when not expecting a visit.

As this is a case of child neglect as well as non-accidental injury, the social worker would want to inspect the entire home: the kitchen to check on what food is in the fridge and the cupboards, and their bedrooms to see what standard of care is being provided for the children and whether there are any differences in provision between the children's bedrooms or what the adults provide in their bedroom for themselves. Because there have been suspicious injuries to the children that have never been adequately explained, there is also a need to inspect the adult bedroom and the bathroom for any signs of other people/men living with the children. The worker would conduct this part of the visit with great sensitivity and know the difference between neglect and poor provision due to poverty, and would do all she can to provide whatever material help the family needs.

The intimate practitioner knows that they have to see the older children on their own and would reflect very hard on whether doing so in a room in the family home is sufficient, given that their mother, the suspected abuser, is in the home. They would conclude that it is not fair or reliable to just see the children alone at home and would decide to also see them separately in school. They would find creative ways of communicating with them, including taking them for a car ride from time to time, because they know from experience how children find it easier to talk when in motion in the car and they are not positioned face to face with the worker. If English is not the first language for this family, the social worker would arrange interpreters. If any of the children are disabled, the worker would ensure that appropriate communication resources are provided. Their knowledge would include awareness of how the children are highly likely to experience them as a powerful figure in their lives. The children know that their social worker has privileged information about them from what they have told the worker, from what other professionals have said and from what the worker has skilfully and authoritatively been able to glean from their parents. The intimate practitioner understands the meaning and power of their role as a transitional participant in the children's lives, because, of all the professionals they have contact with, they are the one person who is linked to all the key professionals and people in their family. The worker uses this knowledge and their relationship with the children to great therapeutic effect by containing their anxieties and helping them to feel safe and more whole again. The children are touched in every sense by the worker's generosity.

While in the house and face to face with the parents and children, the worker would be reflecting hard in action, monitoring their level of professional insecurity here and now in this visit/encounter and checking out with themselves whether they are avoiding doing anything they should be doing. This would include being sensitive to covert physical resistance by the parent, posing the question to themselves: 'This is an announced visit, is the home and where the child and I are at this moment, placed in this room, a manipulation to block me from properly seeing and relating to this child?' They would be focusing hard on sensing the atmosphere in the home and what their intuition and feelings can tell them about the children's experience and how the parent interacts with them. They would know this necessitates a deep sensitivity to non-physical resistance and pathological communication and ask themselves: 'What is being projected on to me at this moment; what is it I am feeling these parents do not want me to do? Are there any signs that I am feeling careless or neglectful towards the children when in their parents' presence?' If the answer is yes, and the worker recognizes that they have been too passive and insufficiently child-centred, they would adjust their approach accordingly and reclaim the initiative straightaway by relating in meaningfully intimate ways with the children.

The worker doubts it is true when the mother says her boyfriend is not living there. They would know that some couples who are poor claim social security as single people and tell the authorities the man is not living at home. They would let the mother know that they know this and insist that it is essential for them to know who is living with the children and to include the father or father figure in the protection work. The worker would understand how traditional constructions of masculinity prevent many men from seeking and accepting help and would be proactive in engaging with the man. They would know too that many men can speak with emotional truth about themselves and would gather their story of fatherhood and family life, observe them with their children and reach a view on the risks and resources they represent to the children and their partner and work with them accordingly.

If it feels safe enough to carry through with asking to inspect the rooms, touch the child and relate to the children on their own, then the worker would take a deep breath and request to do so. If it doesn't feel safe enough, immediately after the visit, they would make contact with their social work manager, either by phone or face to face in the office, and they would jointly make a return visit that day. As these children have been on a child protection plan for several months, none of these tasks and processes connected to seeing them moving around, professionally touching them, relating to them on their own and so on should come as a surprise to the older children or the parent(s)/carers. It would all have been set out in the child protection plan, which would have been drawn up through the process of authoritative, negotiated child protection.

The plan would be intimate too in its understanding of the impact on the parent(s) of the abuse and trauma they suffered in childhood and how this results in them relating in highly ambivalent ways to the worker as an authority figure. The worker would use this insight and their relationship with the parents to provide skilled therapeutic support for them, which can repair the impact of their trauma and develop their self-worth and parenting skills. Because these are involuntary service users, the worker would expect conflict and displays of physical and non-physical resistance. They would have the wisdom, confidence and skill to use good authority to insist that the key measure of safety for the children has to be more than the claims made by the parents to have acquired strengths. They would leave the parents in no doubt that it is essential for them to see actual evidence of how these strengths have evolved into demonstrations of protection of the children, over time.

On their return to the office, the social work manager, who is attuned to intimate practice, would provide containment for the worker through emotional listening, enabling them to talk about what they have just been through. They would enable the worker to explore what they did, their feelings and express that which they are not fully aware of. They would also engage in embodied listening, enabling the worker to recognize their fear of being contaminated by the home or children, paralysed by dogs, and inwardly raging, potentially aggressive and violent adults. Only now, through this process, can the full weight of what the worker experienced in the home emerge, signs of pathological communication be detected, what they did and did not do, what they avoided doing, and whether their practice was mobile and tactile enough and sufficiently focused on the children to really know whether they are safe. This containing supervisory relationship would also explore the worker's use of personal authority and their internalized authoritative voice, helping them to reach new levels of self-understanding, which builds their internal resources and capacity to cope with using personal authority as, or even more, effectively in the future.

The worker would feel no shame if it was decided that they have to go back to the home, nor would they be judged or blamed by managers for not getting it right first time. Managers would understand that because it is based on the perils and vulnerabilities that are always part and parcel of human beings relating to one another, intimate child protection is, by its very nature, an imperfect human science. The fact that child safety can never be guaranteed and the scope that always exists for workers to be hoodwinked, avoid and miss things would be fully understood.

If things should go wrong in a case and a child tragically dies, there would be a commitment from management for the social work team and entire multi-agency system to learn from it. There would be no blame of the individual worker but a concerted effort to learn and improve systems and practice for next time. These wise managers would realize that becoming aware of avoidance and owning up to it and the stupid things that get said and done in the heat of difficult encounters on home visits, and in other spaces, should be a matter for professional pride. It would be understood that it is in those unscripted moments of Freudian slips and absurdity that important learning can occur about family dynamics and the children's experience in that case. And there would be general learning here too for the social work team about the effects of particular contexts such as the home and even particular rooms in it on workers' experiences and practice. This demonstrably deep respect for the complex and difficult nature of practice would be part of a management style that would enhance the self-confidence, reputation and authority of frontline workers. The respectful relations of authority and organizational culture would enhance the capacity of practitioners to use good authority in similar ways with their service users. The worker would be able to practise effectively because their managers, supported by policy makers, have ensured that their workload is manageable and they have organized the system in a manner that allows them to have the time they need to be able to complete thorough, investigative assessments and do quality, longer term, relationship-based work.

And at the end of the day, having written it all up at the computer, the intimate practitioner would travel home in their car with the CD player turned up loud, oscillating between singing along to a favourite tune, joyful in the knowledge of those they have helped today, who smiled and thanked them for all they had done, and shouting loudly at those people who have given them grief today, getting it out of their system. And the next morning, they will make the return journey, readying themselves to perform to their professional best and be the courageously skilled intimate child protection practitioner that they are all over again.

Bibliography

Adey, P. (2009) *Mobility*, London: Routledge.

Allen, A. and Morton, A. (1961) *This is Your Child: The Story of the National Society for the Prevention of Cruelty to Children*, London: Routledge & Kegan Paul.

Bachelard, G. (1969) *The Poetics of Space*, Boston: Beacon Press.

Bailey, R. and Brake, M. (1975) *Radical Social Work*, London: Edward Arnold.

Barber, J.G. (1991) *Beyond Casework*, Basingstoke: Macmillan – now Palgrave Macmillan.

Barlow, J. and Schrader MacMillan, A. (2010) *Safeguarding Children from Emotional Abuse: What Works?*, London: Jessica Kingsley.

Bauman, Z. (2000) *Liquid Modernity*, Cambridge: Polity Press.

Beckett, C. (2003) The language of siege: military metaphors in the spoken language of social work, *British Journal of Social Work*, **33**(5): 625–39.

Beckett, C. (2007) *Child Protection: An Introduction*, London: Sage.

Behlmer, G. (1982) *Child Abuse and Moral Reform in England 1870–1908*, Stanford: Stanford University Press.

Bell, M. (2002) Promoting children's rights through the use of relationship, *Child and Family Social Work*, 7: 1–11.

Beresford, P., Adshead, L. and Croft, S. (2007) *Palliative Care, Social Work, and Service Users*, London: Jessica Kingsley.

Berry, J. (1972) *Social Work with Children*, London: Routledge & Kegan Paul.

Bion, W. (1962) *Learning from Experience*, London: Heinemann.

Birmingham Safeguarding Children's Board (2010) *Serious Case Review Report on the Khyra Ishaq case*, http://www.lscbbirmingham.org.uk/downloads/Case+14.pdf.

Bower, M. (ed.) (2005a) *Psychoanalytic Theory for Social Work Practice*, London: Routledge.

Bower, M. (2005b) Working with families who see help as the problem, in M. Bower (ed.) *Psychoanalytic Theory for Social Work Practice*, London: Routledge,

Bowlby, J. (1951) *Child Care and the Growth of Love*, Harmondsworth: Penguin.

Bowlby, J. (1988) *A Secure Base: Parent-Child Attachment and Healthy Human Development*, London: Routledge.

Brandon, M., Schofield, G. and Trinder, L. (1998) *Social Work with Children*, Basingstoke: Macmillan – now Palgrave Macmillan.

Brandon, M., Belderson, P., Warren, C. et al. (2008) *Analysing Child Deaths and Serious Injury Through Abuse and Neglect: What Can We Learn?*, Nottingham: DCSF.

Broadhurst, K., Wastell, D., White, S. et al. (2010a) Performing initial assessment: identifying the latent conditions for error at the front-door of local authority children's services, *British Journal of Social Work*, **40**(2): 352–70.

Broadhurst, K., Hall, C., Wastell, D. et al. (2010b) Risk, instrumentalism and the humane project in social work: identifying the informal logics of risk management in children's statutory services, *British Journal of Social Work*, **40**(4): 1046–64.

Brown, H.C. (1997) *Social Work and Sexuality: Working with Lesbians and Gay Men*, Basingstoke: Macmillan – now Palgrave Macmillan.

Brown, L., Callahan, M., Strega, S. et al. (2009) Manufacturing ghost fathers: the paradox of father presence and absence in child welfare, *Child & Family Social Work*, **14**(1): 25–34.

Buckley, H. (2003) *Child Protection Work: Beyond the Rhetoric*, London: Jessica Kingsley.

Buckley, H., Whelan, S. and Horwath, J. (2006) *Framework for the Assessment of Vulnerable Children and their Families*, Dublin: Trinity College Children's Research Centre.

Butler, I. and Williamson, H. (1994) *Children Speak: Children, Trauma and Social Work*, Longman: London.

Butler-Sloss, Lord Justice E. (1988) *Report of the Inquiry into Child Abuse in Cleveland 1987*, London: HMSO.

Calder, M. (2008a) Risk and child protection, in M. Calder (ed.) *Contemporary Risk Assessment in Safeguarding Children*, Lyme Regis: Russell House.

Calder, M. (ed.) (2008b) *Contemporary Risk Assessment in Safeguarding Children*, Lyme Regis: Russell House.

Calder, M. (ed.) (2008c) *Carrot or Stick?: Towards Effective Practice with Involuntary Clients in Safeguarding Children Work*, Lyme Regis: Russell House.

Calder, M. (2008d) A framework for working with resistance, motivation and change, in M. Calder (ed.) *Carrot or Stick?; Towards Effective Practice with Involuntary Clients in Safeguarding Children Work*, Lyme Regis: Russell House.

Calder, M. and Peake, A. (2001) Evaluating risks and needs: a framework, in M. Calder, A. Peake and K. Rose (eds) *Mothers of Sexually Abused Children: A Framework for Assessment, Understanding and Support*, Lyme Regis: Russell House.

Casement, P. (1997) *Further Learning from the Patient: The Analytic Space and Process*, London: Routledge.

Cohen, S. (2001) *States of Denial: Knowing about Atrocities and Suffering*, Cambridge: Polity Press.

Coleman, N. and Harris, J. (2008) Calling social work, *British Journal of Social Work*, **38**(3): 580–99.

Connell, R.W. (2005) *Masculinities*, 2nd edn, Cambridge: Polity Press.

Connolly, M., Crichton-Hill, Y. and Ward, T. (2005) *Culture and Child Protection: Reflexive Responses*, London: Jessica Kingsley.

Cook, A. (2008) Knowing the child: the importance of developing a relationship, in B. Luckock and M. Lefevre (eds) *Direct Work: Social Work with Children and Young People in Care*, London: BAAF.

Cooper, A. (2005) Surface and depth in the Victoria Climbié inquiry report, *Child and Family Social Work*, **10**(1): 1–9.

Corby, B. (2005) *Child Abuse: Towards a Knowledge Base*, Maidenhead: Open University Press.

Cresswell, T. (2006) *On the Move: Mobility in the Modern Western World*, London: Routledge.

Dale, P., Davies, M., Morrison, T. and Waters, J. (1987) *Dangerous Families: Assessment and Treatment of Child Abuse*, London: Tavistock.

Dalrymple, J. and Burke, B. (2006) *Anti-Oppressive Practice: Social Care and the Law*, Buckingham: Open University Press.

Daniel, B. and Taylor, J. (1999) The rhetoric versus the reality: a critical perspective on practice with fathers in child care and protection work, *Child & Family Social Work*, **4**(3): 209–20.

Daniel, B. and Taylor, J. (2001) *Engaging with Fathers: Practice Issues for Health and Social Care*, London: Jessica Kingsley.

Daniel, B. and Taylor, J. (2005) Do they care? The role of fathers in cases of child neglect, in J. Taylor and B. Daniel (eds) *Child Neglect: Practice Issues for Health and Social Care*, London: Jessica Kingsley.

Dant, T. (2004) The driver-car, *Theory, Culture and Society*, **21**(4/5): 61–80.

DCFS (Department for Children, Schools and Families) (2009) *Common Assessment Framework*, http://www.dcsf.gov.uk/everychildmatters/strategy/deliveringservices1/caf/cafframework/.

DCFS (Department for Children, Schools and Families) (2010) *Working Together to Safeguard Children*, London: TSO.

De Montigny, G. (1995) *Social Working: An Ethnography of Front-line Practice*, Toronto: University of Toronto Press.

DfES (Department for Education and Science) (2004) *Engaging Fathers: Involving Parents, Raising Achievement*, London: DFES.

DH (Department of Health) (1988) *Protecting Children: A Guide to Social Workers Undertaking a Comprehensive Assessment*, London: TSO.

DH (Department of Health) (2000) *Framework for the Assessment of Children in Need and their Families*, London: TSO.

DHSS (Department for Health and Social Security) (1974a) *Report of the Committee of Inquiry into the Care and Supervision Provided in Relation to Maria Colwell*, London: HMSO.

DHSS (Department for Health and Social Security) (1974b) *Non-accidental Injury to Children*, Circular LASSL (74) 13, London: HMSO.

DHSS (Department for Health and Social Security) (1995) *Messages from Research*, London: TSO.

Dingwall, R., Eekelaar, J. and Murray, T. (1983) *The Protection of Children: State Intervention and Family Life*, Oxford: Basil Blackwell.

Dobash, R.E. and Dobash, R.P. (1992) *Women, Violence and Social Change*, London: Routledge.

Dominelli, L. (1997) *Anti-racist Social Work : A Challenge for White Practitioners and Educators*, 2nd edn, Basingstoke: Macmillan – now Palgrave Macmillan.

Douglas, M. (1966) *Purity and Danger*, London: Routledge & Kegan Paul.

Douglas, M. (1992) *Risk and Blame: Essays in Cultural Theory*, London: Routledge.

Driver, E. and Droisen, A. (eds) (1989) *Child Sexual Abuse: Feminist Perspectives*, Basingstoke: Macmillan – now Palgrave Macmillan.

Dubowitz, H., Black, M., Kerr, M. et al. (2000) Fathers and child neglect, *Archives of Pediatric Adolescence Medicine*, **154**(2): 135–41.

Egeland, B. (2009) Taking stock: childhood emotional maltreatment and developmental psychopathology, *Child Abuse & Neglect*, **33**(1): 22–36.

Evans, T. and Harris, J. (2004) Street-level bureaucracy, social work and the (exaggerated) death of discretion, *British Journal of Social Work*, **34**(6): 871–95.

Featherstone, B. (1999) Taking mothering seriously: the implications for child protection, *Child and Family Social Work*, **4**(1): 43–53.

Featherstone, B. (2003) Taking fathers seriously, *British Journal of Social Work*, **33**(2): 239–54.

Featherstone, B. (2004) *Family Life and Family Support: A Feminist Analysis*, Basingstoke, Palgrave Macmillan.

Featherstone, B. (2009) *Contemporary Fathering*, Bristol: Policy Press.

Featherstone, B. and Evans, H. (2004) *Children Experiencing Maltreatment: Who Do They Turn To?*, London: NSPCC.

Featherstone, B., Scourfield, J. and Rivett, M. (2007) *Working with Men in Health and Social Care*, London: Sage.

Featherstone, M., Thrift, N. and Urry, J. (2005) *Automobilities*, London: Sage.

Ferguson, H. (2001) Social work, individualisation and life politics, *British Journal of Social Work*, **31**(1): 41–55.

Ferguson, H. (2003a) Welfare, social exclusion and reflexivity: the case of child and woman protection, *Journal of Social Policy*, **32**(2): 199–216.

Ferguson, H. (2003b) Outline of a critical best practice perspective on social work and social care, *British Journal of Social Work*, **33**(8): 1005–24.

Ferguson, H. (2004) *Protecting Children in Time: Child Abuse, Child Protection and the Promotion of Welfare*, Basingstoke: Palgrave Macmillan.

Ferguson, H. (2007) Abused and looked after children as 'moral dirt', *Journal of Social Policy*, **36**(1): 123–39.

Ferguson, H. (2008) Liquid social work: welfare interventions as mobile practices, *British Journal of Social Work*, **38**(3): 561–79.

Ferguson, H. (2009a) Performing child protection: home visiting, movement and the struggle to reach the abused child, *Child & Family Social Work*, **14**(4): 471–80.

Ferguson, H. (2009b) Anthony Giddens, in M. Gray and S. Webb (eds) *Social Work Theory and Methods*, London: Sage.

Ferguson, H. (2010) Therapeutic journeys: the car as a vehicle for working with children and families and theorising practice *Journal of Social Work Practice*, **24**(2): 121–38.

Ferguson, H. (2011) Mobilities of welfare: the case of social work, in M. Buscher, J. Urry and K. Witchger (eds) *Mobile Methods*, London: Routledge.

Ferguson, H. and Hogan, F. (2004) *Strengthening Families Through Fathers: Issues for Policy and Practice in Working with Vulnerable Fathers and their Families*, Dublin: Department of Social, Community and Family Affairs.

Ferguson, H. and O'Reilly, M. (2001) *Keeping Children Safe: Child Abuse, Child Protection and the Promotion of Welfare*, Dublin: A&A Farmer.

Ferguson, I. and Woodward, R. (2009) *Radical Social Work in Practice*, Bristol: Policy Press.

Finkelhor, D. (1984) *Child Sexual Abuse: New Theory and Research*, New York: Free Press.

Floresch, J. (2002) *Meds, Money and Manners: The Case Management of Severe Mental Illness*, New York: Columbia University Press.

Forrester, D., Kerhaw, S., Moss, H. and Hughes, L. (2008a) Communication skills in child protection: how do social workers talk to parents?, *Child and Family Social Work*, **13**(1): 41–51.

Forrester, D., McCambridge, J., Waissein, C. and Rollnick, S. (2008b) How do child and family social workers talk to parents about child welfare concerns?, *Child Abuse Review*, **17**(1): 23–35.

Frank, A. (2004) *The Renewal of Generosity: Illness, Medicine, and How to Live*, Chicago: University of Chicago Press.

Froggett, L. (2002) *Love, Hate and Welfare: Psychosocial Approaches to Policy and Practice*, Bristol: Policy Press.

Garland, D. (1985) *Punishment and Welfare: A History of Penal Strategies*, Aldershot: Gower.

Garrett, P.M. (2003) The trouble with Harry: why the new agenda of 'life politics' fails to convince, *British Journal of Social Work*, **33**(3): 381–97.

Garret, P.M. (2004a) Social work's 'electronic turn': notes on the deployment of information and communication technologies in social work with children and families, *Critical Social Policy*, **24**(4): 529–53.

Garrett, P.M. (2004b) More trouble with Harry: a rejoinder in the 'life politics' debate, *British Journal of Social Work*, **34**(4): 577–89.

Garrett, P.M. (2009) *Transforming Children's Services? Social Work, Neoliberalism and the 'Modern' World*, Buckingham: Open University Press.

Giacomantonio, G. (2003) Notes from behind the couch, *The Couch*.

Giddens, A. (1985) *The Nation-State and Violence*, Cambridge: Polity Press.

Giddens, A. (1992) *The Transformation of Intimacy*, Cambridge: Polity Press.

Giddens, A. (1994) *Beyond Left and Right: The Future of Radical Politics*, Cambridge: Polity Press.

Gill, T. (2007) *No Fear: Growing up in a Risk Averse Society*, London: Calouste Gulbenkian Foundation.

Gilligan, R. (1998) The importance of schools and teachers in child welfare, *Child and Family Social Work*, **3**(1): 13–25.

Goffman, E. (1959) *The Presentation of Self in Everyday Life*, New York: Doubleday.

Goldberg, A.I. (1990) *The Prisonhouse of Psychoanalysis*, Hillsdale, NJ: Analytic Press.

Halgreen, T. (2004) Tourists in the concrete desert, in M. Sheller and J. Urry (eds) *Tourism Mobilities: Places to Play, Places in Play*, London: Routledge.

Haringey (2008) *Serious Case Review, Child 'A', Executive Summary*, Haringey Local Safeguarding Board, November, www.haringey.gov.uk/childa.htm.

Haringey (2009) *Serious Case Review, Executive Summary*, Haringey Local Safeguarding Board, March, www.haringey.gov.uk/childa.htm.

Hayes, D. and Spratt, T. (2009) Child welfare interventions: patterns of social work practice, *British Journal of Social Work*, **39**(8): 1575–97.

Healy, K. (2005) *Social Work Theories in Context*, Basingstoke: Palgrave Macmillan.

Hearn, J. (1998) *The Violences of Men: How Men Talk About and How Agencies Respond to Men's Violence to Women*, London: Sage.

Herman, J. (1992) *Trauma and Recovery*, London: Pandora.

Hicks, S. (2000) Sexuality, in M. Davies (ed.) *The Blackwell Encyclopaedia of Social Work*, Oxford: Blackwell.

Hinshelwood, R.D. (1991) *A Dictionary of Kleinian Thought*, London: Free Association Books.

Hoggett, P., Mayo, M. and Miller, C. (2006) Relations of authority, *Organisational and Social Dynamics*, **6**(2): 224–40.

Holland, S. (2004) *Child and Family Assessment in Social Work*, London: Routledge.

Hollis, F. (1964) *Casework: A Psychosocial Therapy*, New York: Random House.

Hooper, C. (1992) *Mothers Surviving Child Sexual Abuse*, London: Routledge.

Horwath, J. (ed.) (2010) *The Child's World: The Comprehensive Guide to Assessing Children in Need*, London: Jessica Kingsley.

Housden, L. (1955) *The Prevention of Cruelty to Children*, London: Cape.

Houston, S. (2004) Garrett contra Ferguson: a meta-theoretical appraisal of the 'rumble in the jungle', *British Journal of Social Work*, **34**(2): 261–7.

Howe, D. (2005) *Child Abuse and Neglect*, Basingstoke: Palgrave Macmillan.

Howe, D. (2008) *The Emotionally Intelligent Social Worker*, Basingstoke: Palgrave Macmillan.

Howe, D. (2009) *A Brief Introduction to Social Work Theory*, Basingstoke: Palgrave Macmillan.

Howe, D., Brandon, M., Hinings, D. and Schofield, G. (1999) *Attachment Theory, Child Maltreatment and Family Support*, Basingstoke: Macmillan – now Palgrave Macmillan.

Ingold, T. (2000) *The Perception of the Environment: Essays on Livelihood, Dwelling and Skill*, London: Routledge.

Ingold, T. (2004) Culture on the ground, *Journal of Material Culture*, **9**(3): 315–40.

Ingold, T. (2007) Footprints through the weather world: walking, breathing, knowing, unpublished paper, via personal communication.

Ivanoff, A., Blythe, B. and Tripodi, T. (1994) *Involuntary Clients in Social Work Practice*, New York: Aldine de Gruyter.

Jackson, L. (2000) *Child Sexual Abuse in Victorian England*, London: Routledge.

Jacobucci, L. (1958) Nancy's ride, *Child Welfare*, **37**(8): 7–12, reprinted in E. Holgate (ed.) (1972) *Communicating with Children*, London: Longman.

Joffe, H. (1999) *Risk and 'The Other'*, Cambridge: Cambridge University Press.

Jones, D. (2003) *Communicating with Vulnerable Children*, London: Gaskell.

Jones, K. with I. Powell (2007) Situating person and place: best practice in dementia care, in K. Jones, B. Cooper and H. Ferguson (eds) *Best Practice in Social Work: Critical Perspectives*, Basingstoke: Palgrave Macmillan.

Kahr, B. (2009) Psychoanalysis and sexpertise, in C. Clulow (ed.) *Sex, Attachment and Couple Psychotherapy: Psychoanalytic Perspectives*, London: Karnac.

Kanter, J. (2004) *Face-to-Face with Children: The Life and Work of Clare Winnicott*, London: Karnac.

Keeping, C. (2008) Emotional engagement in social work: best practice and relationships in mental health work, in K. Jones, B. Cooper and H. Ferguson (eds) *Best Practice in Social Work: Critical Perspectives*, Basingstoke: Palgrave Macmillan.

Kempe, C.H., Silverman, F.N., Steel, B.F. et al. (1962) The battered child syndrome, *Journal of the American Medical Association*, 181: 17–24.

Kempe, R.S. and Kempe, H.C. (1978) *Child Abuse*, London: Fontana.

Kern, S. (1983) *The Culture of Time and Space (1880–1918)*, London: Weidenfeld & Nicholson.

Kesserling, S. (2006) Pioneering mobilities: new patterns of movement and motility in a mobile world, *Environment and Planning A*, **38**(2): 269–279.

Kimmel, M. (1994) Masculinity as homophobia: fear, shame and silence in the construction of gender identity, in H. Brod and M. Kaufman (ed.) *Theorizing Masculinities*, London: Sage.

Kitson, D. and Clawson, R. (2007) Safeguarding children with disabilities, in K. Wilson and A. James (eds) *The Child Protection Handbook*, London: Elsevier.

Kohli, R. (2007) *Social Work with Unaccompanied Asylum Seeking Children*, Basingstoke: Palgrave Macmillan.

Koprowska, J. (2010) *Communication and Interpersonal Skills in Social Work*, Exeter: Learning Matters.

Kramer, S. (2009) Think before you tick, paper to the Child Protection at a Crossroads conference, Tavistock Clinic, London, February.

Lamb, M.E. (1997) Introductory overview, in M.E. Lamb (ed.) *The Role of the Father in Child Development*, 3rd edn, Chichester: Wiley.

Lamb, M.E. (2001) Male roles in families 'at risk': the ecology of child maltreatment, *Child Maltreatment*, **6**(4): 310–13.

Lamb, M.E. and Lewis, C. (2004) The development and significance of father-child relationships in two-parent families, in M.E. Lamb (ed.) *The Role of the Father in Child Development*, 4th edn, Chichester: Wiley.

Lamb, M.E. and Tamis-Lemonda, C. (2004) The role of the father: an introduction, in M.E. Lamb (ed.) *The Role of the Father in Child Development*, 4th edn, Chichester, Wiley.

Laming, H. (2003) *The Victoria Climbié Inquiry*, London: TSO.

Laming, H. (2009) *The Protection of Children in England: A Progress Report*, London: TSO.

Laurier, E. (2004) Doing office work on the motorway, *Theory, Culture and Society*, **21**(4/5): 261–77.

Laurier, E., Lorimer, H., Brown, B. et al. (2008) Driving and 'passengering': notes on the ordinary organization of car travel, *Mobilities*, **3**(1): 1–23.

Lefevre, M. (2008) Knowing, being and doing: core qualities and skills for working with children and young people in care, in B. Luckock and M. Lefevre (eds) *Direct Work: Social Work with Children and Young People in Care*, London: BAAF.

Lefevre, M. (2010) *Communicating with Children and Young People: Making a Difference*, Bristol: Policy Press.

Leigh, S. and Farmer, A. (2008) Critical best practice in child protection: intervening into and healing child abuse, in K. Jones, B. Cooper and H. Ferguson (eds) *Best Practice in Social Work: Critical Perspectives*, Basingstoke: Palgrave Macmillan.

Lewis, N. (2001) The climbing body, nature and the experience of modernity, in P. Macnaughten and J. Urry (eds) *Bodies of Nature*, London: Sage.

Littlechild, B. (2005) The nature and effects of violence against child protection social workers: providing effective support, *British Journal of Social Work*, **35**(3): 387–401.

Lloyd, N., O'Brien, M. and Lewis, C. (2004) *Fathers in Sure Start*, National Evaluation of Sure Start (NESS) Institute for the Study of Children, Families and Social Issues, Birkbeck, University of London.

London Borough of Brent (1985) *A Child in Trust: Report of the Panel of Inquiry Investigating the Circumstances Surrounding the Death of Jasmine Beckford*, London Borough of Brent.

London Borough of Greenwich (1987) *A Child in Mind: The Report of the Commission of Inquiry into the Circumstances Surrounding the Death of Kimberley Carlile*, London Borough of Greenwich.

Lonne, B., Parton, N., Thomson, J. and Harries, M. (2009) *Reforming Child Protection*, London: Routledge.

Luckock, B. (2008a) Safeguarding children and integrated children's services, in K. Wilson and A. James (eds) *The Child Protection Handbook*, London: Elsevier.

Luckock, B. (2008b) Living through the experience: the social worker as the trusted ally and champion of young people in care, in B. Luckock and M. Lefevre (eds) *Direct Work: Social Work with Children and Young People in Care*, London: BAAF.

Luckock, B., Lefevre, M. and Tanner, K. (2007) Teaching and learning communication with children and young people: developing the qualifying social work curriculum in a changing policy context, *Child and Family Social Work*, **12**(2): 192–201.

Lyons, G. and Urry, J. (2005) Travel time use in the information age, *Transport Research A*, **39**(2/3): 257–76.

Marsh, S. and Pancevski, B. (2009) *The Crimes of Josef Fritzl: Uncovering the Truth*, London: HarperElement.

Merleau-Ponty, M. (1962) *Phenomenology of Perception: An Introduction*, London: Routledge & Kegan Paul.

Miller, D. (2001a) *Home Possessions*, Oxford: Berg.

Miller, D. (2001b) *Car Cultures*, Oxford: Berg.

Miller, D. (2008) *The Comfort of Things*, Cambridge: Polity Press.

Miller, D. (2010) *Stuff*, Cambridge: Polity Press.

Milner, J. (2004) From 'disappearing' to 'demonized': the effects on men and women of professional interventions based on challenging men who are violent, *Critical Social Policy*, **24**(1): 79–101.

Monckton, Sir W. (1945) *Report on the Circumstances which led to the Boarding-out of Denis and Terence O'Neill at Bank Farm, Minsterly and the Steps taken to Supervise their Welfare*, Cmd 6636, London: HMSO.

Morris, K. (2010) Children in need: the challenge of prevention for social work, in P. Ayre and M. Preston-Shoot (eds) *Children's Services at the Crossroads: A Critical Evaluation of Contemporary Policy for Practice*, Lyme Regis: Russell House.

Morris, K., Hughes, N., Clarke, H. et al. (2008) *Think Family: A Literature Review of Whole Family Approaches*, London: Cabinet Office.

Morrison, T. (2010) Assessing parental motivation to change, in J. Horwath (ed.) *The Child's World: The Comprehensive Guide to Assessing Children in Need*, London: Jessica Kingsley.

Munro, E. (1999) Common errors in reasoning in child protection work, *Child Abuse and Neglect*, **23**(8): 745–58.

Munro, E. (2002) *Effective Child Protection*, London: Sage.

Munro, E. (2004) The impact of audit on social work practice, *British Journal of Social Work*, **34**(8): 1075–95.

Munro, E. (2005) Improving practice: child protection as a systems problem, *Children and Youth Services Review*, **27**(4): 375–91.

Munro, E. (2010) Learning to reduce risk in child protection, *British Journal of Social Work*, **40**(4): 1135–51.

National Assembly for Wales and Home Office (2001) *Framework for the Assessment of Children in Need and their Families*, London: TSO.

NSPCC (National Society for the Prevention of Cruelty to Children) (1897) *Annual Report*, London: NSPCC.

NSPCC (National Society for the Prevention of Cruelty to Children) (1901) *Annual Report*, London: NSPCC.

NSPCC (National Society for the Prevention of Cruelty to Children) (1904) *Inspector's Directory*, London: NSPCC.

NSPCC (National Society for the Prevention of Cruelty to Children) (1910) *Inspector's Directory*, London: NSPCC.

NSPCC (National Society for the Prevention of Cruelty to Children) (1936) *Annual Report*, London: NSPCC.

O'Connell, J. (2002) Travellers in Ireland: an examination of discrimination and racism, in R. Lentin and R. McVeigh (eds) *Racism and Anti-Racism in Ireland*, Dublin: Beyond the Pale Publications.

O'Hagan, K. (1997) The problem of engaging men in child protection work, *British Journal of Social Work*, **27**(1): 25–42.

Oliver, M. (1983) *Social Work with Disabled People*, Basingstoke: Macmillan – now Palgrave Macmillan.

Oliver, M. (1996) *Understanding Disability: From Theory to Practice*, Basingstoke: Macmillan – now Palgrave Macmillan.

Orwell, G. (1962) *The Road to Wigan Pier*, Harmondsworth: Penguin.

Packman, J. (1981) *The Child's Generation*, London: Blackwell & Robinson.

Parton, N. (1985) *The Politics of Child Abuse*, Basingstoke: Macmillan – now Palgrave Macmillan.

Parton, N. (1996) Social work, risk and the blaming system, in N. Parton (ed.) *Social Work, Social Theory and Social Change*, London: Routledge.

Parton, N. (2006) *Safeguarding Childhood: Early Intervention and Surveillance in a Late Modern Society*, Basingstoke: Palgrave Macmillan.

Parton, N. (2007) Safeguarding children: a socio-historical analysis, in K. Wilson and A. James (eds) *The Child Protection Handbook*, London: Elsevier.

Parton, N. (2008) Changes in the form of knowledge in social work: from the 'social' to the 'informational', *British Journal of Social Work*, **38**(2): 253–69.

Pearson, G. (1975) *The Deviant Imagination*, London: Macmillan.

Pearson, R. (2009) Working with unco-operative or hostile families, in L. Hughes and H. Owen (eds) *Good Practice in Safeguarding*, London: Jessica Kingsley.

Peckover, S. (2002a) Supporting and policing mothers: an analysis of the disciplinary practices of health visiting, *Journal of Advanced Nursing*, **38**(4): 369–77.

Peckover, S. (2002b) Focusing upon children and men in situations of domestic violence: an analysis of the gendered nature of British health visiting, *Health and Social Care in the Community*, **10**(4): 254–61.

Pelton, L. (1978) Child abuse and neglect: the myth of classlessness, *American Journal of Orthopsychiatry*, **48**(4): 608–17.

Piper, H. and Stronach, I. (2008) *Don't Touch!: The Educational Story of a Panic*, London: Routledge.

Pithouse, A. (1998) *Social Work: The Social Organisation of an Invisible Trade*, Aldershot: Ashgate.

Preston-Shoot, M. (2007) Whose lives and whose learning? Whose narratives and whose writing? Taking the next research and literature steps with experts by experience. *Evidence and Policy*, **3**(3): 343–59.

Preston-Shoot, M. and Agass, D. (1990) *Making Sense of Social Work: Psychodynamics, Systems and Practice*, Basingstoke: Macmillan – now Palgrave Macmillan.

Reder, P., Duncan, P. and Gray, M. (1993) *Beyond Blame*, London: Routledge.

Robb, M. (2004) Exploring fatherhood: masculinity and intersubjectivity in the research process, *Journal of Social Work Practice*, **18**(3): 395–406.

Rooney, R. (1992) *Strategies for Work with Involuntary Clients*, New York: Columbia University Press.

Rose, W. (2010) The assessment framework, in J. Horwath (ed.) *The Child's World: The Comprehensive Guide to Assessing Children in Need*, London: Jessica Kingsley.

Rosselin, C. (1999) The ins and outs of the hall: a Parisian example, in I. Cieraad (ed.) *At Home: An Anthropology of Domestic Space*, New York: Syracuse University Press.

Ruch, G. (2005) Relationship-based practice and reflective practice: holistic approaches to contemporary child care social work, *Child & Family Social Work*, **10**(2): 111–23.

Ruch, G. (2007a) 'Reflective practice in contemporary child care social work: the role of containment', *British Journal of Social Work*, **37**(4): 659–80.

Ruch, G. (2007b) 'Thoughtful' practice: child care social work and the role of case discussion, *Child and Family Social Work*, **12**(4): 659–80.

Saunders, P. (1990) *A Nation of Home Owners*, London: Unwin Hyman.

Schofield, G. (1998) Inner and outer worlds: a psychosocial framework for child and family social work, *Child & Family Social Work*, **3**(1): 57–67.

Schofield, G. and Brown, K. (1999) Being there: a family centre worker's role as a secure base for adolescent girls in crisis, *Child & Family Social Work*, **4**(1): 21–31.

Schön, D. (1983) *The Reflective Practitioner*, New York: Basic Books.

Scourfield, J. (2001) Constructing men in child protection work, *Men and Masculinities*, **4**(1): 70–89.

Scourfield, J. (2003a) *Gender and Child Protection*, Basingstoke: Palgrave Macmillan.

Scourfield, J. (2003b) Reflection on gender, knowledge and values in social work, *British Journal of Social Work*, **32**(1): 1–15.

Scourfield, J. (2006) The challenge of engaging fathers in the child protection process, *Critical Social Policy*, **26**(2): 440–9.

Sheller, M. (2004) Automotive emotions: feeling the car, *Theory, Culture and Society*, **21**(4/5): 221–42.

Sheller, M. and Urry, J. (2006) The new mobilities paradigm, *Environment and Planning A*, **38**(2): 207–26.

Shepard, M. and Pence, E. (1999) *Coordinating Community Responses to Domestic Violence: Lessons from Duluth and Beyond*, London: Sage.

Sinclair, R. and Bullock, R. (2002) *Learning from Past Experiences: A Review of Serious Case Reviews*, London: DH.

Small, J. (1986) Trans-racial placements: conflicts and contradictions, in S. Ahmed, J. Cheetham, and J. Small (eds) *Social Work with Black Children and their Families*, London: Batsford/BAFF.

Smith, M. (2003) Gorgons, cars and the frightful fiend: representations of fear in social work and counselling, *Journal of Social Work Practice*, **17**(2): 154–62.

Smith, R. (2008) *Social Work and Power*, Basingstoke: Palgrave Macmillan.

Spratt, T. (2000) Decision making by senior social workers at point of first referral, *British Journal of Social Work*, **30**(5): 597–618.

Spratt, T. (2001) The influence of child protection practice orientation on child welfare practice, *British Journal of Social Work*, **31**(6): 933–54.

Spratt, T. (2008) Identifying families with multiple problems: possible responses from child and family social work to current policy developments, *British Journal of Social Work*, **39**(3): 435–50.

Spratt, T. and Devaney, J. (2008) Identifying families with multiple problems: possible responses from child and family social work to current policy developments, *British Journal of Social Work*, **39**(3): 418–34.

Stanley, J. and Goddard, C. (2002) *In the Firing Line: Power and Violence in Child Protection Work*, London: Wiley.

Stanley, N. and Manthorpe, J. (eds) (2004) *The Age of the Inquiry*, London: Routledge.

Stevenson, O. (1963) The understanding caseworker, *New Society*, 1 August, reprinted in E. Holgate (ed.) (1972) *Communicating with Children*, London: Longman.

Sudbery, J. (2002) Key features of therapeutic social work: the use of relationship, *Journal of Social Work Practice*, **16**(2): 149–62.

Taylor, C. (2008) Humanitarian narrative: bodies and detail in late-Victorian social work, *British Journal of Social Work*, **38**(4): 680–96.

Thompson, N. (1993) *Anti-Discriminatory Practice*, Basingstoke: Macmillan – now Palgrave Macmillan.

Timms, N. (1964) *Social Casework*, London: Routledge.

Trevithick, P. (2003) Effective relationship-based practice: a theoretical exploration, *Journal of Social Work Practice*, **17**(2): 163–76.

Trevithick, P. (2005) *Social Work Skills: A Practice Handbook*, 2nd edn, Maidenhead: Open University Press.

Trotter, C. (2006) *Working with Involuntary Clients*, Sydney: Allen & Unwin.

Turnell, A. and Edwards, S. (1999) *Signs of Safety: A Solution and Safety Oriented Approach to Child Protection Casework*, London: Norton.

Turnell, A. and Essex, S. (2006) *Working with 'Denied' Child Abuse: The Resolutions Approach*, Buckingham: Open University Press.

Turner, V. (1969) *The Ritual Process: Structure and Anti-Structure*, London: Allen Lane.

Turner, V. (1974) *Dramas, Fields, and Metaphors*, Ithaca, NY: Cornell University Press.

Urry, J. (2007) *Mobilities*, Cambridge: Polity Press.

Walker, S. (2004) Community work and psychosocial practice: chalk and cheese or birds of a feather?, *Journal of Social Work Practice*, **18**(2): 161–75.

Ward, A. (2008) Opportunity-led work with children, in B. Luckock and M. Lefevre (eds) *Direct Work: Social Work with Children and Young People in Care*, London: BAAF.

Webb, S. (2006) *Social Work in Risk Society*, Basingstoke: Palgrave Macmillan.

Weld, N. (2008) The three houses tool: building safety and positive change, in M. Calder (ed.) *Contemporary Risk Assessment in Safeguarding Children*, Lyme Regis: Russell House.

Williams, A.B. (1997) On parallel process in social work supervision, *Clinical Social Work Journal*, **25**(4): 425–35.

Winnicott, C. (1963) *Child Care and Social Work*, London: Bookstall Publications.

Winnicott, D.W. (1953) Transitional objects and transitional phenomena, *International Journal of Psychoanalysis*, **34**(2): 89–98.

Winnicott, D.W. (1957) *The Child and the Outside World*, London: Tavistock.

Winnicott, D.W. (1971) *Playing and Reality*, London: Routledge.

Wooton, B. (1959) *Social Science and Social Pathology*, London: George Allen and Unwin.

Zelizer, V. (1985) *Pricing the Priceless Child: The Changing Social Value of Children*, New York: Basic Books.

Index

Printed and bound by CPI Group (UK) Ltd, Croydon, CR0 4YY